SECURITY, TRADE, AND ENVIRONMENTAL POLICY

A US/European Union Transatlantic Agenda

SECURITY, TRADE, AND ENVIRONMENTAL POLICY

A US/European Union Transatlantic Agenda

edited by

Charles Bonser
Indiana University

KLUWER ACADEMIC PUBLISHERS
Boston / Dordrecht / London

Distributors for North, Central and South America:
Kluwer Academic Publishers
101 Philip Drive
Assinippi Park
Norwell, Massachusetts 02061 USA
Telephone (781) 871-6600
Fax (781) 871-6528
E-Mail <kluwer@wkap.com>

Distributors for all other countries:
Kluwer Academic Publishers Group
Distribution Centre
Post Office Box 322
3300 AH Dordrecht, THE NETHERLANDS
Telephone 31 78 6392 392
Fax 31 78 6546 474
E-Mail <services@wkap.nl>

Electronic Services <http://www.wkap.nl>

Library of Congress Cataloging-in-Publication Data

Security, trade, and environmental policy : a US/European Union transatlantic agenda / edited by Charles Bonser.
p. cm.
Includes bibliographical references.
ISBN 0-7923-7785-0 (alk. paper)
1. Security, International. 2. International economic relations. 3. Environmental protection--International cooperation. 4. United States--Foreign relations--European Union countries. 5. European Union countries--Foreign relations--United States. I. Bonser, Charles F.

JZ5588 .S43 2000
327.7304--dc21 99-085693

Printed on acid-free paper. Printed in the United States of America
Printed in the United States of America

TABLE OF CONTENTS

FOREWORD: BACKGROUND OF PROJECT

The end of the 20th century finds the Atlantic Alliance partners in evolution toward a new relationship in the key policy arenas of regional and international security, international trade and competition, and the need to deal effectively with environmental and public health problems associated with an expanding global marketplace. The problems associated with these issues has no doubt put a strain on relations between Europe and North America. This has been exacerbated by internal preoccupations on both continents that have reduced communication opportunities, and led to misunderstandings on both sides of the Atlantic. It is clear to both the leadership of the European Union and the United States that this potential estrangement is not in the interests of either continent.

In response to this situation, in December 1995, the Clinton Administration and the European Union initiated a series of efforts under the framework of a "New Transatlantic Agenda." The purpose of these efforts was to strengthen the communication and ties between the EU and the United States in a variety of functional areas. The effort has been largely successful in improving the situation. While agreements may not always be forthcoming, at least communications are more open.

In an effort to contribute to this dialog, in the summer of 1997, the Indiana University School of Public and Environmental Affairs (SPEA), as part of its 25th Anniversary Celebration, co-sponsored an international conference on transatlantic public policy issues with the École Nationale d'Administration (ENA) in Paris, France. The themes of the conference were, "Development and Security Issues for the EU and the U.S. in the 21st century" and "The Next Generation of World Trade Issues." In addition to members of our own faculty and staff, we included several content experts and public policy leaders in the program from both Europe and the United States.

The conference was quite successful, and many of the participants argued strongly that we should continue this type of joint activity on transatlantic policy issues. As a result, SPEA and ENA developed a plan that would continue these programs, but that would bring several other public policy/administration academic programs in Europe and the U.S. into the process.

A second colloquium on transatlantic issues was held at Indiana University in Bloomington, Indiana, September 30–October 2, 1998. This time the topic was: "Globalization and the Environment." Participating in that colloquium, in addition to ENA and SPEA, were: the German government's Bundesakademie (Bonn, Germany); the University Pompeu Fabra (Barcelona); the National School of Administrative Sciences (Speyer, Germany); the Netherlands School of Government; the Erasmus University School of Social Sciences (Netherlands); the Instituto Nacional de Administracão (Lisbon, Portugal); and the Fondazione Eni Enrico Mattei (Milan, Italy). Once again, the participants included both faculty and outside experts from the various countries involved. The style of this colloquium—and our preference for future meetings—was a round table format that limited attendance to about 60 persons, and allowed plenty of time for informal exchanges.

At the conclusion of the Bloomington colloquium, institutional representatives of the organizations participating in the colloquium met and decided to take steps to institutionalize this relationship by establishing the "Transatlantic Consortium for Public Policy Analysis and Education." A draft agreement was subsequently developed and will be acted on when the group once again meets, May 23–26, 2000, for a colloquium in Maastricht, The Netherlands.The theme chosen for that colloquium is, "Globalization and Regionalization: A Paradoxical Challenge for Public Policy." A program committee is presently developing program detail for the colloquium.

As of November 1999, the institutions working together to establish a more permanent relationship are:

SPEA and the Kelley School of Business, Indiana University
Maxwell School, Syracuse University
LBJ School, University of Texas
School of Public Affairs, University of Southern California
John F. Kennedy School, Harvard University
School of Public Affairs, American University
École Nationale d'Administration, Paris, France
Erasmus University, Rotterdam, The Netherlands
Leiden University, The Netherlands
Netherlands School of Government
Federal Academy of Public Administration, Bonn, Germany
National School of Administrative Sciences, Speyer, Germany

Center for European Integration, University of Bonn, Germany
Instituto Nacional de Administracão, Lisbon, Portugal
Fondazione Eni Enrico Mattei, Milan, Italy
University Pompeu Fabra, Barcelona, Spain
Danish School of Public Administration, Frederiksberg, Denmark
Scuola Superiore della Pubblica Amministrazione, Rome, Italy

The papers presented in this volume were originally presented at the Paris and Bloomington conferences. They were subsequently updated, where necessary, to include new information or circumstances. Plans call for future colloquia of the group to publish their results. For current information on the consortium being planned, visit the web page:<http://www.spea.indiana.edu/ids>.

Charles F. Bonser
Dean Emeritus
School of Public and Environmental Affairs
Indiana University
Bloomington, Indiana
U.S.A.

Section I: International Security Issues for the European Union and the United States

INTRODUCTION, SECTION I

Charles F. Bonser
Dean Emeritus
School of Public and Environmental Affairs
Indiana University
Bloomington, Indiana

It is clear that the collapse of the Soviet Empire at the beginning of this decade has led to what President Bush called, at that time, a "New World Order." Although no one as yet has defined exactly what that means, it obviously includes the fact that the United States has emerged as the only true super power in the world, at least militarily. If there were any doubts to that fact, the events of the last decade removed them. In the 1991 Gulf War, the U.S., with minimal support from some of its NATO allies, destroyed one of the largest military forces in the world with an aerial bombardment and a one-week invasion. In the Kosova air war intervention in 1999, the U.S. flew 90 percent of the NATO missions and drove the Serbian military out of Kosova without a single Alliance casualty.

The other components of that new world order, however, are still taking shape. For the first few years after the fall of the Berlin Wall, the North Atlantic Treaty Organization (NATO) remained in a state of shock. It was in danger of becoming an organization in search of a mission, and the anxiety that situation created permeated the halls of the NATO headquarters in Brussels. The Gulf War, and particularly the NATO Bosnia and Kosova interventions, at least temporarily, brought a new sense of purpose to the organization. The common enemy was no longer the Soviet Empire, and the purpose of the Alliance seemed to shift away from just the defense of its member nations. Now an additional enemy appears to have become "chaos," caused by regional instabilities in places considered to be in the Atlantic Alliance's vital interests. If this is indeed the new mission, however, it requires a NATO quite different than the NATO that was designed to confront the Soviets in a land war in Central and Eastern Europe.

The situation became even more unusual when, in the summer of 1997, the members of the Atlantic Alliance decided to extend an invitation to join NATO to three of our former Warsaw Pact adversaries—the Czech Republic, Hungary, and Poland. In June of 1999, after two years of preparatory work, the three nations formally joined the alliance, much to the dismay of the Russians. The fate of several other Eastern European nations, who had also requested to join NATO, remains undetermined. During this period the Alliance also assisted in the development of the other Eastern and Central European nations into the NATO-associated "Partnership for Peace" organization. To top it all off, as the 20th century draws to an end, NATO troops find themselves in common peace-keeping operations in the Balkans with Russia and other former members of the Warsaw Pact. These events cited in this paragraph would have been considered unimaginable as recently as 1988.

There is still much to be worked out between the United States and its European partners as they attempt to redefine and reconstruct the international security architecture that served post–War Europe and the United States so well. What are the criteria that will determine whether or not NATO will take military action in defense of its interests? What should be the nature of any independent European defense capability, and how should it relate to NATO? How far eastward should NATO advance as it considers new members? What should be the criteria and requirements for NATO membership? What should be the security role of the Partnership for Peace (PFP) nations and how shall they interact with NATO? How can the Russian Federation play a positive role in Europe in its relationship with the PFP and NATO?

The Maastricht Treaty of the EU came into force in 1993. In addition to its important economic measures, the Treaty set the objective of "the implementation of a common foreign and security policy , including the eventual framing of a common defense policy." The EU's Amsterdam Treaty that was implemented in May of 1999, added the concept of "common strategies" to the EU nations' pursuit of "common positions."

The events in the Balkans during the last five years of the 20th century, and particularly the Kosovo action, convinced many Europeans that the European Union needed to step forward to try to implement this foreign policy and independent military goal. The consensus was that it would be separate from, yet coordinated with, NATO to take action in cases where the United States might not wish to be involved. At their Cologne Summit in June, 1999, the EU leaders chose former NATO Secretary General, Javier Solana Madariaga, to become the

EU's first High Representative for a common foreign and security policy. To paraphrase Henry Kissenger's famous comment, there is now someone to answer the phone when the U.S. wants to discuss foreign policy with the European Union.

The EU leaders determined that they must have the capacity for autonomous action, independent of NATO, and backed up by credible military forces; the means to decide to use them; and a readiness to do so, "in order to respond to international crises without prejudice to actions by NATO." This—theoretically at least—offers the possibility of EU-led crises management that includes both NATO and non-NATO (Ireland, Sweden, Finland, Austria) European Union nations. The EU military "forces" will apparently be organized under the auspices of the Western European Union—an independent defense cooperation forum established in the 1950s, that has been an "organization in waiting" for several years. The WEU will now be brought into the European Union.

Until recently, the U.S. view of an independent EU military capability, outside of NATO, was unclear. If anything, both the departments of State and Defense seemed skeptical if not opposed to the idea. They now have apparently come to grips with the reality that the Europeans want their own defense "identity." The shift in Britain's support in favor of merging the Western European Union with the EU may have tipped the balance. The issue now is how this will be accomplished and precisely what will be the relationship of this European defense force to NATO. So far the matter has been obscured by "eurospeak" on the part of the European Union and by platitudes from the Americans.

On the European side, the operations of the Kosovo air campaign also brought home to the Europeans the fact that their miliary was still designed to fight a land war on the European continent with the Soviets, as compared with the Americans who had shifted philosophy and operational capability toward more flexible projection forces. In addition, their military technological capability lagged far behind the United States. Not only do they presently need to rely on the U.S. military for heavy lift (the ability to move men and equipment by air and sea) and for military intelligence capability (particularly satellites and telecommunications), the EU countries will need to make substantial investments in stealth and other assets of modern warfare if they are to have a credible projection force. Whether they possess the political will and ability to shift budget priorities (e.g., away from their "Common Agricultural Policy" and other social programs) in this direction remains to be seen. Many in the U.S. are skeptical.

THE SECTION ONE PAPERS ON INTERNATIONAL SECURITY

Against this backdrop, the papers in the first section of this book deal with this changing international security situation, and pose questions that must be dealt with by the U.S., NATO, and the EU as we move into the new century. These papers are particularly enlightening because they reveal the underlying logic, philosophy, and prejudices of both leading American policymakers and their European counterparts.

The authors of the papers in this section originally presented their views at a colloquium on the "U.S.-European Transatlantic Agenda for the 21st Century," co-sponsored by the French government's École Nationale d'Administration and the Indiana University School of Public and Environmental Affairs, in Paris in the summer of 1997. The authors have subsequently reviewed and updated the papers they presented at that colloquium.

In the lead paper, U.S. Senator Richard Lugar, arguably the U.S. Congress' most thoughtful and influential foreign policy expert, points out that over the past 50 years, the U.S., with greater or lesser degrees of enthusiasm, has supported every previous initiative to achieve greater political and economic unity among European nations. As in these past instances, the U.S. supports the European Union's move to further political union by its creation of a unified common foreign and security identity. We also should support, in his view, the expansion of the EU to include central and eastern Europe.

Given this philosophy, it is no surprise that Senator Lugar also supports the further expansion of NATO eastward. He regards NATO enlargement and the expansion of the European Union as separate but parallel processes in support of the same overall objective, which is a broader, deeper transatlantic community. Such an enlarged and updated NATO will have major implications for economic and financial reform. In his words, "Europe remains central to the health of the American economy. Europe and the United States produce over half the world's goods and services. On an annual basis, American bilateral trade with Europe exceeds $250 billion. America's direct investment in Europe also exceeds $250 billion and is greater than in any other region of the world. To protect this considerable investment, Europe and the United States must ensure that we are as successful in dealing with post–Cold War security challenges as we were in dealing with the challenges of the Cold War."

He also argues that "The accession of Poland, Hungary, and the Czech Republic to NATO eliminated immoral and destabilizing dividing lines in Europe and extended stability into a region long troubled by conflict. A stable and peaceful Europe will benefit all of Europe, including Russia and non-NATO countries. NATO enlargement provides an opportunity for the Alliance to be proactive in shaping a stable strategic landscape in Europe."

The paper then goes on to list and discuss three goals he believes the U.S. should set forth for the future of NATO. These are :(1) the enforcement of Article 10 of the Washington Treaty to remain open to the accesssion of additional members, and a formal review of all applications for memberships; (2) expansion of focus beyond threats from the east to the threats facing NATO from the South and elsewhere in the post–Cold War era; and (3) the upgrading of our allies' ability to project power and to operate "out of area."

In the final section of his paper he discusses the Kosovo conflict, and analyzes mistakes made and lessons learned. He observes: "The Western alliance's commitment to achieving democracy in Yugoslavia in the aftermath of war must be as strong as the resolve exhibited during the bombing campaign. NATO forces expelled Serbian troops from Kosovo at great expense and loss of life. We must not now lose the opportunity to bring stability and democracy to the Balkans simply because we lack the attention span or the imagination to finish the job."

LawrenceKorb, of the Council for Foreign Relations, tackles the matter of trying to provide structure to the "new world order" referred to by President Bush. He suggests that the U.S. and Europe made a mistake at the end of the Cold War by not celebrating and providing a very clear break between the Cold War and the new era. "Without this sense of closure, the current security situation is more confusing than it needs to be." The second characteristic of this new era is that economic power is becoming more important relative to military power, and in that light, the tremendous economic growth in Asia has consequences for security and stability in both Europe and the United States. Finally, Korb argues that the nation-state, "the bedrock of international politics for centuries," is changing in contradictory ways. At the same time as we are witnessing the expansion of such supranational organizations as the EU, NAFTA, and the World Trade Organization, we also are witnessing a proliferation of nation-states, and the emergence of transnational groups like organized crime or political/social terrorists that are not responsible to any nation or supranational body.

The upshot of this situation, is that "communism has been replaced by chaos as the real enemy"of the Transatlantic Alliance. The task of the Alliance then becomes to establish rules that prevent this chaos from emerging. These must include expecting nations to protect human rights, and to adhere to international conventions dealing with weapons of mass destruction. Those that violate these rules should be denied economic aid and the advantages that flow from participating in the international economic system.

If military operations become necessary, Korb believes they should be multinational, and not be undertaken without United Nations authorization. He would support the creation of a UN peacekeeping force.

The third paper in this section, by Ambassador Gilles Andréani, of the French Ministry of Foreign Affairs, looks at the question of whether the U.S. and Europe are going to maintain common security interests over the next ten years or so. The major security issues he sees facing Europe in the decade to come are:

1. Instabilities linked with the transition process that their "southern neighbors" are going to experience—those southeast of the Mediterranean. The transition from the Arab-Muslim world into modernity, toward a market economy and democracy.
2. The incorporation of Eastern Europe, including Russia, into the European Security structures.
3. Global issues that concern the proliferation of terrorism and organized crime.

His question is, "Are these subjects enough to form a common agenda for the United States and Europe comparable to the defense of the territory of the Alliance before the Soviet threat for nearly 50 years?" His answer is, "yes and no." Yes because there are parallel interests in all of these matters. But "there are things that are taking place a little differently" such that, in respect to our common agenda, joint action must be determined based on the particularities of each case—"The problem is to decide what the political, institutional, and military conditions must be of a relationship between Europe and the U.S. that allows us to agree as much as possible each time on what we should do to settle the security problems that we will face in the next century."

Ambassador Andréani then explores the several actions and programs that the Europeans have been taking over the past few years to deal with these threats to security. But he concludes that some of these problems are "beyond the scope" of the Europeans to solve without the help of the Americans. If fact, he argues, the EU and the U.S. need each other. The question, then, is "What can the U.S. do? What is the condition that will allow us in each individual case to find a political agreement between Europeans and Americans and act accordingly?"

His answer is that in order for (NATO) to function, "we need to develop within NATO political mechanisms that allow for Americans and Europeans to be willing to develop a common policy, in any given crisis . . . The political condition which must allow us to arrive at this result depends fundamentally and largely on the capacity of Europeans to become organized on a political level. I think that a Europe that is fragmented, divided, one that hesitates to act, is a bad political partner for the U.S. It is in the event that the Europeans succeed in forming a collective point of view that they can present to the U.S. in a coherent manner, dialogue with them and arrive at a truly common position, that the Europeans will form a true partner for the U.S. I think that this is the schema toward which we must aim, and this is the schema which we have in mind behind our vision of a more balanced NATO in which Europeans are less fragmented but speak more with one voice in order to reach common positions with the U.S."

The next four papers, by Lt. General Thomas Montgomery, head of the U.S. Mission to NATO (1995-98); Guido Lenzi, of the Western European Union; and Colonel Jens Zimmerman, of the German Ministry of Defense, consider the reorganization/reform of NATO and the further development and integration of the European Union defense identity, including the Western European Union, with NATO.

General Montgomery's paper discusses the changes in NATO as a result of the Eastern Europe realignment. These include the processes and procedures that will truly make the NATO-Partnership for Peace organization a viable operating relationship. The establishment of the Euro-Atlantic Partnership Council and the enhancement of the twenty-seven-member Partnership for Peace Program will result in increasing opportunities for "forging a closer political and security relationship with the Alliance as a whole as well as with individual Allies."

NATO's military command has taken "three bold steps" to "bring the Partner nations inside NATO fences." These include involving military staff of the Partner nations in the daily staff work that will plan and execute Partnership for Peace exercises and operations; inviting Partner nations to assign senior military representatives to NATO headquarters; and reorganizing the military command structure to better meet NATO's future military requirements and prepare it to accept the additional force contributions of new members.

General Montgomery also supports the creation of a European Security and Defense Identity (ESDI). He does suggest that "I have difficulty envisioning any major operation in which the United States would choose to remain on the sidelines, but I would remind you that United States supports the development of a ESDI as long as it is developed *within* NATO, and not outside of it. We understand Europe's desire to be a strategic partner, rather than remaining strategically dependent on the United States, but the truth is that a separate strategic capability requires a solid political and financial commitment that Europe has been hesitant to assume."

He does express some concern about a possible future watering down, in the face of expanding NATO missions, of "the essential ingredient of NATO's Strategic Concept," its commitment to the collective defense of member nations. "I am a little concerned that, with the proliferation of new missions, the Alliances emphasis and capability for Collective Defense might start to slowly erode. If the Alliance is to prosper into the 21st century we must never lose sight of the importance of maintaining the very basic and essential military capabilities required to execute NATO's primary Collective Defense mission."

Guido Lenzi argues that the challenges of the new international situation do not need "new architecture," but they do require a "a revitalization of existing international organisms like the Council of Europe and the OSCE." He expects the WEU will be at the intersection of NATO's destructuring and downsizing, and the European Union's upsizing and increasing its responsibilities. He suggests that the ESDI can help keep the transatlantic relationship together, but it must be ensured that consultative processes, visibly comparing notes as often as possible so that there is a process of progressive adaptation.

Colonel Zimmerman believes the challenge of today is to extend stability in and for Europe. He thinks this will require two elements: intensified integration and improved cooperation. The future security structure in Europe cannot be created from scratch. "We must rather bring together the existing institutions and processes, especially the NATO, EU, WEU, and OSCE and we must succeed in managing their interaction and complimentary approach."

Against this backdrop, he argues, establishing the security structure in Europe means to push ahead with four developments:

1. We need a NATO that can react flexibly to the new challenges by preventive and proactive crisis management, by transfer of stability and by cooperation. At the same time the Alliance must retain its collective defense capability.
2. We must continue the process of opening this new NATO to the East while maintaining the necessary balance between this process and a security partnership with Russia and Ukraine.
3. We must give the transatlantic link between Europe and North America a new foundation.
4. Europe must become a political union with a more efficient common foreign and security policy. Europe must develop its own ability to take strategic action within the Alliance.

On the issue of the further integration of both the EU and NATO, the Colonel points out that integration is about transferring stability by opening the Alliance and the European Union to "independent and sovereign nations which are committed to democracy, market economies, and shared values. The enlargement processes of NATO and European Union are thus interrelated and overlapping activities. Taking full advantage of their inherent conceptual and political interrelation will lead to synergistic effects in giving Central and Eastern Europe a Euro-Atlantic perspective."

His paper expands in some detail on both of these issues and on the policy and operational steps that need to be taken.

A major issue, then, as stressed by all three authors, is clearly not just how these institutions will change, but how the relationships between the organizations will evolve. This then will affect the transatlantic relationship and, ultimately, the security of the European continent.

Ambassador Marshall Brement's paper looks at the post–Cold War world from a historical perspective. He points out that "in the years since 1989, we have not only had the breakup of the communist system; we also have had the dissolution of the colonial/imperial system which was prevalent in Europe for centuries.". . . Furthermore, it is important to remember that these changes happened not just in the period from 1945 to 1989, but over a much longer timeframe.

Brement suggests there were four major changes in Western Europe from 1945–1989. They were:

1. the commitment to democracy and democratic systems;
2. the commitment to a market economy;
3. the commitment to the giving up of national sovereignty to supranational organizations and to the integration of Europe; and
4. the acceptance and encouragement of the presence of the United States on the European continent as a major actor.

He argues that the vast changes in Europe and the United States after 1945 were primarily responsible for the cataclysmic changes that began in 1989. After an intriguing review of these events, the Ambassador concludes with the observation: "The problem we face, then, is to bring the perceptions of the American people about their government, and the place of the United States in the world today, in line with the realties of the post–Cold War world. We will need strong presidential leadership to accomplish that task."

In the next two papers, Eric Danon, of the French Ministry of Foreign Affairs, and Immo Stabreit, the German Ambassador to France, raise the issue of non-military threats to European security. *Danon* indicates that the dialog between Europe and the United States on such issues as terrorism, drug trafficking, and organized crime is still in the beginning stages. Part of the reason for that situation is that "there has not been a very elaborate theoretical and doctrinal reflection on non-military threats, as there has been for military questions." Europe and the U.S. have different conceptions, for example, on the issue of drug control and terrorism. In the years ahead, the two entities will have develop and put in place a common basis of thought on all non-military threats if they are to make progress in their control. This will not be an easy matter to accomplish. Even within the EU, there are differences between the member states in the extent of the problems, and how they regard and deal with them. This makes it difficult to reach consensus within the EU, and then makes it difficult for the EU to negotiate with the U.S. on joint programs.

The non-state nature of these crimes is also a problem in developing programs for their alleviation. Perpetrators operate across state boundaries, often committing crimes in one state while their base of operations is in another. This complicates the states' ability to set up police networks and networks of justice cooperation. Danon argues for the establishment of U.S./EU forums to begin to discuss these questions, just as we have international forums for such topics as nuclear disarmament and conventional weapons control. As a second stage, he suggests approaching the matter of operational cooperation. Of course, this will not be easy, given the proclivity of police and justice systems to treat these issues in a confidential, essentially bilateral manner. He concludes by observing: "that these non-military threats are going to rise in importance. If we do not want them to put our societies at risk, we are going to have to find a number of quick responses. The US and the European countries are interested, above all, in not becoming destabilized by these problems. We therefore need to find new ways of working together on these issues."

Ambassador Stabreit is very concerned about the problem of organized crime, and "its great machine," the drug trade. "In my 35-year career, I have seen organized crime getting very close to the top and trying to infiltrate governments in a number not insignificant in both the developed and the underdeveloped world. Now we are told that there are approximately 130 groups of organized crime in Russia. The problem is that organized crime, in a way which has not yet happened in the same way in any other country of the developed world, has penetrated parts of the administrative apparatus or is cooperating with it."

He is concerned that the level of organized crime is rising rapidly, and that the citizens of our countries believe that their governments are ineffective in dealing with the situation, or are—even worse—infiltrated by the criminals. He supports Eric Danon's argument that we must have more international cooperation between police and justice systems if we are to bring the problem under control.

Ambassador Stabreit also feels strongly that Europe and America are in danger of drifting apart, now that the Cold War is over. He believes this would be very negative for both continents. "I think it is very important that on both sides of the Atlantic we do not become strangers to each other on account of the different speeds and directions into which our societies develop. So we have to work on this by increasing student exchanges, increasing exchanges between our political leaders and increasing the coverage of global issues in the press."

The next two papers, by Stanley Sloan of the U.S. Library of Congress and Senator Xavier de Villepin, of the French Senate, focus on somewhat different aspects of the Transatlantic Agenda. Senator Villepin places "great importance" on the future of the transatlantic relationship, and states that it is "among the top priorities of French diplomacy." His paper examines three alternative scenarios by which the relationship could develop in the next century, and comes down on the side of "the third scenario, [which] predicted an equitable European/U.S. partnership characterized by a strong and balanced relationship."... He argues that "we must do everything to prevent the first bleak scenario that would see the U.S. and Europe give exclusive priority to their domestic problems and move apart from one another."

His paper discusses several aspects of the economic/international security scene that reinforce his view that "we face the same threats, and it is clear that it is only through joining our efforts that we will be able to attack these threats at their roots and do what we can to free the future generations from them." These include NATO reform and enlargement, the evolution of the EU and the launching of the European Monetary System and Common Currency, the establishment of the World Trade Organization, and the need for a multinational framework for dealing with our common problems. He concludes by stating: "The U.S. will find tomorrow in the EU a more and more solid partner. We must not pass up this opportunity, which is perhaps historical, to build for tomorrow a veritable partnership which, through its dynamism and the synergies that it will form, will allow the transatlantic relationship—which is already exceptional—to be more global and more efficient."

Stanley Sloan, while recognizing the evolution of the international system of institutions, argues that policies cannot be legitimized based on international objectives. The nation states are still required to provide legitimacy to international policy based on national objectives and perspectives. He points out: "we all know that we need to distinguish between the objective of trying to create European unity, trying to construct a European security and defense identity, and the reality that neither of these currently exist. . . . even an optimist ought to project at least another 50 years before we could expect to see anything emerging that might even resemble the Swiss Federation." (The model some point to as the "end game" of the European Union.)

Discussing the role of NATO in the 21st century, Sloan expects that it will remain primarily a collective defense organization, even though its main function at this time is promoting defense cooperation, a positive activity that promotes stability. But, "Article V does remain the core of the Alliance."

He sees NATO moving forward on expanding its membership. He quotes Dean Achesson, who told Congress, the North Atlantic Alliance "is conceived rather in the spirit of growth, of development, of progress and what we seek is to pursue the opportunity for a living heritage of freedom to continue to grow."

The final paper in Section I is by Senator Paul Girod, Vice President of the French Senate. *Senator Girod* states in his comments that in the new century, "the rank of the European continent will depend a great deal on the energy and enthusiasm of this transatlantic dialogue." He recognizes the contribution of former U.S. Secretary of State, Warren Christopher, in proposing a new Transatlantic Agenda in June of 1995. The initiative then moved forward politically with at the European/American summit in Madrid in December 1995. "The perspectives which Mr. Warren Christopher had outlined were ambitious, because beyond the questions of security, he initiated the development of a transatlantic zone of free trade. He had thus evoked the creation of an entire regime of investments and more subtle definitions of rules to expand the access to the market, encouragement of investment in information technologies, the elimination of commercial barriers and the opening up of the sky through air treaties."

With regard to the future development of NATO, Senator Girod states that the integration of Poland, the Czech Republic, and Hungary in 1999 probably mark the beginning of the founding of a new world. But this is a world in which dangers are far from being completing erased. "The transatlantic dialogue, in the ensemble of its dimensions, constitutes an essential framework for our two continents to decide on a common future. . . . Our ambition is to offer our inhabitants a better world, and to the entire planet the example of democracy which is both mature, relaxed, sure of itself and open to all of the preoccupations of the world's citizens."

Commentary

During the conference at which the original version of these papers were presented, there was a very lively discussion among the participants. Some of these comments provide clarification of views, and some are enlightening about attitudes and opinions. Those presented here provide a flavor of the discussion, without identification of the speaker or editorial comment.

Question for Senator Lugar

You talked about Ukraine and the Baltic states which I think are very problematic areas. U.S. policy has been to effectively isolate Belarus, while Ukraine and Poland issued a statement that we should not isolate Belarus. I would appreciate your comment on that matter. My second question is in regard to the Baltic states and whether or not some sort of alternative security system could be developed, say involving the OSCE, in mediating between Russian and NATO?

Senator Lugar's Answer (edited)

Let me respond to the second question first by saying that I would encourage such initiatives with regard to the Baltic states and certainly some have been suggested by Scandinavian countries. . . . I think the United States has an obligation to speak out on that because essentially the Baltic states are (approaching) the United States. . . . So we would encourage European initiatives quite apart from any undergirding or encouragement that we give.

I think the question of Belarus is not one in which the United States, as a matter of foreign policy, is attempting to isolate Belarus. Quite to the contrary, I've visited the country along with my former colleague Senatpr Sam Nunn of Georgia with regard to persuading Belarussians to work with us to get missiles, ICBMs, out of the country; to work on housing for Belarussian officers, which was one of the quid pro quos for moving the missiles and for other assistance likewise that was of use to them. I thought that we had a very good relationship and so did our administration for a period of time . . . . They are not a candidate for NATO. No one is suggesting that, they do not suggest it nor do we. I think we in the United States at least hope that they will move as have other newly independent states toward democratic institutions at some near point.

Comment

What is this Transatlantic Agenda? I find that it manifests itself in different ways. It can be interpreted as simply a matter of generalities, of unproved cooperation among established Allies linked to the program of NATO enlargement or of increased enlarged institutions of free trade. General endorsements of better cooperation and of improved trade relations cannot be objected to, but is there an actual policy project?

I think the answer to this is yes. . . . It is a second term Clinton Administration project, extremely ambitious to . . . lay down the foundations of a new international system and to add to the reputation that Mr. Clinton deservedly has as an extraordinarily skillful politician. . . . His purpose, as the National Security Council Chairman Sandy Berger has said, is first to reaffirm the United States as "a European Power." It is next to build an undivided, peaceful and democratic Europe. That is not to help build— but it is to build an undivided, peaceful and democratic Europe permanently linked to the United States.

NATO expansion is a step in this plan. An indispensable step, according to Mr. Berger again, a sweeping, broad, historic strategic objective which in the end it is hoped will prove an achievement comparable to the Marshall Plan. . . . The fundamental criticism that I would make of it, on its conception, is that it results from that unfortunately widespread tendency or impulse today to create an image rather than a reality. It incorporates historic American tendencies towards global integration, global federalism under American leadership or on the American example which can be traced back to at least to those of Woodrow Wilson. . . .

The contrast that I would draw between this program and the program that it would emulate—the great consolidation of the Alliance at the end of 1947 and the beginning of the 1950s—the difference is that then there was an international crisis. Then the Allies wanted consolidation.

The judgment that I would have to make of this new program, the Clinton Administration's program, is that it is spiritually, if I may use the expression, empty. This is because it is fundamentally unserious, unrealistic in terms of what the Allies really want of the real conflicts of interest that exist with the Allies and essentially designed for the sake of image.

Question to Yves Boyer

I noticed that you said that the great challenges of our society today on the international scale (terrorism, organized crime) could not be undertaken by a structure like NATO. On that note, allow me to disagree. It must be noted that one-fifth of NATO's budget goes to scientific and environmental affairs. There even exists a committee called the "Committee on the Changes of Modern Society," and this committee is in charge of actions in all domains of social life. I am sure that, when it becomes necessary, when their governments ask them for it, the delegates of this committee will add to the agenda certain additional points concerning the new threats that have already been evoked. I cannot go too far into the details, but in any case, these subjects are already on the agenda.

Answer:

When I said that the challenges such as terrorism, etc., would perhaps be poorly undertaken by NATO, I meant that, due to the nature of these problems, they call for methods of settling that involve the armed forces, perhaps, in which case NATO would be quite appropriate, but that (also) calls in customs, the police, diplomats, economic measures, etc., of all kinds, and for which NATO does not hold a secure role. What especially bothers me is that NATO is a regional organization. Its field of action is clearly defined by the Treaty of Washington. And what are trying to do right now? Are we selling ourselves surreptitiously a new organization, under American leadership, of course, which would make we Europeans in charge of these problems? . . . The North Atlantic organization is a regional organization whose field of action has been well defined. It seems to me that certain measures or certain desires expressed by our American friends are moving in the direction of a considerable expansion of NATO's zone of action and influence.

Question to Lawrence Korb

Among the principles, (Korb) seemed to put the UN very much in the forefront and relied a lot on the UN. I would like to venture a different viewpoint and ask for his comments about the recent experience in Europe (which) has shown precisely that it was the inefficiency of the UN system trying to intervene in ex-Yugoslavia which, after many failures, that led to NATO taking over with some fairly historic developments.

Answer

As regards to the UN in Bosnia, remember the first statement on Bosnia was, "The hour of Europe is at hand." Europe was going to do it first and then that did not work. Then the United Nations was asked to do more than it was capable of doing. It was asked to do peacekeeping when there was no peace to keep. I think we ask too much of the United Nations and then we blame the UN for the resolutions that we passed. I think the United Nations, while it has not been perfect, has gotten blamed for things it shouldn't have and I think we've learned a lot. My point was that regardless of whether it's NATO or whatever group that does the operation I think one of the standards is that you need to have the UN authorization to do it. The reason I like that precedent is if Russia decides to go into what it calls the 'near abroad' we can say, 'look before we went into the Gulf, before we went into Bosnia we had UN authorization and if you think it is that critical, you need to come to the UN.' That way I think we will prevent them from taking advantage of instability in one of the former republics.

Question

How do you think the cost (of NATO expansion) will affect the public debate?

Korb Answer

I think that the cost issue will be a major factor in the debate in the U.S. Senate. Senators are liable to say, 'Well, wait a second. Why should we pay any of the costs of harmonizing or integrating the Eastern European militaries because look at what we spend on defense and look at the fact of all the troops we still have in Europe and look at the situation in Japan where the Japanese do provide a tremendous amount of support.' . . . Somebody said that if you are adding three, four, or five states, doesn't that expand the area that you need to defend? How will we defend it with a budget that is smaller than it was when NATO was small? I think that will come up and that will be kind of another interesting side.

Boyer Answer

In answer to the question concerning the costs of expansion, I would say that NATO's and the EU's expansion to the East can be seen as taking place within a measure of stabilization of the situation in Europe. And I would say that the Europeans of the EU are going to pay a significant amount in terms of the expansion of the EU, so we could imagine quite clearly a kind of distribution of tasks between the Americans who would pay the most for the expansion concerning NATO and the European Union would support the enormous cost, much higher than those of NATO's expansion, of the Central and Western European countries who might become members of the EU. It is a kind of distribution of the responsibility.

Comment

I can say two things about Bosnia. First, I would like to remind you that during the entire crisis, from the beginning in the middle of 1991 until 1995 . . . I am sorry to say to our American friends, I do not want them to think that I am anti-American, but I seem to remember that all of the European attempts to resolve the crisis were systematically, and I am weighing my words, torpedoed by the State Department. Thus, we can say that the Europeans were useless; they did not want to take action, perhaps, but on the other hand it would be interesting to reconstruct the history of the crisis, and in the history of the crisis we would see that we were perhaps not always supported as we should have been by our American friends.

Question

My question is for Mr. Lawrence Korb who drew our attention to Turkey at the end of his remarkable presentation. One year ago, under the initiative of the French Institute of Criminology and of the geopolitical club to which I belong, which is the "forum of the future," two days of international studies on the new forms of crime took place. Among those present were a delegate of the American administration on the war against drugs, the Russian Army General who commands special troops formed to counter the new forms of crime, the General of the Turkish division who commands the same kind of troops in Turkey, and Admiral Lacoste, who was the director of our foreign security service. Keeping with what we learn in military school, the first day was devoted to studying the circumstances, and next to seeking solutions. We learned that Turkey was the country at the center of an observation and lock-up plan of the most serious crimes: weapon trafficking, fission materials, organized crime such as the Mafia, etc. And during the second day, our distinguished speakers concluded that, on the European and even the world scale, that Turkey's necessary integration had to be positioned immediately within this plan of listening to, locking up and fighting organized crime. I think that this appeal has not been met; could Mr. Korb tell us what he wants to do about this and give us his recommendations?

Korb Answer

I think you've probably made my point better than I did as to why it's important for Turkey to be a part of Europe. Because a lot of these problems cannot be solved without Turkey. I think it is important to bring Turkey into Europe. My point is, Turkey is pivotal because the Islamic world has two models: the Turkish model—which is the separation of church and state, and the Iranian model. It is important for the Turkish model to be accepted by the Islamic countries. If they come into Europe I think that there is more hope for that. After all, the Turks are saying, "We were OK to be in NATO" when you had this common enemy and you were worried about the Soviet Empire, but now you don't seem to care. I think that the United States and Europe need to work very carefully on the Turkish situation to make sure that they become part of this new international order.

Comment

I cannot stop myself from commenting on what William Bellamy (Minister/Counselor for Political Affairs, U.S. Embassy, Paris, France) said when he said "we support the EU, it is great that it is developing, but it must certainly not become a power block." It must not become a "powerless block," either. It must have the ability to defend its interests. Today the EU extends a lot of influence and what we might call power, outside its territory. It is a powerful organization. It is a powerful entity in the commercial domain, in the political domain, and none of this is a hostile project to the U.S. It is possible that, in signing the Maastricht Treaty, the Europeans signed an objective to extend this power into the domain of foreign policy, and security and defense. They must do so, and it is a good thing. There is no hostility in this toward the U.S. And we cannot say "yes, we support you, you are not becoming a power block."

The EU is already an instrument of power and it will become more of one in the future. I think that our entire problem is to make sure that it involves a process that takes into consideration the long-lasting Atlantic Alliance and the degrees of common interest which is very high between the U.S .and the EU. That is our objective. And we will not solve this problem simply by denying it, and by saying "the EU cannot become a powerhouse," because, in many ways, it already is.

I wanted to say this in response to William Bellamy's presentation, with which I agreed, by the way.

Mr. William Bellamy

I did not want to suggest that Europe does not have the right to form a block, and even less that Europe does not have the right to defend its interests. In fact, I cited the example of the common defense of Europe in economic matters and in other domains. This is normal. I think that for the U.S., the question is rather "must Europe form saying that it must rival the U.S., to resist what we call hegemony, domination? Must we speak of Europe in negative terms, in order to justify its construction?" That is still not the case. That happened, and the Americans usually react against this tendency.

Question

We (France and the U.S.) are both great powers, at least we have the attitudes of being great powers. We both have universalist and democratic projects, and we are both very proud of our independent actions and distrustful, too, perhaps too often, of the other's independent action. And Mr. Andréani said quite rightly that we have shared identical interests and also parallel interests. But what is often troubling about the diplomacy between France and the U.S. is that we also have a parallel diplomacy rather than a shared diplomacy.

I wonder if the day has not come for France's greatness, because I think that it is very important for French identity to see itself as great, to continue now much more often by sharing the responsibilities and by an increased comparison to the U.S.— instead of this annoying habit of distinguishing itself from the U.S, at times in a manner that is, I believe, quite often vexing in the eyes of the Americans.

Response of Mr. Gilles Andréani

I think that you are right, but here I think we must ask ourselves about France's European objective. France has made, with no possible turning around, the choice of channeling the essential part of its influence, both in the world and on the diplomatic scene, by Europe. That is not the case exclusively in regard to its cooperation with the U.S. I think that it is simply measuring the reality that most of this planet's problems, certainly with the exception of some, are not answerable in a bilateral Franco-American cooperation.

First, it is an imbalanced cooperation by its very nature. And second, our vision of the way we must work is to try and arrive at common European positions and objectives, and then to arrive at something in common with the U.S. When William Bellamy said "what we don't want is for Europe to position itself as a rival to the U.S.," I think that he is right. It is not the objective to have on this planet two big elephant-types who go around not knowing the other exists in a world that is fragile, complex, in which it is better to act together than separately. I think that our vision of things is more of arriving at a Euro-American team, at something that is coordinated. But naturally that implies many fulfilled conditions, which is not necessarily the case currently.

The first is that the Europeans are beginning to agree to intervene together and try and form an opinion that they must then attempt to debate with the U.S. That implies, too, that the U.S. is receptive, and, this is not to criticize the U.S., but all of our countries, as I have said, are more autocentric. They have less space and less energy to devote to—this is true especially of the U.S.—that most of the work has been completed and that the rest is pretty secondary. So, I think that we must reform common work habits, in the definition of common strategies between the U.S. and Europe, concerning issues different from those of the Cold War.

Now, the truth is that in this world in which the U.S. is the sole global power, it is very difficult to convince them that it is profitable for them to do that. They are entirely convinced on the theoretical level. I believe William Bellamy when he says, "but the Clinton Administration wants Europe to develop into a global partner." That is entirely true. But then, from subject to subject, when they say "we would love to do something together, for example regarding the Middle East peace process, we would like to coordinate our views with yours" and we send positions to the U.S.; we try to move closer to them. . . . This is a very important subject for the U.S. I can understand it when they say "it is already hard enough with Congress, etc., to develop an American position, and, in any case, we are key players in this affair, why would we go get involved with the Europeans?

In other words, I think that there is an American desire to have a global partner; a stronger and more coherent Europe. There is also a European desire to act symbiotically with the US. But I would say that the force of habit, the weight of interests make it difficult to achieve. So, naturally, we must change this. We must try and achieve this. But it is true that when we list the subjects, it is very difficult to find a subject with common interests, a comparable degree of implication, and in which the respective weight of Europe and the U.S. allows for true cooperation.

There are not many issues which bring all of these things together, and it is too bad, because this is what we must strive for.

Comment

As a German, I could remain in my corner and follow this Franco-American debate with much interest. But I would like to emphasize something and bring us back to the fact that this discussion we are holding, which is a well-known discussion, is extremely theoretical because we are pretending that this European identity exists. But this identity is a project, a program, and we Europeans are breaking our backs to make it a reality, and it is entirely logical in the logic of the process of European integration.

So if a day comes when we succeed in obtaining this identity, because the political willingness of the Europeans allows us to call it a European identity, we will be able to verify if this really results in the unfavorable consequences about which we have been speaking or is it that, as a consequence of the transition process, we also taught Americans and Europeans to live with it, and I think we must do this.

U.S./EUROPEAN SECURITY POLICY FOR THE 21ST CENTURY

Senator Richard G. Lugar
United States Senator from Indiana

Last April, Senate Majority Leader Trent Lott asked me to speak on his behalf at a ceremony in the U.S. Capitol commemorating the 50th anniversary of the North Atlantic Treaty Organization (NATO). The event was a celebration of NATO's victory in the Cold War and the Alliance's decision to invite new members to join the Alliance for the first time since 1980. I took the opportunity to lay out my vision of NATO in the next century. The future of NATO is bright if it adapts to post–Cold War Europe.

Europe remains central to the health of the American economy. Europe and the United States produce over half the world's goods and services. On an annual basis, American bilateral trade with Europe exceeds $250 billion. America's direct investment in Europe also exceeds $250 billion and is greater than in any other region of the world. To protect this considerable investment, Europe and the United States must ensure that we are as successful in dealing with post–Cold War security challenges as we were in dealing with the challenges of the Cold War.

On April 29, 1998, the United States Senate gave its advice and consent to the Protocols of Accession for Poland, Hungary, and the Czech Republic to become members of the Washington Treaty. The resolution of ratification was approved by an overwhelming vote of 80–19. In my opinion, the Senate took advantage of an historical window of opportunity to take steps that will secure European peace and stability and lock in the freedom and independence won in the revolutions of 1989 and the collapse of communism.

The more distant we are from the days of the fall of the Berlin Wall and the collapse of communism, the clearer it becomes that we have entered a new era. The revolutions of 1989 not only led to the collapse of communism ,but also to the end of the peace orders established after two world wars. What is at stake now is order and stability in Europe as a whole. And that is why American interests are involved.

It is clear that NATO cannot by itself solve all of Europe's problems. But without a stable security framework, we run the risk that reform and democracy in Eastern and Central Europe will not persist but will instead be undercut by destructive forces of nationalism and insecurity. The failure of democracy in the East could not help but have profound consequences for democracy in the continent's western half as well. If history teaches us anything, it is that the United States is always drawn into such European conflicts because our vital interests are ultimately engaged.

The accession of Poland, Hungary, and the Czech Republic to NATO eliminated immoral and destabilizing dividing lines in Europe and extended stability into a region long troubled by conflict. A stable and peaceful Europe will benefit all of Europe, including Russia and non-NATO countries. NATO enlargement provides an opportunity for the Alliance to be proactive in shaping a stable strategic landscape in Europe.

I believe the United States must set forth three goals in discussions over the future of NATO: (1) the enforcement of Article 10 of the Washington Treaty to remain open to the accession of additional members, and a formal review of all applications for memberships; (2) expansion of focus beyond threats from the East to the threats facing NATO from the South and elsewhere in the post–Cold War era; and (3) the upgrading of our allies' ability to project power and to operate "out of area."

NATO'S OPEN DOOR

During Senate debate on enlargement, I listened carefully to those who suggested that there was no threat to the United States and NATO and thus we should not expand the Alliance. They suggested there will be plenty of time to expand the Alliance should a new enemy or threat appear on the horizon. I strongly disagreed.

We have learned that the weapons used in Desert Storm were envisioned, planned, and first produced in the 1970s. Thus, the systems which allowed us to triumph in the Persian Gulf are 20 or 25 years old. The organization and infrastructure to meet future threats must have a similar "root structure." We must begin to construct an Alliance which can meet future, undetermined threats.

One cannot expect an Alliance to be shelved during times of peace and simply dusted off when threats emerge. The Alliance must begin to lay the foundation that will prepare us to meet an uncertain future. In my mind, expanding the zone of peace and security in Europe and adding three new, willing members will contribute to that preparedness.

NATO's "open-door" policy toward new members established by Article 10 of the Washington Treaty, has given countries of Central and Eastern Europe the incentive to accelerate reforms, to peacefully settle disputes with neighbors, and to increase regional cooperation. Hopes of future membership in NATO has been a tremendous driving force of democratization and peace in Eastern and Central Europe, including former Warsaw Pact nations.

To retract the "open-door" policy, as some have suggested, would risk undermining the tremendous gains that have been made across the region. The result of a "closed-door" policy would be the creation of new dividing lines across Europe. Those nations outside might become disillusioned and insecure and thus inclined to adopt the competitive and destabilizing security policies of Europe's past.

NATO's decision to enlarge in stages recognizes that not all new democracies and applicants in Europe are equally ready or willing to be security allies. Some states may never be ready.

The selection of future NATO members should depend on: (1) a determination by NATO members of their strategic interests; (2) NATO's perception of threats to security and stability; and (3) actions taken by prospective members to complete their democratic transitions and to harmonize their policies with NATO's political aims and security policies.

To reinforce the benefits of Article 10, I believe a comprehensive review of the qualifications of the nine current applicant countries should be conducted under the guidelines laid out in the 1995 NATO Study on Enlargement. A review of this type would further demonstrate that NATO is actively considering a continuation of the enlargement process. Some believe that the Alliance is not interested in further enlargement; a formal review of the type I suggest would go far in reassuring NATO and non-NATO states of the Alliance's plans. Furthermore, a review would provide NATO aspirants with additional incentive to continue democratic, economic, and military reforms. This is in the national security interests of the United States and NATO and should be encouraged.

These actions would also serve to clarify the security expectations of non-NATO members. It would make clear that it is the intention of the United States that NATO remain a serious defensive military alliance and not slip into a loose collective security society. It would suggest that enlargement will be a careful, deliberate process, with consideration of all security interests. Finally, it would draw again on the principle of reciprocity, both to encourage prospective members to align themselves with NATO's values and policies and to signal that threats levied against would-be members will be counterproductive.

OUT OF AREA OR OUT OF BUSINESS

For nearly 50 years, NATO was oriented and organized to defend and respond to an attack from the East. An invasion by Soviet and Warsaw Pact forces was the primary threat facing the Alliance. Since the collapse of the Soviet Union, new threats have replaced the nightmare of Soviet armored divisions crashing through the Fulda Gap. The proliferation of weapons of mass destruction, rogue states, terrorism, ethnic strife, and other potentially destabilizing elements now threaten the Alliance.

It is a basic American interest that the Alliance not only enlarge to help stabilize Eastern Europe but that enlargement be part and parcel of a broader transformation that turns Europe into an increasingly effective strategic partner of the United States in and beyond the continent.

I believe this includes an improvement in the ability of NATO to operate outside the borders of its members. This is not a new mission. The potential for these types of endeavors has been present since NATO's inception. The true core of NATO has always been collective defense, but Article 4 of the Washington Treaty suggests that NATO will consult and can act if the security of any of the parties is threatened. This interpretation was reinforced by John Foster Dulles in May 1949 during Senate consideration of the Washington Treaty. Secretary of State Dulles testified that the occasions for consultation under Article 4 are not merely attacks in the Atlantic area dealt with by Article 5, but threats anywhere to any of the parties, since the parties have interests and possessions throughout the world. So we are not talking about new NATO responsibilities; these types of actions were considered by the members of the Alliance and are supported by language in the treaty ratified by the Senate in 1949.

It is important to remember that participation in non-Article 5 missions is not obligatory and each NATO member is free to make an independent decision regarding participation in those missions. The United States and other NATO members are able to decide on the basis of their interests and an independent assessment of the situation whether to participate. This is as it should be.

THE CAPABILITY GAP

NATO must also attempt to breach the gap between members' capabilities. The collapse of the Soviet Union and the Warsaw Pact has altered the strategic and military landscape in which NATO forces will operate in the future. The potential for massive tank battles over the plains of Central Europe has been reduced. Instead, military strategists believe the conflicts of the 21st century will require NATO members to rapidly deploy forces over long distances, sustain operations for extended periods of time, and operate jointly with the United States in high-intensity conflicts. NATO's operations in Kosovo provide an excellent example of the preeminence of U.S. forces and the need for our allies to make a substantial investment in their own military capabilities.

NATO developed a truly credible capability to defend itself from threats emanating from Central Europe and the former Soviet Union. But our allies have not moved far enough or fast enough to improve their capabilities to defend against newly emerging threats. In many cases these threats cannot be readily distinguished as either Article 5 or Article 4 threats.

One of the threats NATO faces today concerns destabilization of its southern borders and forces. For example, Turkey's borders are directly threatened by rogue states to its south. NATO has a credible plan to reinforce Turkey in the event of hostilities. Unfortunately, this plan relies heavily on U.S. forces. If the U.S. were unable to provide the military apparatus necessary to implement this plan because of its involvement in operations elsewhere, the reinforcement blueprint would be in jeopardy. European forces simply lack serious power projection capabilities for demanding Article 5 missions, in addition to the potential for meeting Article 4 contingencies.

We must maintain and improve NATO's military force capability to respond to all conceivable missions. Our goal must be to enlarge NATO not simply quantitatively but also by enhancing NATO's strategic strength and military effectiveness. The need for improved European power projection capability becomes self-evident when one considers that the U.S. currently contributes only about one-fifth of NATO's total conventional forces, but provides the vast majority of NATO's usable military capability for power projection missions.

We must reconfigure NATO to deal with the threats of the 21st century by requiring improved allied power projection forces for operating in a seamless web of situations including within NATO's enlarging borders, inside Europe including on its periphery, and outside Europe when the Alliance's vital interests are at stake.

All future U.S. administrations must demand rough trans-Atlantic parity in power projection capabilities and we must not settle for less. NATO is the only institution capable of building these necessary force structures. We must continue to press our European allies on these issues and call for a more equitable burden-sharing arrangement in power projection capabilities.

The Alliance must also revise NATO's Strategic Concept and military structure to make NATO both more politically and militarily relevant to post–Cold War security issues. We must ensure that NATO continues to meet the security needs of all of its members states, including the United States. That should be our primary objective.

THE ROLE OF THE EUROPEAN UNION

Central and Eastern Europe are important to the economic future of the United States and Europe. Although it remains small as a percentage of the European economy, it is arguably the continent's most vibrant region. I believe the United States should encourage its European colleagues to expedite the membership of the new allies within the European Union (EU). Equally, if not more important, the United States should urge the EU, in the strongest possible terms, to consider on their merits the membership requests of key European countries who were not among the first new members of the NATO alliance.

Recognizing that EU membership depends on a process of political and economic integration, the EU should nevertheless hasten the development of trade and investment networks that will strengthen the new democracies and contribute to stability before new applications for NATO membership are considered.

If our common interest is to help our economies benefit from growth in Central and Eastern Europe, then an indispensable part of our strategy must involve questions of security. The EU is an important part of the transatlantic security equation, but America's strong relations with Europe could not have evolved over the past 50 years without the NATO Alliance. Just as the Alliance produced a half-century of peace in Western Europe, an enlarged NATO can spread this peace across the entire continent.

During Senate debate some proposed that NATO enlargement be tied to the expansion of the EU. EU enlargement is highly desirable in its own right, but must not be a condition to NATO membership. It would restrict a Transatlantic Alliance led by the U.S. to the political exigencies of a strictly European organization.

The transfer of security decision-making power to an institution that was unable to develop a common security policy and failed to stop the fighting in the former Yugoslavia would not bode well for the future of European security.

Finally, subordinating NATO to the EU in this manner would make the Alliance not a cornerstone of European security, but an appendage. The role of the U.S., Canada, and Turkey, none of whom are members of the EU, would be significantly diminished in the enlargement process. This potential "back-door" approach to enlargement is fraught with dangers; I prefer the "front-door," the "open-door."

KOSOVO

This past spring, NATO launched offensive military operations for the first time in its history. The potential for conflict in Kosovo had been discussed by observers of the region for years. Despite the pattern of Milosevic's aggression in Slovenia, Croatia, and Bosnia, there was insufficient attention to the powder keg in Kosovo until we reached the crisis stage.

For years the administration and NATO gave insufficient attention to the root cause of the problem in the Balkans—the lack of democracy in Yugoslavia and the presence of a regime with a history of aggression. Rather than depending on uncertain negotiations to patch together a problematic and fragile diplomatic solution, the United States and NATO should have been working much earlier to support democratic forces in Serbia.

President Clinton commenced the war to prevent, or at least deter, the Serbs from using ethnic cleansing to drive the Albanians from Kosovo. The president hoped that subsequently Kosovo could be secured as an autonomous region of Serbia. Within the first few days of Operation "Allied Force," the world witnessed the failure of the first objective. Whether the second objective is possible over the long run given the continued leadership of President Milosevic and other convicted war criminals is subject to severe doubt.

Our objective might have been the end of the Milosevic regime, a democratic Serbia, and an interim government for Kosovo and Serbia administered by NATO nations with a clear chain of command.

In each of the four Congressional meetings I attended where the president was present, I asked: "What if NATO's bombing plan doesn't work even for your limited objectives? What is "plan B"? I pushed the point, along with other lawmakers, that he must prepare alternatives. Military history demonstrates clearly that battles rarely proceed as they are drawn up on paper. Indeed, this one would be no exception.

Milosevic did not back down when the initial NATO bombs began to fall as the administration had hoped. He declared that his objective was the removal of ethnic Albanians and the establishment of a Serbian Kosovo. His troops used terror to expel the majority of Albanian Kosovars, while destroying their houses, confiscating their bank accounts, and seizing or invalidating their identification papers. The Serb forces randomly massacred large groups of Kosovars. A week into the fighting, Milosevic forces had achieved his basic objectives of expelling most of the Albanians and establishing Serbian control of the province.

Meanwhile, Europe had an enormous refugee problem on its hands. At least 850,000 Kosovars were housed in camps in Macedonia, Albania, and other countries. The refugees represented not only a huge expense, but also a potential source of instability for the countries keeping them. The United States and NATO were left to deal with these problems through hasty improvisation.

Being a member of the NATO Alliance does bring certain limitations in exchange for the benefits of additional resources, manpower, and moral credibility. The dynamics of the NATO operation, for example, required the assent of all 19 members for specific military actions. With 19 countries publicly debating the bombing target-by-target, surprise was impossible.

But the United States must recognize that it is more than just another member of the Alliance. We are the leader of NATO, and as such, we must exercise effective persuasion to protect our own interests. Both during previous diplomatic efforts regarding Bosnia and during the Kosovo operation, the Clinton administration has been prone to use alliance disagreement to avoid hard decisions. One of the reasons that President Clinton gave for not even planning for the use of ground forces was that some members of the NATO alliance strenuously objected to ground troops.

But this type of justification usually begs the question. The United States, as the alliance leader, must present a strong and coherent case backed by the weight of American diplomatic and military power to the other members for the action that needs to be taken. In most cases, Alliance members welcome resolute leadership from the United States.

Many members of Congress have worried that Kosovo is a distraction from more fundamental foreign policy concerns and that we should be reserving our military strength for other potential conflicts. Undoubtedly, any decision to use military force must take into account the wider context of our global commitments. But the fact is, in Kosovo, we engaged in the largest war we have had since 1991. The Clinton Administration may have stumbled into the war without a detailed plan, but once engaged, we had to win it.

The Iraqis, the North Koreans, and many others around the world who might challenge us on a regional basis have watched our resolve in Kosovo very carefully. Failing to win the war would provide encouragement for other adventures by those who are a threat to our interests. Winning the war would reinforce for despots around the globe the risks of challenging the United States.

In addition, the credibility and very existence of NATO would be thrown into doubt by a defeat in Kosovo. The first test of NATO's ability to fight an actual war might be its last attempt. For NATO to turn its back on ethnic cleansing on a massive scale in Europe would invalidate the alliance. This is our most important and successful alliance, and one that has maintained stability in Europe for a half-century. We should not forget that two devastating world wars began in Europe. The strength and cohesion of NATO is a fundamental component of preventing conflict in Europe in the future.

NATO: LESSONS LEARNED FROM KOSOVO

One of the primary principles of attack taught at military schools is the use of overwhelming force. NATO's battle plan violated this principle from the outset. Overwhelming force was publicly rejected when the operation began. President Clinton with full forethought gave a speech on the first night of the bombing explaining that we would not use ground troops. He repeated this pledge again and again, and when he was pressed, he rejected even planning for the use of ground troops. These pledges relieved Milosevic from concern that he might face a NATO ground force that would win the war and threaten the existence of his regime.

NATO and the United States thus had limited themselves to exactly the type of strategy that military leaders and historians counsel against. Our battle plan was designed to force concessions through punishment, rather than to achieve objectives by using all military means at our disposal. As in Vietnam, we were seeking to find the "threshold of pain" of our enemy.

The Clinton Administration's strategy expected that NATO bombing would quickly unnerve the Serbian leadership and force them to agree to NATO's terms. This was an unjustifiable leap of faith. Indeed, Milosevic had a different strategy. He moved 40,000 of his best forces to the borders of Kosovo with the intent of ejecting by force the ethnic Albanian majority in Kosovo.

Essentially, this left the success of *our* military operations in the hands of the Serb leadership. Milosevic knew that with no ground forces being contemplated, he could wage a ground campaign in Kosovo with impunity until he saw it in his own interest to negotiate.

This principle is particularly important because democracies and alliances do not have an appetite for open-ended war, even one as limited as the air war in the Balkans. We worry about the expense of war, the potential for casualties, and deployments that take our troops away from their loved ones. We also react with aversion to civilian deaths among our enemy's population. These reactions all are evidence of the strength of our moral society, and none of us would wish for a more ruthless national conscience. But we must have a clear idea of their implications for how we make war. In most protracted conflicts waged on a limited basis, the terms of negotiations will shift against democracies as the war proceeds.

The war surrounding Kosovo presented the incredible irony of two wars occurring simultaneously over the same object but rarely intersecting. NATO's war took place mostly over Serbia where bombs were dropped on petroleum depots, military headquarters, bridges, rail lines, and communication centers. Meanwhile Milosevic's troops were fighting a ground war in Kosovo that in its decisive stages was not deterred or slowed by the NATO air attacks. In early May Milosevic welcomed back his victorious generals from Kosovo, who told him that the war was won!

It was no accident that a more compliant negotiating stance on the part of Milosevic followed a Kosovar Liberation Army offensive that drew Serb forces into the open and subjected them to heavy losses from allied sorties. In other words, movement came after the two wars finally began to intersect and the force being applied had a direct impact on the main instrument of Milosevic's power.

KOSOVO: AFTER "ALLIED FORCE"

With American troops in Kosovo, the U.S. government must ensure that those troops have everything they need to defend themselves and carry out their mission. They should not be restrained by unreasonable terms of engagement that place them at risk.

U.S. troops in Kosovo represent about one-eighth of the NATO peacekeeping force. It is important that the Clinton Administration work hard to ensure that our NATO partners continue to provide the dominant share of troops, refugee assistance, and other expenses arising from NATO's involvement.

The NATO operation in Kosovo should aim to bolster the larger goal of stabilizing the region. Our own interests will be damaged if the Balkans continues to be an unstable powder keg that periodically explodes in violence. The United States should take a longer view and support democratic forces in Serbia that could result in the integration of that country under a new government in Europe.

Along with seven other senators, I wrote to President Clinton in December 1998 urging him to shift focus to a policy of replacing the Milosevic regime with a democratic government committed to the rule of law. We said "Until Milosevic leaves power, he will be able, and willing, to reignite the Bosnian war (with possibly serious consequences for U.S. personnel deployed there), unleash renewed repression in Kosovo, or generate new crises as his needs require. We should not let our understandable concern about managing the crisis of the day outweigh the priority of removing the source of the crisis."

In pursuit of this objective, I am a co-sponsor of the Serbia Democratization Act. It would make the removal of the Milosevic regime and the transformation of Serbia to a democracy a U.S. policy objective, and it would authorize additional economic, diplomatic and informational steps in pursuit of this objective.

The Western alliance's commitment to achieving democracy in Yugoslavia in the aftermath of war must be as strong as the resolve exhibited during the bombing campaign. NATO forces expelled Serbian troops from Kosovo at great expense and loss of life. We must not now lose the opportunity to bring stability and democracy to the Balkans simply because we lack the attention span or the imagination to finish the job.

Democracy-building in Serbia is not a purely altruistic exercise. Without a democratically elected government in Belgrade that is supportive of peace, protective of individual freedoms, and anxious for the economic benefits of European citizenship, American troops could remain for many years in Kosovo and Bosnia. In addition, the United States will almost surely be called upon to expend financial and human resources again to help resolve new Balkan crises.

Despite the media's focus on wars, breakthrough negotiations, or dramatic ultimatums, most foreign policy campaigns are won and lost with mundane and painstaking work before and after crises occur. The Western alliance can win the next Balkan war right now at very small expense by committing itself to Serbian democratization.

American support for the democratic opposition has been minimal because our government gave priority to securing Milosevic's cooperation in solving the most recent crisis, which he had manufactured. Keeping our distance from the opposition was a price we paid for that collaboration. That left Milosevic free to plan the next crisis and free to close down the media, shut out the students, and intimidate the democratic opposition. Even as we advocated democracy, market principles, an independent media, human rights, and the rule of law, our own policies toward the Yugoslav government perversely undercut progress in these areas.

Apart from the "dump Milosevic" theme, the opposition is fragmented and lacks a coherent message. But, it also lacks resources and firm support by the United States and the West. We should try to provide basic operating tools such as fax machines, telephones, gasoline, office space, and office supplies. We should increase radio and television broadcasts to bring objective news coverage to the Serbian people through the Voice of America, Radio Free Europe, and other international news programs. We should seek ways to strengthen the independent media as an antidote to state-run news sources that have facilitated the regime's disinformation. And we should make clear that substantial economic benefits from the West would follow a genuine embrace of democracy in Serbia.

Our assistance should be targeted to: (1) the Alliance for Change, the most promising pro-democracy group; (2) elected municipal leaders who oppose Milosevic; (3) the rural areas, where Milosevic opposition is high; (4) the beleaguered independent media; (5) students groups; (6) trade unions; and (7) other groups committed to democratic change. We should encourage the democratic opposition to create a common resource center through which foreign contributions could be channeled and prioritized.

The administration recently lifted legal restrictions on support for the Serbian opposition groups. The president announced in Sarajevo that $10 million will be available for democracy promotion in Yugoslavia. These funds are welcome, but long overdue. The sluggish government grant-making process could delay these funds for several months. That may be too late.

This is why the work of non-governmental organizations (NGOs), particularly the National Endowment for Democracy (NED) is so important. The NED and other NGOs can gain access to grass roots leaders that government officials cannot easily obtain. They can respond far more quickly, often more effectively, and at less expense than government agencies.

The NED and each of its four core groups have been the most actively engaged NGOs in Yugoslavia: the Republican and Democratic party institutions have been assisting the opposition parties and movements for years; the "Solidarity Center," which is affiliated with the AFL-CIO, has helped to keep trade unions a viable force; and the Center for International Private Enterprise has aided the embryonic private sector. NED, itself, has provided support for the struggling independent media, judicial reform, civil education, and the student movement.

The NED group should immediately implement projects that were suspended during the bombing campaign, use unexpended democracy funds now in the pipeline, and devise new projects that can be implemented quickly. Meanwhile, the Agency for International Development and Department of State should relax time-consuming grant review and approval procedures. Incomplete aid proposals that arrive on time will help the democratic forces more than impeccably designed projects that arrive too late.

Having squandered a decade of opportunity for democracy-building in Serbia, we should not now expect instant gratification. But Serbia has never been more ripe for change. Even without an independent media, the Kosovo debacle has provided irrefutable evidence to large segments of the Serbian people that the Milosevic approach is bankrupt. A focused and immediate democracy-building campaign can prevent the next Balkan crisis and bring hope to this troubled part of the world.

CONCLUSION

NATO is truly a remarkable institution because its member nations have joined together to ensure that their ideals are protected by our collective moral and military strength. And during this 50th year of NATO, the strength of those ideals and our commitment to defend them collectively has been augmented by the Alliance's welcoming of Poland, Hungary, and the Czech Republic and their pledges to stand with us in the promotion and defense of those ideals.

The United States' Senate has advocated the importance of new members for NATO. Our study and debate on extension of membership resulted in an overwhelming affirmative vote only after sober understanding of its collective defense obligations. That debate also focused our attention on three goals for the future of NATO, even as we welcome new members and celebrate an historic half-century of Alliance achievement.

First, NATO's "open-door"policy toward new members as established by Article 10 of the Washington Treaty must be maintained. It has given countries of Central and Eastern Europe strong incentives to accelerate democratic reforms, to settle peacefully disputes with neighbors, and to increase regional cooperation. A closing of this door would result in new dividing lines in Europe. We are hopeful that NATO will provide additional incentives to continue constructive reforms by maintaining strong relations with applicant countries through the Partnership for Peace and conducting reviews of their progress to meet NATO requirements.

Second, although NATO was organized and oriented to respond to an attack from the East, the current threats to NATO come from weapons of mass destruction, terrorism, hostile activities of rogue states, and ethnic strife. The essential core of NATO has been collective defense, but the treaty provides NATO with the ability to act elsewhere if the security of any of its members is threatened. This is not a new NATO responsibility, such activity is supported in the language of the Washington Treaty ratified by the United States Senate in 1949. Participation in these types of missions is not obligatory and has always rested upon the independent decisions of its members.

Third, many United States senators believe that our NATO allies have good reason to improve their capabilities to respond to newly emerging threats that face all of us on both sides of the Atlantic. NATO forces as a whole must be readied to face the newly emerging threats facing our nations. Many in Congress believe that rough parity between the United States and European forces in the ability to project power and sustain these types of operations is a reasonable goal to be affirmed at this Summit. This Alliance must move forward to meet these new threats and admit new members, or it will surely regress to the point where contending nationalisms spark a return to old divisions

We are mindful that NATO has placed much of its future at stake in Kosovo. A large majority of our body affirms that the Alliance must be preserved and that it must be victorious. History will record the strength of our bonds at this crucial moment for our Alliance and the vision we express for the future of NATO even during this time of our greatest test.

DEFINING THE NEW WORLD ORDER

Lawrence Korb
Vice President, Council on Foreign Relations
New York, New York

Let me begin by saying that before we look at security in what has become known as the post–Cold War world, we—the United States and Europe—made a very big mistake at the end of the Cold War by not celebrating the end of the war in the same manner that we marked the end of World War II. Because there were no shots fired, it did not seem appropriate to celebrate. But as you talk to people, on both sides of the Atlantic, there is no real sense of closure. Many people in the United States still compare what we do now in defense to the days of the Cold War because in many ways there was no clear break between the Cold War and this new era. Some see the situation in Bosnia and Kosova as a continuation of the conflicts we had in the Cold War, like Korea. They are markedly different. Without this sense of closure, the current security situation is more confusing than it needs to be.

The first problem that we have in the security field is trying to define this "new world order," as former President Bush called it, because it is different from anything we have ever seen, particularly since the creation of the nation-state. For this first time we don't have a superpower rivalry, and without a nation or a group of nations trying to upset the international balance, it becomes very hard to engage the people in democracies to be very concerned about what's going on in the international arena.

For example, during our last presidential election, in the final debate between Senator Dole and President Clinton there were no questions asked on foreign policy. Finally, in frustration as the debate was about to end, the moderator said, "doesn't anyone have a question about foreign policy?" This young man got up and he asked a question about our trade relations with Japan. This lack of interest can be attributed, at least in the United States, to the lack of a superpower rivalry.

The second characteristic of the new era is that economic power is becoming ever more important and certainly increasing relative to military power. During the Cold War, world leaders focussed on military alliances like NATO, CETO, SENTO and ANZUS. Now it is NAFTA, GATT, APEC—all of these economic groupings. I think it is no accident that one of the reasons President Yeltsin accommodated himself to the expansion of NATO was that he wanted membership in the G7. I think he recognized that, in the post–Cold War world, economic influence is becoming more important than military.

The third characteristic is that wealth is moving to Asia. This has tremendous consequences on both sides of the Atlantic. In the U.S. when we focus on security, it has always been centered in this part of the world. When the United States got involved in Korea, General MacArthur wanted many more forces to deal first with the North Koreans and then the Chinese invaders. General Bradley, then the chair of the Joint Chiefs of Staff, said Korea was the wrong war at the wrong time in the wrong place. In his view and that of President Truman, U.S. interests were centered in this part of the world. Today, you cannot ignore Asia because of the tremendous economic strength in that part of the world. How we deal with the changing dynamics in Asia will have consequences for security and stability, on both sides of the Atlantic.

Finally, the nation-state, the bedrock of international politics for centuries, is changing in several contradictory ways. On the one hand, especially here in Europe, nations are giving powers or sovereignty to the European Union. The big question on people's mind is the common currency and the need to reduce unemployment. Even in our country, with NAFTA and GATT, the United States has given up some of its sovereignty to international bodies like the WTO. This has led to tremendous reaction in the United States. Boutros-Ghali, the former Secretary General of the United Nations, was the least popular person in the U.S. in 1996. It was no accident that President Clinton decided to jettison him during the 1996 campaign because of the concern in the United States over this loss of sovereignty.

At the same time that we're creating these supranational organizations, we're witnessing a tremendous proliferation of nation-states. Since the end of the Cold War, there have been some 25 new states created and nobody knows exactly where the proliferation of new smaller states will stop. Simultaneously, we have witnessed the emergence of transnational groups, like organized crime or terrorists, that are not responsible to any nation or supranational body.

WHO IS THE ENEMY?

In any discussion of security in this new era, the main issue is just who or what is the enemy? I would argue that communism has been replaced by chaos as the real enemy. President Bush's phrase, the "New World Order," certainly captured what we're trying to accomplish—that is, to maintain order into the international environment. But the notion of chaos—and not a distinct ideology—as the enemy is a complex notion, and it is a much more difficult concept to sell to populations.

When General Powell was designing the armed forces of the United States in this new era, he felt that unless the U.S. had specific enemies, the Congress and the American people would not spend very much money on defense. So he made up the six so-called "rogue" states of Iran, Iraq, Syria, Libya, North Korea, and Cuba. They became the enemies against which the United States built its forces. Nonetheless, if you take a look at the *actions* that the United States and the Europeans have taken in the security arena, these are actions to prevent chaos in the international system. The NATO interventions in Bosnia and Kosovo are perfect examples.

If you are trying to prevent chaos, you need to establish rules of international behavior to prevent this chaos from emerging. I think we're beginning to see a number of rules that we would like to see followed as we come into the new millennium. First of all, we expect nations to have a decent respect for human rights, and particularly for the rights of minorities within their populations. I think this was the big mistake that was made when Yugoslavia initially broke up. Before recognizing the component parts, the U.S. and Europe should have received some assurances that the rights of minorities in those various subunits of the former Yugoslavia would be safeguarded. Without that protection, the world ended up giving some groups the *caucus belli* that they were looking for.

Second, you still want to maintain respect for international borders. The first war of the post–Cold War world was the Persian Gulf War against Iraq because Saddam had blatantly violated the border of another member state of the United Nations.

Third, we expect nations to adhere to international conventions, particularly as they pertain to weapons of mass destruction. I have no idea why North Korea signed the nuclear Non-Proliferation Treaty (NPT), but I am glad that they did—because it gave the U.S. and the world legitimacy to take action when North Korea began to develop nuclear weapons. One of the great achievements of the past few years was the indefinite extension of the Non-Proliferation Treaty and the signing of the chemical weapons convention.

Fourth, economic aid and the economic advantages of the international system should be denied to those who violate any of the rules, whether it is aid from any of the international institutions, like the IMF or the World Bank, or just openness to markets. In the United States, we use the most favored nation status as a way to influence behavior of particular nations.

The fifth rule of the new order is that if military operations are necessary, they should not be undertaken without UN authorization. Although this rule was not honored in the Kosovo action by NATO, I think one of the smartest things that Secretary of State Baker did as we were getting ready to take on Saddam in the Gulf was not to allow American naval vessels to intercept ships bound for Iraq until the UN had actually authorized action. The world wants to establish this particular precedent, particularly if Russia should decide to intervene in what it calls the "near abroad."

Sixth, military operations should be multinational in character as they were in Bosnia, Kosovo, Albania, and in the Gulf. Multinational UN operations would be facilitated if an international peacekeeping force were created. Secretary Christopher had a good idea when he proposed creating a West African peacekeeping force under the aegis of the United Nations. The Danes have put forward some very good proposals in this area. The great powers cannot get involved in every ethnic conflict. Our populations would not tolerate it. But preventing disorder in the international system requires having a ready, military force in the background.

Two other developments in the international system are worth mentioning here. First is the move toward professional militaries. I was here in France a couple of years ago to testify before the National Assembly as the French began their steps to move toward a professional military. In this new world order, professional militaries offer tremendous advantages over conscripts because they can be sent into these very ambiguous situations where a clearly defined enemy does not exist.

Second, in Europe and the U.S., the elites are not engaging the publics in foreign policy debates. Jim Hoagland of the *Washington Post* has written very trenchantly how the foreign policy elite gathered in Paris and in Madrid to expand NATO without having engaged the publics. The idea of NATO expansion is something that the elites have set up between themselves and then presented the publics with as a *fait accompli*. In fact, that is one of the arguments that carried the day for NATO expansion—that is, "it may not be a good idea, but we've gone too far down the line for the public to oppose it now." As Tom Freidman pointed out in the *New York Times*, our populations are being taken hostage. It does not have to be that way. The public has to be engaged now more than ever. Paradoxically, the foreign policy elites did not need to engage them as much in the Cold War because the people understood exactly what the stakes were. Now they do not.

In addition to codifying these rules of international behavior, the United States and Europe have the tremendous challenge of incorporating China and

Russia into this new world order peacefully. In order to bring a rising Asian power into the world order in the 20th century, a war with Japan was necessary. It is challenging because many Asian counties do not have the same concept of the nation-state and international law as do the United States and Europe. The United States and Europe have to work together, particularly with China. If China knows they can play the U.S. and Europe off against the other, as they do with Boeing and Airbus, we'll all lose in the end. Similarly with Russia, we must get them to accept NATO expansion without antagonizing them. As we saw during the Kosovo intervention, the Russians are still upset about NATO's addition of Poland, Hungary, and the Czech Republic.

Another challenge for the United States and Europe is Turkey. The Turkish model of separation of church and state in an Islamic country is really the model that the world needs. A strong Turkey will be the key to peace and stability both in the Middle East and in North Africa. The European Union appears to continually raise the bar for Turkey to be admitted each year. If this continues, there could be a tremendous backlash in Turkey.

Finally, the United States and Europe need to share the burden of security more equitably than we do now. This is not 50 years ago when the United States, with 40 percent of the world's GDP, could, in fact, underwrite the security for its allies. Europe must begin to develop projection forces. The large, cumbersome land armies of Europe are simply not appropriate to the new world order. The U.S. and European militaries are much more likely to be involved in the Bosnias, the Persian Gulfs, and the Caucuses, than in responding to a massive land attack.

The U.S. made a terrible mistake in not taking the French up on their offer to rejoin the military arm of NATO, if Europe were given the responsibility for the Southern Command of NATO ("Cinc South"). The United States should have said that if the Europeans want to take control of the Southern Command, they should put naval forces into the Mediterranean. When the Europeans have sufficient forces, they could run the commands. Then the U.S. can take its carriers and the rest of the 6th fleet and move it to the Gulf or the Pacific. We should not have immediately rejected the idea.

It is time for Europe to begin to assume more control over its own destiny. I am concerned that when continued NATO expansion hits the floor of the U.S. Senate, and somebody adds up what the U.S. spends on defense compared with the other 15 nations in NATO, they will find a $100 billion difference. People are going to say that is not an equitable way to handle security. It is time for the Western European Union to begin to take its rightful role. If the European Union, particularly with the common currency, becomes a true supranational organization, it is only appropriate that it begin to develop its own defense policies and be able to take military action on its own. It is therefore gratifying to see the EU now moving in the direction of a "Common Foreign and Security

Policy Identity," with the WEU playing a key role. The appointment of Javier Solana, former Secretary General of NATO, as the EU's first High Representative for a common foreign and security policy, is a major step forward for Europe. The U.S. now has a phone number to call to reach "Europe" on foreign and security policy issues. We will see if they follow up with the force realignments and defense expenditures needed to make a real contribution.

U.S./EUROPEAN SECURITY AGENDA IN THE NEW MILENNIUM*

Gilles Andréani
Ministry of Foreign Affairs
Paris, France

I hold a rather unusual position in the Ministry of Foreign Affairs. I am the Director of the Center of Analysis and Forecasting, which causes me to look beyond the short term, and I want to look at the questions before us from that perspective.

The first of these questions is: "Are the U.S. and Europe going to maintain common security interests in the next ten years or so?" In the past we had a common agenda; are we going to maintain it in the future? From the European point of view, if we look at the challenges that European security is facing, we find three series of subjects.

The first involves the instabilities linked to the transition process that our southern neighbors are going to experience. In the south-east of the Mediterranean this transition will bring the Arab-Muslim world into modernity, toward a market economy and democracy. All of this will be a very difficult transition, filled with many conflicts and tensions, including the Arab-Israeli conflict. Those are among the top challenges that directly affect the security of a country such as France.

The second order of challenges is the incorporation of our eastern European neighbors, including Russia, into the European and Western security structures:

**translation by Daria M. Roche*

a long-term effort of stabilization of central and eastern Europe and of Russia, with several points of tension in a complicated landscape that pose problems for Europeans. The first is the Balkans. We have seen the developments in Bosnia Herzegovina and in Albania. There is also the Caucasus. There are, in addition, certain tensions between neighboring democracies of eastern Europe, that have fortunately been settled or are being settled.

The third series of challenges for European security are, in no particular order, global issues such as non-proliferation, terrorism, and organized crime, as well as crises that could happen elsewhere, outside the immediate geographical area of Europe, but that affect Europe's interests. This can occur in Africa. This can also occur in Asia where Europeans have interests. This is a list of the tensions, the risks with which we might be confronting at the dawn of the next century.

Are these subjects enough to form a common agenda between the U.S. and Europe, comparable to the defense of the Alliance in front of the Soviet threat for nearly 50 years? I would say "yes and no."

Yes, because, indisputably, we have parallel interests in all of these matters, practically identical interests. We have interests in the success of the peace process in the Middle East. We have interests in settling the problems in the Caucasus. We have an interest in fighting against terrorism and proliferation. Thus, we have a mass of common interests that will form an area of understanding and cooperation for a long time between the U.S. and Europe.

However, this is going to be a case-by-case agenda. We must now define a common strategy and common actions in each individual case. This could proceed well. It could proceed from time to time with differing opinions, as to be expected. Our problem is to decide what the political, institutional, and military conditions must be, of a relationship between Europe and the U.S. that allows us to agree as much as possible each time on what we should do to address the security problems that we will face in the next century.

What should we do in order to meet this objective? In this respect, there are things that Europe must do and things that the U.S. must do, and things that NATO must do. So let us take these three in order.

The Europeans have not remained inactive when faced with these challenges. If I take the first one that I mentioned, that is, the transition of countries south and east of the Mediterranean—economic, demographic, and political transitions that these countries are experiencing, transitions that are extremely tense—the Europeans have already responded with a long-term stabilization process. I am thinking primarily of what we have called the "Barcelona process," which basically consists of three issues: of setting a goal of freeing up trade between these countries and Europe, in bringing them significant economic assistance, and in developing a political dialogue with them.

In eastern Europe, the EU has already developed a strategy of expansion for the EU and developed a working partnership with Russia.

In matters of non-proliferation, there are both individual actions of the member states and collective actions within the EU. It has adopted several measures of export control that are among the most rigorous in the world. There is a well-developed anti-terrorist and police cooperation between European countries, and so on.

As Europe is developing a common foreign and security policy, it is trying to ensure that this common foreign and security policy can resort to military means, if it becomes necessary one day. And this can occur in several ways. The problem with that, however, is that for several years, basically since the Maastricht Treaty, the debate has been much more polarized on the institutional questions than on the fundamental questions. In addition, we are momentarily forced to respond to the types of challenges that I have mentioned (in other words, move from a draft army that focusses on collective defense to a projection army whose objective is to allow for the quick dispatching of significant forces out-of-area). We are also trying to develop our own European capabilities, that would allow Europeans to act jointly in certain circumstances. This has been the case with EUROCORPS, and it has been the case with two forces developed with Italy and Spain, called EUROFOR and EUROMARFOR. Have the Europeans done enough in this area? Certainly not.

As far as politics are concerned, I think that we have also made progress. The Europeans are becoming more capable and determined to act than they have in the past. After all, they were involved for three years in the former Yugoslavia on their own , and then under the aegis of NATO (Germany joined them, which was an important new step). Several weeks ago, you witnessed the Europeans, under the direction of Italy, begin a humanitarian aid project in Albania, that helped contain the disorder and dissolution of the Albanian state.

There are things that the Europeans can do. It is clear, however, that they will not be able to do everything, and that some of these problems are beyond their scope and can only be reasonably resolved with the help of the Americans.

This is where I get into the second aspect: "What can the U.S. do?" They must become convinced of two things. The first is that Europe needs them, but also that they need Europe. The U.S. needs a more responsible Europe—one that tries to develop stabilization strategies for its immediate regional environment and that can field more capable and more mobile armed forces. They need this because, if we look at the security challenges in the next century, it is clear that the U.S. has interests in finding one or several global partners capable of helping them resolve global problems. And yet there are not many such partners available for the U.S. And if the Europeans succeed in developing both their military tools and the common willingness to act, they will become the type of global partner that the U.S. needs. I do not think that this global partner can be

Japan, China, or South America. It can only be Europe. The Americans should, hopefully, be convinced that there is reciprocal relationship here; not only do the Europeans need an American presence (and need the Americans to continue to help them settle certain problems that are not clearly within their reach), but also that the Americans can and must count on the Europeans.

What does all of this mean for NATO? General Montgomery has discussed elsewhere in a very detailed manner NATO's current reform, and I do not want to dwell on this. I would just like to say one word on our political perspective when we think of NATO.

NATO has already changed significantly and is going to change even more. As I already said, formerly NATO had to face a predetermined threat in response to which it could allow itself of advance military measures. Those of command knew who was going to intervene in any given crisis. If NATO wants to survive into the next century, it must face a much greater challenge: that of defining the mechanisms that will allow it, in each case, to gather a coalition of countries willing to act, to organize them, and to send them where they are needed. This is much more difficult in miliatry terms. It is also more difficult politically.

As for the military aspect, General Montgomery explains how the NATO reform would allow us to develop more flexible forces, ones that would be capable of functioning in a variable geometry, with equally flexible command structures. All of that is just fine, I do not need to emphasize that.

What about the political aspect? What is the condition that will allow us in each individual case to find a political agreement between Europeans and Americans and act accordingly? For three years in the former Yugoslavia, the Europeans were alone. The U.S. disagreed with their policy, and I must say, they publicly disagreed. This is one thing which we must not allow to re-occur. In other words, in order for everything that General Montgomery describes to work, we need to develop, within NATO, political mechanisms that allow for Americans and Europeans to be able to develop a common policy in a given crisis.

I do not want to be pessimistic, but this will be very difficult to accomplish. It is the French objective. It is an objective shared by all Europeans, but it will be difficult because each of our countries is to look more closely at domestic issues and to be less available for foreign actions. It will be more and more difficult to mobilize the opinions and the political leaders of all of our countries toward exterior actions. And once they have done so, it will be even more difficult, I would say, to arrive at common purpose among ourselves.

The political condition which must allow us to arrive at this result depends largely on the capacity of Europeans to be organized on a political level. A Europe that is fragmented, divided entity hesitant to act, is a bad political partner for the U.S. It is in the event that the Europeans succeed in forming a collective point of view that they can coherently present to the U.S. a dialogue and arrive at a truly symbiotic partnership. I think that this is the vision toward which we must aim, one of a more balanced NATO in which Europeans are less fragmented but speak more with one voice in order to reach common positions with the U.S.

I am not going to go any further in my presentation except to say that we have reached a turning point. But from the perspective of the development of European politics, of the reform of the tools of European defense, of the reform of NATO, it is essential that we reach a common understanding about what our alliance can be, and what our security relationship can be in the next century. If this does not occur, I believe that the hypothesis of America and Europe going off in separate directions is not at all impossible.

NATO IN TRANSITION

Lt. General Thomas M. Montgomery
U.S. Military Representative to the NATO Military Committee (1994–1998)
Brussels, Belgium

In 1997, NATO formally established a historic new relationship with Russia with the signing of the Founding Act on mutual relations, cooperation, and security between NATO and the Russian Federation. It recognizes the necessity of nurturing a special relationship with Russia and establishes a viable mechanism for consultation, coordination, and, to the maximum extent possible, joint decision-making and joint action on common security issues. One feature of this act is a permanent Joint Council. The permanent Joint Council is the principle venue of consultation between NATO and Russia in times of crisis. Just as importantly, this council meets regularly at various levels to discuss all aspects of security issues facing both of the parties. This routine pattern of consultation is built on the principles of transparency and reciprocity. It offers the potential for NATO and Russia to establish a more normal working relationship similar, in fact, to those enjoyed by NATO allies.

The military plays a significant role in this new structure. Under the auspices of this council, the Chiefs of Defense Staff meet at least twice a year and Military Representatives meet monthly. NATO-Russian military to military activities which, until 1997, had been largely dormant, have substantially expanded and will include more practical cooperation at all levels.

Among the numerous areas of cooperation, NATO and Russia have pledged to participate in joint military operations, including peacekeeping operations under the authority of the United Nations or the OSCE. More significantly, if

NATO chooses to employ Combined Joint Task Forces (one of the other new initiatives in NATO) in operations, Russia will participate in them on a case-by-case basis at an early stage.

The Russian Federation has opened a mission in Brussels that also includes a military delegation. NATO followed suit with an information office and a military liaison office in Moscow. Russia has also been invited to establish military liaison missions at NATO's strategic commands at Mons and in Norfolk. All of this is both unique and unprecedented in NATO's history. It clearly demonstrates NATO's transformation and its entirely new approach to its former adversary.

In turn, I believe that this approach will set the right tone for increased security cooperation among all of our European nations. In fact, a substantial contribution to the future of European security cooperation is already ongoing through the successful Partnership for Peace Program (PFP). With the establishment of a Euro-Atlantic Partnership Council and the enhancement of an already robust Partnership for Peace Program, the 27 partner nations will have even more opportunities for forging a closer political and security relationship with the Alliance as a whole as well as with individual Allies.

Some critics have described the enhancement of PFP as merely a consolation prize for those nations not invited to join NATO. This narrow view masks what is a very significant advancement in European security cooperation. Quite simply, Partners are involved in the day-to-day activities of the Alliance to a degree that could not have been previously envisioned. Indeed the Euro-Atlantic Partnership Council, developed in 1997 in full cooperation with Partner representatives, combines the positive political aspects of the North Atlantic Cooperation Council, the old NACC, with the operational experience of Partnership for Peace in a single new cooperative and transparent mechanism in which allies and partners are able to fully address the political and security challenges of the future. The expanded dimension of political consultation offered in this new forum will cover a wide range of issues that warrant greater cooperation between Allies and Partners such as crisis management, defense strategy, defense planning and budgeting, and the counter-proliferation of weapons of mass destruction.

As the U.S. Representative to NATO's Military Committee, I'm pleased to say that the Military Committee developed three bold steps designed to bring Partner nations inside NATO's fences. The most important of these is the establishment of the Partnership for Peace Staff Elements. Partner nations assign their officers to various NATO headquarters where they sit side by side with their NATO counterparts to do the daily routine staff work that is required to plan and to execute Partnership for Peace exercises and operations.

Additionally, we have committed ourselves to examining how these Partnership for Peace Staff Elements could contribute to the work of Combined

Joint Task Forces (CJTF) as we further develop that concept. The significance of this, yet another unprecedented NATO initiative, should not be underestimated. As one Partner officer skeptically remarked when he was first informed of this initiative, "Is NATO really going to let us do this?" The answer is a firm "yes" because former adversaries working together on joint military operations inside a NATO headquarters will go a long way to reverse 50 years of enmity, mistrust, and misunderstanding.

Second, Partner nations have assigned senior military representatives to NATO headquarters, where they regularly meet with the Military Committee to fully participate in the Partnership for Peace process. At a minimum, Partners are included in PFP consultations that aim to reach a common understanding before the Military Committee makes a decision. More importantly, Partners participate in joint PFP decision-making with the Military Committee whenever appropriate and possible.

Third, the Military Committee concluded that the scope of NATO-PFP exercises must be expanded. The current intensity of the exercise program is at both NATO's and our Partner nations' resource limits. Therefore, our emphasis has switched from quantitative goals to qualitative goals whereby we reduce the number of actual member exercises, but we increase the quality of them and the complexity and the sophistication. One might ask how much impact can NATO-PFP exercises have on overall European security. The answer, I think, is plenty. Not only will future exercises be more challenging, but they will concentrate on employing new interoperability objectives that will offer Partners the opportunity to fully develop their capabilities to deploy and operate alongside NATO, using *NATO* doctrine and meeting *NATO* standards.

Another major NATO initiative was that of internal adaptation of NATO's structures. This kept us, I assure you, working through many a Brussels night.

I'd like to address two of the elements that have direct bearing on the future of European security: the new military command structure, and the European Security and Defense Identity (ESDI). The new command structure of NATO is a much more efficient organization and it will reduce the number of NATO military headquarters from 65 down to somewhere around 20. Allied Command Atlantic is comprised of five subordinate commands, including three regional commands and two combatant commands. The combatant commands are specialized—one is a submarine command and the other is a striking command that gives us CJTF capability. All of these commands report directly to the Supreme Allied Commander in the Atlantic in Norfolk.

The really tough work has been on the redesign of Allied Command Europe. It is clear now that the Allied Command Europe's second command level will likely be reduced from the current three regional commands to two regional commands—Allied Forces North headquartered in Brunsem in The Netherlands and Allied Forces South, which will maintain its present headquarters in Naples,

Italy. Allied Forces North will consist of one air component command, one naval command, and three joint sub-regional commands. These are new kinds of headquarters in the structure that in varying degrees, depending on where they are, will have a "joint capability" to organize and to conduct joint operations. All of the land forces will belong to these commands.

Allied Forces South will also have an air and a naval component command. What remains to be determined is the number and the location of joint sub-regional commands in the South. There are some difficulties right now and we are working them with both Turkey and with Spain.

I'm optimistic that the final piece, the design of the third subregions in the South, will soon be resolved. This new structure is intended to be leaner and more flexible to meet NATO's future military requirements, but it will be ready to accept the additional force contributions of new members as well. It will also be more capable of focusing on the increased emphasis on regional cooperation between selected Allies and Partners.

Another important issue is giving form to a "European Security Defense Identity" (ESDI), and thus strengthening the Western European Union. During the 1997 Madrid Summit, the Alliance welcomed the completion of work on the initial steps necessary to enable NATO to share NATO assets with the Western European Union for European-led operations. The United States fully supports this initiative, which will permit our European Allies to accept greater responsibility for leading and employing military force in a small-scale peace support operation in which NATO may not choose to participate.

Furthermore, an increase in European defense capabilities will provide at least two benefits. First, it will strengthen the overall military effectiveness of the Alliance, and second, a stronger European military capability will help convince the American taxpayer that we are not shouldering a disproportionate share of European security. This in turn will help, I think, ensure the enduring American commitment to Europe. European security is just as important to the United States as it was during the Cold War. It is, and I think will remain, an essential tenet of our foreign and defense policy. I cannot envision a time in the foreseeable future when this commitment will diminish. Therefore, I also have difficulty envisioning any major operation in which the United States would choose to remain on the sidelines, but I would remind you that the United States supports the development of a European Security Defense Identity, as long as it is developed in cooperation with NATO.

With shrinking defense budgets and rising weapons procurement costs, it makes no sense to develop a parallel military structure and capabilities. We understand Europe's desire to be a strategic partner rather than remaining strategically dependent on the United States. But the truth is that a separate strategic capability requires a solid political and financial commitment that Europe has been hesitant to assume. Until that commitment is made, NATO will continue to rely on the United States to provide some essential military assets. For example, I'm referring to strategic command, control and communication assets; intelligence gathering; strategic lift and logistical expertise. If the Western European Union is to assume more responsibility for even a modest size "Petersburg Operation," European Allies must commit themselves to increasing their contributions to NATO in these particular areas. Furthermore, the Western European Union must demonstrate that it can employ its own as well as NATO's shared resources and assets in an efficient and a credible manner.

Combined Joint Task Force is another major initiative that we have been working on, and it had been touted as a part of the solution to the strengthening of the Western European Union as well. Indeed CJTFs will be a critical element in the new NATO because they will enable us to respond quickly and flexibly to any of NATO's military missions. They will, however, not be cheap. A fully capable and deployable CJTF headquarters will require substantial investment in modern communications equipment necessary to command and control and direct a major NATO operation. CJTFs will be particularly helpful if the maintenance of European security requires the deployment of military force beyond NATO's borders for an out-of-area operation; understanding that CJTFs are being developed primarily to help NATO perform its own missions. CJTFs may indeed prove useful for WEU led operations. Particularly by providing a command and control structure. In this respect, as NATO develops CJTFs and the Western European Union enhances its capabilities, we must be careful not to create a bifurcation of NATO missions with the WEU having primacy for crisis response and the NATO responsible for collective defense. Such a bifurcation would be unhealthy for both organizations.

NATO has been working on grand ideas for the past few years. My advice for the foreseeable future is that NATO should properly digest the results of Paris, Madrid, and the subsequent addition of Poland, Hungary, and the Czech Republic to the Alliance, so that these grand ideas become grand actions. Enlargement itself will require substantial effort by both new members and by NATO to ensure that new members are prepared to assume the considerable responsibilities of membership.

From the military perspective this will be a challenge but it is one that I believe can be met. The Euro-Atlantic Partnership Council and the enhanced PFP offer tremendous opportunities to contribute to a more secure Europe. But they must be put to the test immediately, especially to allay the concerns of those countries who did not receive first-round invitations.

Let me conclude with a note of caution. It has been suggested that NATO's Strategic Concept will be re-examined in the near future. The essential ingredient of that concept, and of NATO's success, has been its commitment to collective defense of member nations. That's why the Alliance was founded. That's why the Alliance still exists. It is certainly why the nations of Central and

Eastern Europe yearn to join the Alliance. I have no doubt that Collective Defense will be preserved as the bedrock of Alliance policy in any update of our Strategic Concept, but I am a little concerned that, with the proliferation of new missions, the Alliance's emphasis and capability for collective defense might start to slowly erode. To be sure, the assumption of these new missions has been appropriate and they have been well considered. Our success in Bosnia (and Kosovo) is, I think, ample proof of that.

I want to also iterate that the United States is, and should be, fully supportive of the European Security Identity. Let there be no doubt about that. Ultimately, however, if the Alliance is to prosper into the 21st century, we must never lose sight of the importance of maintaining the very basic and essential military capabilities required to execute NATO's primary Collective Defense mission.

THE EU/WEU ROLE IN EUROPEAN SECURITY

Guido Lenzi
Director, Insitute for Security Studies, Western European Union (WEU)
Brussels, Belgium

I will try to be very brief because many things I meant to say have already been said. I will be rather schematic in expressing to you my ideas about some of the new elements that Europeans and Americans have to take into consideration together. It has been said—I won't go over that—that the international situation has changed. The threats and challenges have become extremely ambiguous. Even a new word has been created, "glocalism," a mixture of globalism and localism to describe what is happening everywhere, also in the States and Canada, where a reaction against central government and transnational risks are at play.

These challenges (we're talking here about Article V, non-territorial defense response) are ambiguous, multi-layered and difficult to predict. Therefore, no alliance, no international agreement can pre-establish the response of the international community—not even NATO. The reactions will have to be played on an ad hoc basis; possibly on a preventative basis, in the attempt to prevent events or to contain the first expressions of a crisis before they reach a point where they actually burst into conflict, when as we know, things become very difficult for anybody to tackle and deal with.

It is not a matter, I feel, that can be circumscribed by international law—it is not a matter of architectures anymore. A lot has been said about building new architectures, when we have enough architectures as it is in Europe—indeed, a whole bundle of connections that would need to be disconnected, I would think, to a certain extent. The important thing is to pluralize the reactions, and ensure that the reaction is different every time, coming as it may from a different quarter, with different contributing countries and on the individual merits of every individual crisis.

Some international organisms have to be revitalized and put to better use, like the Council of Europe and the OSCE. There is on the contrary, a tendency to pile everything up onto NATO, for the moment, and eventually on the European Union, whenever it comes to grips with its common and foreign security policy. Now, it has been stated (and I think it is a truism, something we'll have to live with) that the American and European approaches are different to these new crises. There is an obvious re-nationalization of the security responses. National interests are becoming much more relevant in each one of our countries. That is normal. There is nothing pathological about it. On the contrary, it is the spin-off of a much more relaxed international situation, at least in Europe. Nevertheless, the Americans remain in Europe the common denominator and the catalyzer that they have always been, even recently with the reunification of Germany. If it hadn't been for President Bush's determination and for his reassurances to Europeans and Russians alike, things wouldn't have gone as smoothly and as quickly in Europe. The Americans remain important as a coalition builder, as a common denominator, and as a point of reference for the individual European countries.

Now, back in 1991, another important event occurred, that went largely unnoticed. In the autumn of that year, NATO decided on a new strategic concept; a few days later, the European Union approved the Maastricht Treaty. These additions to the policy of these two organizations were both in the same field. NATO is an integrated military structure and the European Union an integrated economic and social structure. Both of them, between November and December 1991, decided to go political and engage in the reunification of Europe, ensure the stabilization of the new democracies. This very generous competition between the two organizations must not now turn into a collision, which may still happen, in many perceptions if not in actual fact. But perceptions and facts are one and the same thing, very often, in security terms.

In August 1996, NATO decided that it would allow WEU to assume the political control and the strategic direction of some missions that NATO would not want to undertake; WEU—no mention of the European Union. There is still a reluctance in America to consider that aspect of the Maastricht proposition by which the European Union and Western European Union should join, get closer together, and establish a functional relationship between themselves.

The markers of these are ongoing processes will be much more clearly established in Amsterdam (the EU Intergovernmental Conference) and Madrid (the NATO Summit), and we'll see better where we're going from there. Now,

ESDI: the acronym is in many a ministerial communique, but many people still wonder, "What is that?" It stands for European Security and Defense Identity. Maybe ESDI is like that "vision thing." Nobody knows what it is but we all know what it is when we don't see it.

That, I think, is something that keeps us together, transatlantically. We both have a vision thing. We both have a messianic role, Europeans and Americans, that we think we can perform in international relations. Shape the world to our image, which is not always easy or straightforward. In any case, there are going to be, I feel, two processes. One from beneath, in which individual countries will come together, on the basis of national interests motivating them to react—Italy, Greece, Turkey, Denmark, Romania, Austria, and Albania, some very strange bedfellows one may think. But they are there together on the basis of this national interest, and that is good. It could have been better, but it's good. There could now be an incremental process, by which WEU may eventually, want to get involved and even the European Union, in some kind of a regeneration process of Albania. Reaction to events may come from the bottom up, and meet an international institutional recognition which will come from above—United Nations, OECD, European Union, NATO—which will legitimize, in a sense, what will come most naturally among Europeans.

This is not the process that Maastricht had established. Of course, according to Maastricht we should be doing things very logically. We're eventually going to have a common foreign defense policy, a common defense and a common army. We tried that in '54 and it didn't work, and I don't think it is going to work very soon now. The important thing is that we do things in ways that are recognizable politically and, therefore, operationally efficient. No operation in this field, in non-Article V interposition missions, can be operationally efficient if it is not politically credible. Otherwise, with the first soldier killed, the solidarity crumbles. We've seen that before. Therefore, it is important that we proceed in both directions, the institutional way (initiated in Maastricht) and in the prognostic sense of Europeans assuming their responsibilities as things happen. Neutrals, non-members of security institutions, can pitch-in on these missions whenever needed. It would be even useful to include Eastern and Central Europeans into the second pillar of the European Union before they are ready for the economic integration. It would be illogical to expect of them that they undertake the three pillars of European integration or be left out of the door.

Now, where does the Western European Union stand? Some claim it cannot exist. It just so happens that the Western European Union is not only here, which in itself would not be enough, but it has two suitors. The Western European Union indicated very explicitly in the ministerial NATO communiques of Berlin in 1996. It also appears prominently in Article J4.2 and others of the Maastricht Treaty. So everybody is calling out its name but it cannot act until and unless it is emancipated by the concurrent political will of these two organizations.

Western European Union is ready to act because it has all it takes. It has the decision-making bodies, it's putting together its own multinational forces, and so forth. Credible or not, we'll have to see. Nobody is credible nowadays; no pudding is credible until you eat it.

The essential thing is that Western European Union is and will find itself at the intersection of NATO's destructuring, downsizing its missions (the CJTF concept is about downsizing the missions), and the European Union upsizing, increasing its responsibilities. At the intersection—you can almost draw it on a graph—at that intersection Western European Union will be activated by these two organizations. So it is there, it's like a bicycle; it doesn't move until you start pedaling. You must know where you're going, because otherwise you fall down again. That is the trick with bicycles.

Finally, the very last thing that needs to be said, is that these international security issues need the involvement of public opinion. It is not like in the past: defending national territory is a constitutional duty; you don't discuss it and you don't dispute it. Cooperative security, instead, is a matter of interposition, non-Article V, non-territorial defense. Why should we go into Albania? It has to be explained. Why should we go into the Great Lakes, in Somalia? It has to be explained to public opinion. You have to acquire the support of the national and international communities. If that has to happen, it is important that these changing modalities are appropriately perceived in Europe and the United States alike.

Therefore, the transatlantic relationship is preserved but it must be ensured that consultative processes are the ones foreseen by Article IV of the Washington Treaty. Article IV, not Article V, Article IV—consultation, comparing notes as often as possible and visibly, so that there is a process of progressive adaptation. Not once and for all, which is not possible, but according to the various contingencies as they happen. American decisionism, racing too far ahead (like it has done in many circumstances lately from "rogue states" to agreements with Russia) will otherwise discourage the Europeans and the Europeans who may go back to sleep like they did for 50 years with the Americans taking care of them. It's cheap and it's effective and we would thank you very much.

CHALLENGES FOR EUROPE IN THE NEW CENTURY: A GERMAN PERSPECTIVE

Colonel Jens Zimmerman
Federal Ministry of Defense,
Bonn, Germany

Before looking East, as suggested by our panel theme, I would like to recall what the challenges are for Europe as a whole. The very challenge of today and tomorrow is the extension of stability in and for Europe. To this end we need a comprehensive and political and conceptual approach focusing on two major elements. These are: intensified integration and improved cooperation. The future security structure in Europe cannot be created from scratch. Rather, we must bring together the existing institutions and processes, especially the NATO, EU, WEU, and OSCE, and we must succeed in managing their interaction and complimentary approach.

A purely eurocentric view would risk neglecting the Atlantic dimension of European security. Past history proves that the fate of America and Europe is intertwined. Hard to imagine a single security related issue either of us faces, that we would not be much better off facing it together. That is all that you can say about an alliance.

Against this background, establishing the security structure in Europe means to push ahead with four developments:

1. We need a NATO that can react flexibly to the new challenges by preventive and proactive crisis management, by transfer of stability and by cooperation. At the same time, the Alliance must retain its collective defense capability.

2. We must continue the process of opening this new NATO to the East while maintaining the necessary balance between this process and a security partnership with Russia and Ukraine.
3. We must give the transatlantic link between Europe and North America a new foundation.
4. Europe must become a political union with a more efficient common foreign and security policy. Europe must develop its own ability to take strategic action within the Alliance.

Now, keeping this in mind, let's follow the program impetus of looking East. What are the requirements? First, there is a requirement of listening to the desires of 100 million people in Central and Eastern Europe. They have been suppressed and deprived of their natural rights of freedom, democracy, and a market economy for a long time. They now want to join the same structures of values and institutions that enabled Western Europe to overcome its own legacy of conflict and division and to reach prosperity. They want to join the Alliance and the European Union for the same reasons that we remain staying in them. Keeping this Western club closed would be apolitical, unhistorical, and immoral. All European countries have the same legitimate interest and right to choose their own security arrangements.

The second requirement is maintenance of stability in and for Europe. This century alone proved sufficiently how destructive instability in the region has been for the whole of Europe and the world. There is still uncertainty about the democratic development in some countries. Domestic reforms need to be consolidated and the civil control of military must further be promoted and neighborhood stability must be reached.

This stability in Central and Eastern Europe is in everybody's interest. It cannot be maintained without Russia. Russia remains a great European power and must be constructively involved in the creation of a new Euro-Atlantic security order gaining from stability at its western border. All states have the greatest stake in ensuring that Russia continues its development toward democracy and economic reform. Europe needs Russia as a responsible partner, especially with regard to future coalition efforts that may be required in managing security in and beyond Europe.

Another key factor of stability and security for the continent is an independent democratic and stable Ukraine, with respected territorial integrity and borders. Ukraine is mastering a difficult balance which geography and history have placed upon her—a balance between economic restructuring and social stabilization on the one hand, and Western orientation and Eastern confidence-building on the other. To meet these requirements our concept must be both political and a comprehensive. It must be a concept of integration and cooperation. The overall aim is to create in Europe a zone of unique stability and prosperity by improved political, economical and military cooperation, and by the integration of democratic states.

What integration is all about is transferring stability by opening the Alliance and the European Union to independent and sovereign nations which are committed to democracy, market economies, and shared values. The enlargement processes of NATO and European Union are thus interrelated and overlapping activities. Taking full advantage of their inherent conceptual and political interrelation will lead to synergistic effects in giving Central and Eastern Europe a Euro-Atlantic perspective.

Let me expand a little bit more on NATO opening and European Union enlargement. The new NATO will complete its internal adaptation. NATO added three new states in 1999, and will keep the door open to those who were not among the first candidates. By the way, to start with a small number of states seems at least to me very important in order to enhance the credibility of enlargement being an open process. The new NATO is forging a security partnership with Russia on the basis of the Founding Act that was signed in Paris in the summer of 1997.

This document, far from being a simple formula, must be a program for practical cooperation as already commenced in the NATO missions IFOR, KFOR, and SFOR in the former Yugoslavia. The new NATO will establish a proper framework for enhanced partnership of a new quality with the Ukraine. In response to the legitimate concerns of those who will not or will not yet join, the Alliance will continue to try to further develop the growth and potential of the Partnership for Peace as well as the Euro-Atlantic Partnership Council.

I would like to underline that PFP is not, also in the German perception, a substitute for NATO enlargement or a mere mechanism to breathe new life into NATO. On the contrary, it is the most ambitious military cooperation effort ever undertaken by any alliance in history. PFP is an element of the European security structure in its own right. It counteracts existing feelings of insecurity and promotes the process of political, economic, and social reform. In doing so the Alliance becomes a mighty bolster to democratic structures not yet consolidated. Its focus on civil control of the military is effective and its requirement of settling border disputes with neighbors is an excellent barrier against resurgence of historical conflict.

PFP enhancement needs to be complimented by intensified regional, sub-regional, and bilateral activities. The elements of this seconding strategy strengthen the political and conceptual link between NATO opening and EU enlargement. The process of EU enlargement aims at both deepening and widening. Deepening is the guiding principle for the continuous Intergovernmental Conference which concluded in June 1997 at the Amsterdam summit meeting. The reforms—aiming essentially at more effective decision-making procedures, majority voting, representation of the member states, subsidiarity, more transparency and closer involvement of the citizens—need to be concluded satisfactorily to prepare for the widening process and the enlargement negotiations.

To meet security requirements, the European Union, in its irreversible process toward a true political union, must also become a security and a defense union. This means, in the first place, making common foreign and security policy more efficient, attaining a greater capacity for external action, strengthening the operational role and capability of the WEU, and integrating the WEU step-by-step into the European Union. Emphasis has to be given to the fact that even after completion of EU-WEU merger, Article V responsibility for collective defense will remain with the Alliance as already stipulated in the actual Brussels Treaty.

Arms control is also fundamental for stability in and for Europe. For Russia it is of primary interest to adapt the arms control regime in Europe in a way that reflects the fundamentally changed security order in our continent. We share this interest. It is a legitimate requirement and a political and strategic necessity for all of us. A modern arms control regime as a key element of future European stability must be guided by a cooperative understanding of common security, rather than by old thinking in terms of Soviet-NATO confrontation. Such an arms control regime must reflect both NATO's and Russia's need and willingness to pursue flexible crisis management on the one hand, and a security partnership on the other. It must not be framed exclusively in terms of defense against a defined enemy.

With regard to the Treaty on Conventional Forces in Europe, this means we will have to get rid of all elements that still reflect the outdated confrontational approach. Moreover, we will have to elaborate on those which are valid for a new cooperative approach. In other words, we must shift the conceptual emphasis from numerical balances and quantitative reductions to commonly accepted strategic requirements in combination with confidence-building constraints on reciprocal bases.

The future timetable is impressive. Everything already has been addressed. The NATO summit in July 1997 was a historic event—not just on enlargement but on future European security and stability. The opening of NATO is first and foremost, a political and not a financial issue. It will be measured in far reaching *political and strategic options* for the new millennium and not in budgetary terms.

DIMENSIONS OF CHANGE IN THE POST–COLD WAR WORLD

Ambassador Marshall Brement
Chair of Security Studies, George C. Marshall Center
*Garmish, Germany**

The revolution of 1989 marked the end of the Cold War. It was also the end of the era that began with World War I and the Treaty of Versailles—an era of unparalleled violence and revolution. We now have good reason to believe that the major conflicts that tore Europe apart during that era causing millions of casualties and untold damage are a thing of the past. It is literally impossible for us, for example, to imagine a future war between Germany and France—two countries that fought three bloody wars against each other in three-quarters of a century.

In the years since 1989, we have seen not only the breakup of the communist system, but with the end of the Russian Empire, the final dissolution of the imperial systems that had dominated major parts of the world for centuries. From what has happened since 1989, it is clear that those who said the Soviet system was an imperial system and that the Soviet Union was an empire, were quite right.

But even going further than that, it is fair to state that 1989 marked the end of a period of 500 years or more, beginning with the Renaissance and the emergence of the scientific and cultural revolutions that spawned the enlightenment in France and Great Britain and that ultimately led to the

---

**presently at University of Virginia, Government and Foreign Affairs, Charlottesville, Virginia*

American and the French revolutions. In every country in Europe during those 500 years there raged disputes between what Sir Michael Howard has called "The Party of Movement" and "The Party of Order."

The "Party of Movement" he defines as the party of the enlightenment, the party whose thoughts were perhaps best expressed in the words of Thomas Jefferson, in the American Declaration of Independence, when he said: "we hold these truths to be self-evident, that all men are created equal and that they are endowed by their creator with certain inalienable rights and that among these are life, liberty and the pursuit of happiness," the latter being a wonderful Jeffersonian euphemism for private property.

In opposition to the democratic philosophy of the "Party of Movement" were ranged the forces composing the "The Party of Order"—the conservative forces that were the bedrock of European politics for centuries. This party based its political appeal on blood, on race, on soil, on tribe, on tradition, and on religion. We sometimes tend to forget that it was this party that was in control in much of Europe and of the Western world right up until World War II. In 1939 on the continent of Europe, for example, the only democratic states were France, the Scandinavian countries, the Benelux countries, and Great Britain. In 1940 there were only three such democratic European countries—Sweden, Switzerland, and Great Britain.

So when we think of all the enormous changes that we have been living through, it is important to remember that the roots of these cataclysmic events took place not just in the period from 1945 to 1989, but in a much longer timeframe. What we have had in Europe since 1989 has been the ending of one civilization and the beginning of another—a major revolution. The roots of this revolution were contained in four major transformations that took place in Western Europe from 1945–1989. They were:

1. the commitment to democracy and democratic systems;
2. the growing belief in the benefits of a market economy;
3. the giving up of many important aspects of national sovereignty to supranational organizations, such as the EC and NATO, organizations which are the instruments putting Europe on the road to political and economic integration; and
4. the acceptance and encouragement of the presence of the United States on the European continent as a major actor in European affairs.

Again, keep in mind that all four of these transformations were very problematic, if not unimaginable, to the people of Western Europe in 1945. No major political thinker in the post-war period would have hazarded a prediction that within less than five decades the tenets of liberal democracy would sweep the field on the European continent.

Similarly, market economics did not have much in the way of intellectual justifiers in Europe in the post-war period. There were, at that time, a few people—von Hayek, Schumpeter, and others—who did present a rigorous philosophical justification for the free market system. But for the most part, intellectuals in Europe and elsewhere, having only recently come out of the Great Depression and the greatest war in human history, believed that the market was not an adequate tool to deal with the economic problems of the twentieth century; that the only way to construct a rational order was by the imposition of various state systems and controls on economic activity. After all, the only two countries in Europe or North America that had major economic growth throughout the 1930s were the Soviet Union and Nazi Germany.

As for the integration of Europe, the EC in Brussels makes decisions daily that impinge on the sovereignty of the nations of Western Europe, telling their citizens what they can eat, what they can wear, and what is permissible for them in a thousand different areas. And when European armed forces engage in combat, as they have recently in the former Yugoslavia, they do so by and large under a NATO unified and integrated command. This was unimaginable in 1945. In fact, if any leading politician had suggested just after the World War II that, within 20 years, major steps toward political and economic integration were going to take place in Western Europe, he would have been dismissed as a visionary, or even a crackpot.

Similarly, the idea that the United States would soon become, for all practical purposes, a European power was unimaginable in 1945. The major problem that President Truman and his advisers faced at that time was how to demobilize a ten million-man army without disrupting the American economy. The American tradition of non-interference in the affairs of Europe was expected to continue in the post-war world. The great powers of Europe, especially Great Britain, were expected at that point to continue dealing with the Continent's security problems, as they had for the past centuries. The American foreign policy tenet of non-involvement was part of a tradition best expressed by George Washington in his farewell address when he said (and every American was reminded of this in countless fourth of July orations) that Europe is a corrupt place and that we in the new world should basically stay out of the affairs of Europe, lest we become corrupted ourselves.

Only with this in mind can we have an adequate framework for examining the enormous changes that have taken place on the European continent since 1989, changes that have been astounding in both their scope and their rapidity. Obviously, there is not enough space here to deal with each of those changes except in a shorthand fashion, but as I have suggested, their sum total is nothing short of revolutionary.

We can begin with the demise of the Marxist-Leninist system and the emergence of some two dozen new states on the European continent. In addition, a number of important old states have emerged with new borders—the most prominent of which are, of course, Germany and Russia. In thinking about

Russia, it is important to keep in mind that this giant country has never had borders that match its current borders nor western borders of this general shape since 1653, when Russia absorbed Ukraine.

Since 1989 we have seen the dissolution of two multi-ethnic states which were creatures of the Versailles Conference—Czechoslovakia and Yugoslavia—and the dissolution of a product of World War I, the Bolshevik system in Russia. We have also witnessed the disappearance of the Russian empire that preceded it.

So we have now had three different European models of how multi-ethnic states can dissolve. First of all, there is the excellent model of a good national divorce—i.e., the one that has taken place in Czechoslovakia. No marriage counselor could wish for a better model of how to divide marital resources with as little acrimony as possible.

Second, we have a moderately good model, the Soviet Union. Given the state of the Soviet Union in 1991, with its enormous armed forces and its 30,000 nuclear weapons, it is quite striking that, although there has been considerable violence within the former USSR, that violence has been basically on the periphery. In that sense, the dissolution of the Soviet empire matches, in the kinds of violence that it has evoked, the conflagrations that we've seen in the breakup of other empires. Such violence has been considerable, but it has largely been on the periphery—in India and Africa, for example—and not in the center, not in the heartland of the empire. There have been very few Russians killing Russians, and for that, we all have every reason to be very thankful.

Third, we have had just a terrible model of multi-ethnic dissolution, that of Yugoslavia, which broke apart in unspeakably brutal violence, much of which could have been avoided. Space does not permit a close examination of this phenomenon, but what is crystal clear is that the horrors that we have witnessed are the precursors of horrors yet to come and that the Balkans will remain a running sore in Europe for decades.

Getting back to our list of revolutionary changes, we've seen the dissolution of the Warsaw Pact, of COMECON, and various other hegemonic tools by which the Soviet Union maintained its primacy in Central and Eastern Europe and the political and economic independence of all those countries. In fact, one of the unexpected bonuses of the end of the Cold War is that countries like the Czech Republic, Slovakia, Hungary, and Poland have moved from "Eastern Europe," where we had placed them when they were satraps of the USSR, to where they really belong geographically—i.e., Central Europe.

And, as opposed to dissolution, we have witnessed the unification of one country, the major country in Central Europe, and that is, of course, Germany. More than that, we've seen a unified Germany in NATO, which is probably one of the, if not the, greatest diplomatic achievements of the twentieth century. Again, this is not something that anyone would have anticipated could happen in this century. After his summit with Khruschev in Vienna in 1961, for example, President John F. Kennedy, talking to his advisors, said, "It seems silly for us to be facing an atomic war over a treaty preserving Berlin as the future capital of the reunited Germany, when all of us know that Germany will probably never be reunited." So the sudden bloodless reunification of Germany would have been a surprise to John F. Kennedy, as it was to all the rest of us. That it happened so fast and relatively smoothly is something for which we should, again, all be thankful. But we have less reason to be thankful for the fact that since 1989, we have also seen the emergence of unbridled nationalism and nationalistic manifestations that had lain dormant under the Cold War glacier for decades. That glacier has fortunately melted, but lo and behold, many of the snakes underneath have somehow survived and managed to thaw and emerge virulently alive. Disputes that security experts had largely forgotten about, but which were cancers to indigenous peoples whose memories went back for generations, emerged to trouble us in the new post–Cold War world in which we now live.

The changes that have taken place in Russia since 1989 have, of course, been enormous. While there is only space to discuss a few of them, perhaps the most profound among them has been the strengthening of the regions of Russia at the expense of the center in Moscow. Russia, because of its geography and economy, throughout its entire thousand-year history, has always been a country that has been ruled from the center with an iron hand. This was the way Russia, and then the Soviet Union, was maintained. The strengthening of the regions that has occurred since 1991 raises the strong possibility that the Russia we see today will not be the Russia that will be in existence 20 years from now.

Right now, even at the periphery, there is Chechnya, which is independent in everything but name, although many Russians would deny that. There are other regions with similar tendencies which make it very difficult to see how Moscow, given its current circumstances, can maintain its economic control over the regions, or even its geographic definition in the form in which it exists today. This, of course, gives rise to enormous problems in the security arena, problems that could affect all of us.

Within Russia, the *nomenklatura*, the same elite group that used to rule the USSR, has taken advantage of the opportunity of the breakup of the Soviet state to grab power economically. In some senses this "old boy network" has provided the economic glue which keeps the system together. These people know each other and, inefficient and corrupt though they may be, can still get things done on occasion. How long that can last is a real question.

We've also seen the emergence of a self-directed bureaucracy in Moscow, a bureaucracy which sets its own goals and which has nobody exerting the kind of control over it that is needed in any society. Keep in mind that the Communist party of the Soviet Union served a number of legitimate functions, the most important of which was control. The legal system of the Soviet Union was entirely subservient to the Party. The whole process of control, and of making the society coherent, was accomplished through the Communist party apparatus. That apparatus has completely disappeared and this disappearance is, in my view, the principal reason for the emergence of the Mafia in the Soviet Union—something that not a single Soviet expert predicted, or even conceived was possible.

It is very difficult to imagine how the whole situation of crime, corruption, and the Mafia that has made Russia into what has been called the "Wild East," is going to be resolved. I talk with a lot of Russians and they all are brilliant in depicting the problems facing their country. But I have yet to meet the Russian who can come up with a plausible solution to these problems.

Crime and corruption are particularly difficult to deal with in Russia, not just because of the disappearance of the Communist Party, but also because of the tremendous weakening of the instruments of control since Soviet times. Those organizations that had that task—primarily the legal system, the KGB, and the internal police—are now very weak. The officials and officers manning these institutions are overworked and underpaid and their morale is abysmal. The result is that Russia is now suffering from all the problems of corruption that afflict many of the most underdeveloped countries.

On the positive side, for the first time in ten centuries, the Russian people are free to do what they want, to say what they want to say, to print what they want to print. This is an enormous achievement, but it impinges on the emerging quarrels between local governments and the center in Moscow. The freer the local authorities become, the less attractive it is for them to obey the dictates of Moscow. This is particularly true for those regions that have great natural resources or are located at great distances from the capital.

The revolutionary changes that we have witnessed in Europe in the post-1989 period have been mirrored in the United States. As we look back on the Cold War, we see that, just as in Europe, it hid from our view major developments that had taken place in the United States, but which were essentially not visible to us because they were obscured by the security concerns involved in our rivalry with Moscow.

Those people, however, who have expressed concern about a possible turn by the United States toward its traditional policy of "isolationism" in the wake of the Cold War are off the mark. The United States is now and will remain a global power. It has security interests throughout the globe, and will continue its substantial trade with all the regions of the world. The possibility that the United States will fold itself back into a fortress North America and get out of the world's economic system is simply not within the realm of possibility. This thesis has no credibility.

However, there is at the same time no gainsaying the fact that the tradition of looking inward that characterized the foreign policy of the United States until the

Japanese attack on Pearl Harbor is more prevalent today than it was at the height of the Cold War. The phenomenon that has taken place is, in my view, quite a natural one. The Cold War, if I may be permitted a metaphor from physics, put the United States into an "excited quantum state" focusing on our rivalry with the Soviet Union, which took place primarily in Europe, i.e., a different quantum state than the one we would be in normally. When the threat from the outside went away, as it has since the end of the Cold War, the United States simply went back to its normal state, which is less eurocentric than before. This is not necessarily an adverse development.

The reader, of course, needs no reminding that the United States is not just a European power—it is also a major Pacific power. During the Cold War the United States had a maritime strategy that tasked our navy in the event of war to move into the Norwegian fjords and to defend ourselves north of Iceland. With the end of the Cold War there is an obvious need for a new maritime strategy. We have to have one because, in fact, when we say the United States is a Pacific power, in fact, means that it is a naval power. Given our geographic position and the immensity of the Pacific, we have to be.

One of the striking changes that has emerged in our defense posture since the end of the Cold War is that now U.S. forces abroad are numerically equal in both the Atlantic and the Pacific. We have 100,000 troops in the Atlantic and 100,000 troops in the Pacific. That is an enormous difference from the situation that existed during the Cold War.

The United States has emerged as the single superpower, simply carrying forward the powerful military machine that it developed during the course of the Cold War. Europe had, and still has, the possibility of becoming a second superpower, but it has no temptation to do so. France, Germany, Italy, and the United Kingdom alone have a combined population that is larger than that of the United States; a GNP that is equal to that of the United States; a glorious military tradition (much more of a military tradition, in fact, than the United States); the needed nuclear capability and military technology; and, some would argue, the geopolitical necessity to become a superpower. The reason they have not done so is that they think it too expensive. With the same GNP as the United States, their expenditures on defense, taken together, are about 33 to 40 percent of that of the United States.

During the war in the Persian Gulf, where the interests of Europe are even greater than those of the United States in terms of dependence of Persian Gulf oil, the Europeans provided 10 percent of the amount of troops and resources that the United States provided. A similar situation occurred in Bosnia, where 31 of the 33 satellites used by NATO were provided by the United States, and later on during the Kosovo air war.

The fact is that the United States is now politically, economically and culturally comfortable with a $260 billion defense budget. This means that

Washington is now comfortable with levels of expenditure on defense which match what we were ordinarily paying during most of the Cold War. This degree of comfort has nothing to do with an outside threat. One of the best examples of this took place when a hurricane destroyed McDill Air Force base in Florida, a base which our Presidential Base Commission had already targeted for closure. President Bush, however, immediately pledged to rebuild it from the ground up. This had nothing to do with defense needs. What he was worried about, of course, were the Florida primaries and how Florida was going to vote in the general election. Military bases mean jobs and jobs mean votes.

It can be no surprise that four-and-a-half decades of the Cold War have changed the United States in a fundamental way. In the 1996 presidential election campaign, the only criticism the Republicans leveled at President Clinton in foreign affairs was that he was not spending enough on defense, even though we all agreed that there was no conceivable threat to the United States about which we should be concerned. Senator Dole made a point of stressing that, if elected, he would increase spending on defense readiness. But it's hard to see why one needs readiness if there's no perceived threat—readiness for what?

One of the net results of this $260+ billion defense budget is that it is providing us with the wherewithal to carry out a genuine revolution in military affairs. In the Persian Gulf war and in Bosnia and the Kosovo air war the United States therefore had a tremendously preponderant position as compared to our allies. Furthermore, with roughly one-third of the defense budget going to research and development, and with half that amount, say $30–45 billion, devoted to fueling the revolution in military affairs—in communications, command, control, computers, lasers, information warfare, and so forth—the difference between the United States and its allies grows exponentially. Every year the United States spends on this one area of the military roughly the total national defense budget, of say, Germany or France or England. There is thus no chance of any nation, friend or enemy, catching up with the United States in this critical area at the cutting edge of military affairs for decades to come.

As noted, we have seen a major shift in the American security outlook from the Atlantic to the Pacific in the United States since the end of the Cold War. This shift is not just a shift on the part of Washington policymakers. It is part of a major demographic shift as well. More than 40 percent of the students at the University of California at Berkeley are of Asian origin. Hawaii is largely Asian. We've seen an inevitable movement toward Asia in our thinking and this is being felt more and more in the Congress.

One of the great contributing events of the 1989 revolution was when 2,000 Germans began crossing the border from East Germany to West Germany per day, some of them travelling in circuitous directions through Hungary and Czechoslovakia. The United States is now absorbing many more than 2,000 legal and illegal immigrants a day coming from Latin America. This is having, and will continue to have, profound effect on the security outlook of the United States. One of the major developments in this respect is the North America Free Trade Agreement (NAFTA). In addition, we have serious persons actually calling for bilingual education in America (which in my view is a terrible idea). But terrible or not, it illustrates the major trend in the United States moving the security outlook of our nation away from Europe.

There is, however, a countervailing force in this regard—i.e., the fact that the entire generation of security specialists raised during the Cold War are very eurocentric and determined to keep the United States functioning as, in effect, a European power. They see the instrument for accomplishing this as the North Atlantic Treaty Organization.

The Cold War was itself eurocentric. At the highest levels of our government, we were focused on the transatlantic alliance. There exists, in other words, what the Marxists would call a fundamental contradiction between the specialists in the United States, who are very much transatlantic in outlook, and the mood or the tendency in the United States which is moving inward, southward, and westward.

One of the strongest reasons the United States has fought hard for the expansion of NATO is the fact that these specialists, for perfectly honorable and good reasons, would like to pin the United States to Europe—because they think that this is the right thing to do. The only institutional way to accomplish that is through NATO, keeping it as strong and robust as possible.

As noted earlier, the last presidential campaign in the United States was truly remarkable for its lack of foreign affairs content. There was absolutely no criticism on the part of the Republicans of a president who, some of us thought, was open to criticism on foreign policy questions. It was a campaign in which, as Larry Korb has mentioned, we saw the rather plaintive moderator in the presidential debates plead for somebody "to please ask a foreign policy question." When he finally found someone in the audience to do so, that person asked not a foreign policy question, but a trade question.

So we went through an entire debate cycle, three debates, without a single foreign policy question put to the principal candidates for president. You have to go back to 1936 in the United States to find another campaign so devoid of foreign policy. This is in spite of the fact that the conduct of foreign and national security policy is the most important function of an American president, and must occupy a large share of his time.

In sum, we have gone through a major revolutionary change in our national security structures and in the international security system since the end of the Cold War. But the institutions we have available to us to deal with these new problems are the ones that were developed during the Cold War period. The first problem we face, then, is to adapt those institutions to the realties of the post–Cold War world—both in the United States itself and in our relations with a much transformed Europe. This will not be easy. We will need strong presidential leadership and the best efforts of leading political philosophers and specialists in the foreign affairs field to accomplish that task.

NON-MILITARY THREATS TO THE ALLIANCE*

Eric Danon
Former Deputy Director for Security Affairs, Ministry of Foreign Affairs
Paris, France

I have been given the opportunity to say a few words on what could become a dialogue between the EU and the U.S. concerning the rather difficult questions of non-military threats, also called global or transnational threats, according to the importance they are accorded. These are principally terrorism, illicit drugs, and organized transnational crime. We can add other threats to these (e.g., certain trafficking of people), but we can also be content, at first, with an approach to these three first threats that I have cited.

The dialogue between the European Union—and, more globally speaking, Europe—and the U.S. on these questions is still in the beginning stages. For years military threats have been in the forefront, both on the theoretical level and on the practical level, in the organization of defense. What is going on in response to non-military threats? Well, there is nothing comparable yet today, even though these threats constitute perhaps the most difficult problems. There are three issues I would like to bring up very briefly. The first, as I said, is that there has not been a very elaborate theoretical and doctrinal reflection on non-military threats, as there has been for military questions. Hence the difficulty to work today on these questions. There is not, for example, a uniformly registered definition of terrorism. There is difficulty, according to the countries, in defining organized crime. There are different conceptions, both political and cultural, of

translation by Daria M. Roche

the drug problem. In short, today, in our efforts to establish a true dialogue, we are lacking a kind of common basis of thought which, undeniably, will have to be developed and put into place in the years to come.

The second problem is that the EU has a hard time getting all 15 members to agree on the policy to uphold on these questions. For the non-specialists, I remind you that the fight against these threats is treated in what is called the third pillar of the EU. That is, a system in which all of the countries must agree in order for something to be done. This does not come out of what we call community competence in which the countries weigh less individually, after a time, than the organization of the Union in its entirety. This is a difficulty that is obviously very important for establishing a relationship between the Union and the U.S., but also with other countries in the world, since these questions are not treated in the Union in a clear and harmonious manner.

Within the Union, you have numerous differences of opinion on the relative approaches to these questions. For example, the drug question is the object of differing opinions between France and The Netherlands. The question of terrorism is the object of differing opinions between France and Spain. The question of the Mafia and of organized crime poses problems between France and Italy. In short, there are problems coming to agreement together and, since this difficulty exists, it resurfaces, obviously, as I said, in the capacity to establish a common foreign policy on these questions and thus to establish this dialogue with other entities, such as the United States.

Finally, there is a third difficulty that stems from the nature of these threats themselves. The problem is almost easily conceptualized when these threats come from the states. When one state supports terrorism, when one state supports drug traffickers, we know pretty much how to treat the question in the classical geopolitical frameworks. But when the threat reveals itself to be coming from outside the states, and is revealed as something that ignores boundaries, bypassing the states, putting societies at risk not in terms of security but in terms of stability, we have a problem responding to it. That is, our societies have a hard time finding state-like responses to non-state-like threats. This difficulty is found particularly in the matter of setting up police networks or networks of cooperation of justice.

Thus, starting out from these difficulties, what does it seem possible to do in the coming years in this transatlantic dialogue? Well, it is pretty simple. We must arrive at a common approach to the phenomena and then set up an operational and practical cooperation that works.

On the common approach, there is today a lot of work to do to bring together the American and the European concepts concerning these questions. I take for example the question of drugs. The U.S. has today a concept in which there is a delegation of responsibilities among the states: this is the phenomenon of authentification. This is a concept which, today, is very far removed from the

European concept on the question of drugs. These are very different and distant elements that we are going to have to join together over time through a system of common thought.

I could give comparable examples regarding terrorism, because the U.S. has not been affected by terrorism as have European societies: the IRA in England, the ETA in Spain, the Corsicans for France, etc. And, thus, the U.S. has, to this day, a culture of terrorism radically different from the European culture. Americans have a vision of terrorism driven or supported by states, but not an approach of internal or socially driven terrorism, as is the case in the European societies. There, too, we are going to have to discuss things a long time before we harmonize our positions.

With regard to organized crime—perhaps because the Mafias have appeared in the U.S. too, and in forms often fairly comparable to European forms—the concepts are closer.

In short, we have a lot of work to do to bring these concepts closer together. This work is made all the more difficult because there are no specialized forums today in which to discuss these questions, as there is with other policy issues. This lack of opportunity for jointly discussing these questions is one of the principle difficulties we find in the transatlantic dialogue. With other organizations trying to fill this void, there is presently a kind of dispersal of debate throughout the world, which does not help in the clarity of resolving these problems.

But the question is even more difficult. The operational services of justice and of the police tend to consider that multilateralization of cooperation goes contrary to their effectiveness. That is, the police and justice services prefer, in treating these issues, to treat them in a confidential manner, essentially bilateral between services. Thus, there is a problem to resolve: this squaring of the circle. How do we bring several countries together, in a same common objective, to fight against these threats, with judicial and police services that prefer inter-service relations to be extremely discreet and bilateral?

There is another difficulty in our operational cooperation, which is that the very concept of repression or of judiciary cooperation is currently very different between the U.S. and the European countries. The difficulties can be seen almost every day, in the concept, for example, of extradition in judicial matters, or in the difficulty of cooperation between services (such as American police services or the CIA and their French equivalents). There is simultaneously a very long tradition of bilateral cooperation, for example, between France and the U.S., concerning drugs, but very big difficulties in reaching common concepts at a multilateral level.

These are some elements of the debate. I do not wish to give these points a geopolitical scope that is stronger than they need, but I think that as military threats become progressively blurred, and the question of geostrategy based on nuclear dissuasion is almost behind us, these non-military threats are going to rise in importance. If we do not want them to put our societies at risk, we are going to have to find a number of quick responses. The U.S. and the European countries are interested, above all, in not becoming destabilized by these problems. We therefore need to find new ways of working together on these issues.

THE CHANGING WORLD PARADIGM AND THE U.S./EUROPEAN AGENDA

Immo Stabreit
German Ambassador to France
Paris, France

Let me begin by making a very short statement on where we stand. I think that in European history we have a certain periodicity. You can trace this back a few hundred years. You have periods of between 15 or 20, sometimes 25 years of rapid change, upheaval, wars, revolution. Then the system settles down and quiet reigns for between 30 of 40 years. After that—as I like to say—the volcano gets active again. That the quiet periods should last about 40 years is of course by no means an accident. After 40 years the majority of the people then alive do not have an immediate personal recollection of the last period of upheaval. The desire for change becomes almost irresistible, untrammeled by recollections of previous wars and revolutions.

Now the European system has in essence become the world system. We had the last great explosion of the volcano between 1914 and 1945. This is a period which I think you have to see as a unit, because there never was any real peace following World War I. There could not be any peace with the "peace" we had. The industrialized world proved incapable of dealing with the social and economic consequences of World War I. In 1945 the situation again froze. The dividing line now ran between the two remaining major world powers, the Soviet Union and the United States. There were attempts to change the borderlines between the systems, notably in Berlin and Korea, but by and large the world remained divided along lines which had been established by the victorious armies in 1945. Then, after 40 years, a new period of change and upheaval started, and it started in 1985 with Gorbachev taking charge of the Soviet Union. When Gorbachev took over he was calling for reform, but he wanted to reform communism which proved to be an impossible task. As the Russians say: "The hunchback is corrected only by the grave." What in fact he did was to set into motion an avalanche of events which buried not only the communist system but also himself under it. So the period of big change started in 1985 and I think we are still in the midst of it. It will probably take us well into 2005 or 2010. 1 may not live to see the year 2010, but I am sure it will be a very different place from what it is today. I am almost sure, and I certainly hope that the changes will be peaceful ones.

Now there is something new complicating this process. In 1945 the world distinguished itself from the world 80 years before much less than the world of 1985 distinguished itself from the world of 1945. If you go back 80 years, say from 1995 to 1865, almost all of the technical and scientific inventions which dominated the world in 1945 had already been made, with the notable exception of the internal combustion engine and the airplane. The railroad was certainly there, artificial fertilizer had been invented, electricity had been invented, the telephone and telegraph were to come very soon. Science was exploding. Of course, the two World Wars made for an enormous technological acceleration because of the efforts of research into war technology or war-related technologies. The Cold War pushed this development even further. In both World Wars, but certainly in the World War II and during the Cold War, the civilian spin-off of this scientific and technological effort was gigantic and it has brought about a world which is changing with breathtaking speed, not on account of social or economic changes, but because of technology.

Many people feel dizzy with this process; they feel disoriented and there are very deep fears with which we have to cope in political life. We have to deal with these challenges in Europe and we have these challenges in common with the United States. One of these challenges is organized crime. Because of the enormous mobility of human beings and the rapidity of information exchange, organized crime has become a major danger for all of us. And, of course, if you talk of organized crime, you talk about drugs, and if you talk about drugs, you talk about precisely that incapacity to cope with a rapidly changing environment which makes so many people, and in particular young people, reach for a Nirvana. The great machine of organized crime today is the drug trade. In addition, we have to face terrorism and we have ecological problems which we also have in common, albeit in different degree.

I have worked in the public service for 35 years, and I have seen—please do not ask me for specifics, but I could give you specific instances—organized crime getting very close to the top and trying to infiltrate governments in a number of not insignificant states in both the developed and the underdeveloped world. There is organized crime in Russia today on an unprecedented scale. Of course, there was organized crime in Russia even under Stalin. But then basically the ruling communist elite kept the spoils of power for itself and saw to it that crime would be kept down and not challenge them in their seizure of the national wealth. This is now different. When the top "family" disappeared, which had been carving up the cake of the national product by themselves and doing all the trafficking for themselves, the other "families" began to blossom. Now we are told that there are approximately 130 organized crime groups in Russia. The problem is not just that the police and the courts are not able to cope with them because they are understaffed and underpaid. The problem is that organized crime, in a way which has not yet happened in the same way in any other country of the developed world, has penetrated parts of the administrative apparatus or is cooperating with it.

I think that here we have something that is an immediate threat to us as well. As a matter of fact, this is probably the most immediate threat we are facing together. I remember very well that our good friend Mr. Free told me that for the first time the Russian Mafia had been appearing on the East Coast of the United States in Atlantic City. The way they acted was adding something new to the well-known image of the Italian Mafia. Indeed, it is said that in comparison with the new guys, the old Italian Mafia "looked like a nuns' convent." So, even for the United States, the problem of organized crime in the formerly communist states, which are struggling to build democracies and shed off the remnants of the old systems, has now become a burning problem.

The amount of organized crime we have in Germany, and in particular in the new Bundeshinder, including crime rings which have their roots in Russia but also in other formally communist states, is absolutely depressing. Our police force at this point in time is not organized in a way to deal with such massive attacks, because, among other things, it is structured locally. We do need the international cooperation that we do not have yet in the necessary dimensions and that we do have to get. The amount of crime in our countries—and, in particular, organized crime, which is especially brutal—could become a political problem, as citizens expect protection against crime from their governments.

Now you will say, "Are you distrustful of your own democracy?" Of course I am not, because Germany today has a very stable democratic system. So does the United States, and so have other states of the western community. But having said this, I do see certain developments which, if we continue to let them happen, could well destabilize our societies. None of us is immune to challenges to our governmental systems, our democratic systems. And one of the biggest challenges today is organized crime, which is thriving on drug trade and which disposes of enormous amounts of money. Money, as we know, opens doors and it shuts mouths. The level of crime is rising above a certain mark, and particularly if the citizen has the feeling that the authorities of his country, freely elected authorities, are helpless and unable to protect him any more, or, even worse, have become infiltrated, then we could be very quickly in trouble.

Turning away from this subject, I would like to end with another consideration which I think is important. We now have what the French would call a "décalage" as far as the relations between Europe and the United States are concerned—a want of synchronism in terms of societal developments and of technological developments. That is not astonishing, as America has become the trendsetter. In France this is very often bitterly resented in cultural and civilizational terms. But I think it is a fact, whether we want to accept it or not. Therefore, I think it is very important that on both sides of the Atlantic, working from the United States and from Europe, we do not become strangers to each other on account of the different speeds and directions into which our societies develop. We have to do this particularly among what you would call the elites. We have to maintain a very high level of familiarity.

I am worried when I see that there are very few American students coming to Germany any more. There used to be many more 30 years ago, when we had in general many more students from foreign countries than we have now. I do not know whether this is the same in France and in other countries. I *do* know that knowledge of Europe is diminishing in the United States because, among other reasons, the interest in the outside world is diminishing as American citizens not feel less threatened by world events. Not too long ago I spent a couple of days in Columbus, Ohio, reading the local newspaper, the *Columbus Dispatch*. It's a good paper, if you want to be informed about what is going on in the United States. But there is not very much, as a matter of fact, hardly anything about the outside world. It is all about trials, judicial questions, local issues, family drama, and so on.

So we must work on this. We also have to work much more on Franco-German relations, maintaining and enhancing the mutual knowledge between the French and the Germans and in particular of their language. It is a task to which we have to devote attention every day, like a bicycle which you have to pedal and keep moving forward if you do not want to fall down. It is really one of the most important things that we have to keep on our mind. This is why I believe we have to use all possibilities of mutual exchanges. It is very sad if for two years we have hardly had any members of the U.S. Congress visiting Germany. Now lately, fortunately, there have been some delegations. These exchanges and these contacts would have to extend to all levels of society so that we do not lose sight of each other and we do not become, as I said, strangers to each other. It is like a marriage. You have problems, you iron them out. But once you begin to look at each other and you say, "Hey, why did I marry that woman?" or "why did I marry that man?" this could be the beginning of the end.

ASSUMPTIONS ABOUT THE U.S., THE EU, NATO, AND THEIR IMPACT ON THE TRANSATLANTIC AGENDA

Stanley Sloan
Senior Specialist, Congressional Research Service
U.S. Library of Congress, Washington, D.C.

I propose in this paper to discuss, from an American perspective, the assumptions and assertions that influence the way that I look at foreign policy events at the end of this decade. I will conclude with a few comments about the European-American agenda for the 21st century.

My job for the Congressional Research Service (CRS) is to provide the Congress with objective and non-partisan research and analysis. Our job at CRS is not to be advocates but to be analysts. But these comments are my personal view, although they are not too different from what I would be willing to tell members of the U.S. Congress.

Let me start with my assumptions. I will first organize my assumptions and assertions into a brief discussion of how I see the international system. Second, I will make offer observations about Europe. Third, I will make some observations about the United States, and fourth, observations about NATO.

My first assumption is about the international system. In the international system we have seen dramatic change over the last decade. One thing has not changed, and that is the fact that the international system still functions based on nation-states making decisions on a national basis and then acting on those decisions. We have international organizations that help us channel and structure some of these nation-state decisions and relations among nation-states. But it is very important to understand that, in fact, the system still works based on sovereign nation-states. I believe this will continue to be the reality for the foreseeable future. Nation-states will continue to be the primary instrument of action and organization in the international system.

Those who are engaged in political action will try to change that political reality and I think many of those attempts will be important and constructive attempts. The process of European integration is an attempt to change that fundamental reality. But we should make a distinction between understanding political action and understanding political analysis. When we analyze the international system, it is important not to mistake political objectives of moderating nationalism with the analysis of how the system actually works. Although international affairs are increasingly characterized by globalization and by interdependence, the legitimization of policy still has to be accomplished on a national basis. It is very difficult, not just in the United States but also in European countries, to legitimize policies based on international objectives.

Let me move on to some assumptions and assertions about Europe. I believe that the process of unification of Europe will continue in the future. But I think it's important to apply what I've said about the international system to an understanding of what is happening in Europe. Sometimes in the United States, when we listen to the rhetoric about European unity, there is a danger that we will confuse the rhetoric with the reality. Sometimes it sounds to the untrained ear that in fact European unity is already here. That a European security and defense identity already exists. But we all know that is not true. We all know that we need to distinguish between the objective of trying to create European unity, trying to construct a European security and defense identity, and the reality that neither of these currently exists.

I think that it is important to look at Europe, as always, in historical perspective. The process of European unity now is some 50 years underway. You can look at what has been accomplished and say it's a very substantial accomplishment. But if you look at the objective of moving toward some kind of more coherent political unity, I would say even an optimist ought to project at least another 50 years before we could expect to see anything emerging that might even resemble the Swiss Federation. The only problem I have with the Swiss model is that the one way that Switzerland has managed to hold all of the cantons together is by pursuing a policy *toward* the rest of the world that isolates Switzerland's confederation *from* the rest of the world. That certainly is not a model that Europe can afford to follow, either in terms of European interest or in terms of the Transatlantic Agenda.

My assumption about the United States is that, following the Cold War, we entered an escapist period in U.S. history. The United States is now emerging from this escapist period of its history. During this escapist period we saw the first Clinton administration come to office saying, "it's the economy, stupid." It based almost all of its actions in its first year on a somewhat unilateralist approach. It found out very quickly it does not work. Two years later we elected a Congress in the United States that tried the same approach. They discovered it didn't work.

I believe the United States is now moving toward an approach of globalization. I don't know exactly what shape or form this will take, but we are emerging from our period of escapism. We will continue in the future to see indications of both isolationist and unilateralist tendencies. Those will continue to be part of the American political culture, but they will not be the dominant way the U.S. relates to the rest of the world. They will produce hiccups, tremors, and difficulties from time to time, but they will not dominate U.S. policy.

I find it interesting to look at public opinion polls even though one must take them with a grain of salt. American public opinion polls during this period of escapism did not show nearly the degree of isolationism or unilateralism that American political leaders demonstrated. There has remained a reservoir of good will among the American people toward U.S. involvement in the world and U.S. cooperation with other nations. Some of the more interesting polling data on American attitudes toward NATO enlargement revealed that those Americans—a fairly solid majority—who support NATO enlargement do so because they believe it will expand cooperation with other countries. This may seem very idealistic, but it gives American political leadership a fairly strong foundation from which to act.

Let me move on to some assumptions and assertions about NATO in a little more detail. Even though I think many people have not observed it closely, the evolution of the Alliance started in the early 1990s, has continued since that time, and actually has made very substantial progress. The fact is that—even with all of the evolution and all of the work that has been done within the Alliance—the fact is that NATO is still perceived quite differently by different people. It reminds me of the Indian fable about the blind men trying to describe an elephant, based on where they touch the animal. That is pretty much the way we've been looking at NATO over the last several years. I think that we are now moving toward more of a consensus concerning the totality of the elephant that we call NATO. But there still are many different perceptions out there.

I'll give you my interpretation of the elephant. My interpretation of what NATO is and where it is going is that NATO does remain a collective defense organization—Article V does remain the core of the Alliance. But the fact is, Article V is not the principal preoccupation of the Alliance. The fact is (and when I first used this expression in a study for Congress a lot of people reacted negatively to it), Article V and collective defense have been put in the back pocket of the Alliance. That does not mean it has been put away completely. If you have something in your back pocket it's available, it's fairly close, it's accessible but you don't use it. At the moment we really don't need to use it. We are focusing Alliance energies on other activities.

What are those other activities? One strength that carried through from the Cold War to the present day is the ability to use the Alliance to promote defense cooperation. I think the main function of the Alliance today is to promote defense cooperation. Defense cooperation, which was used in the Cold War for deterrence and defense, we are using today for two somewhat different purposes.

The first purpose is a very practical one. The world still remains a dangerous place—the end of the Cold War did not mean an end to original sin. Unfortunately we may have to use force in the future to deal with challenges to our interests. We've already found that in Bosnia and Kosovo, and we will probably find it again in the future. The fact is that maintaining defense cooperation in NATO supplemented by political cooperation and consultation means that policymakers of the member countries will have options that they wouldn't otherwise have. If we weren't to maintain this defense cooperation, we would not be able to mount the kind of coalition operations that are possible with NATO. It doesn't guarantee that political action will be taken, that political decisions will happen, but it does provide the options. I don't think that you can ask much more from the organization.

There is another thing that happens with defense cooperation that I think is undervalued and that is that defense cooperation also projects stability. This is particularly important in terms of the developing relationship between NATO and Russia. I think that there is a potential for defense cooperation not only to change perceptions but also ultimately to change political realities. There has been a lot of talk about the relationship with Russia and NATO enlargement and many have said that there is a danger that NATO enlargement will destroy arms control. I'm going to take a somewhat different perspective on this and say if we destroy arms control, but we do it in the right way, it will be a good thing.

That sounds rather strange to say. Defense cooperation, on the spectrum of relationships among states, is much further along the line on the cooperative side of the scale than is arms control. A lot of our arms control relationships with Russia are based on Cold War assumptions. I'm not sure that we want to persist with all of these assumptions. Trying to move toward a relationship with Russia that is characterized by defense cooperation rather than Cold War-based arms control is moving the Russia relationship to an entirely new level. That doesn't mean we've gotten there, but that should be our objective: to replace the confrontationally founded arms control relationships with Russia with relationships based on political/military cooperation.

Let me conclude by focusing on the future agenda. First, the short-term agenda. I have three items on that agenda. One is NATO enlargement and the ratification process in the United States. The second, very briefly, is on Bosnia and what happens after the mandate for the Stabilization Force (SFOR) runs its course. The third is what do we do after this very creative and sometimes difficult period that we are going through with NATO.

The first question: enlargement—there are still questions about where we're going. My assumptions are, after we incorporate the three new members into the Alliance, NATO may eventually add Slovenia and Romania. Where the Alliance goes after that is an open question.

The second issue will be whether the European Union is willing to move ahead with EU enlargement at a sufficient pace to keep this process in parallel with the process of enlarging the Atlantic Alliance.

There is a wild card here, and that is one I mentioned earlier, Bosnia. We still don't have a coherent answer in the Alliance to what happens in Bosnia after SFOR's mandate runs out. The same problem is there for Kosovo and the entire Balkan region. The United States government, in my opinion, does not have a coherent answer to these questions. We even have differences that are only barely hidden by the public statements of our leading officials within the Administration and the Congress.

Finally, I will conclude with a brief comment about NATO and the need to move from creativity to consolidation. We've gone through a period in which a lot of new institutions, consultative frameworks, and procedures have been developed in the Alliance relationships with a variety of countries. The fact is the system is facing overload and all of the NATO officials I talk to say there are more meetings than any one person can go to in any one day. Following this very creative period there's a real need for the Alliance, even while it is dealing with Kosovo and Bosnia, even while it considers further enlargement, to start consolidating and to make effective use of all of the processes, procedures, and institutions that have been created. So the next few years will have to be a period of consolidation in the Alliance after going through a long period of creativity and turmoil.

I am very optimistic about the future of the Alliance. I am not blindly optimistic because in fact we always have problems to deal with. Those of us who work on these issues wouldn't have jobs if there were no problems, so I am thankful that there are some problems that we can address. But I am struck by one element of continuity about NATO. If you look at the North Atlantic Treaty, you will see that it is a marvelous document. There is very little in that document that could offend anyone, including Russia. I like to think back to the words that Secretary of State Dean Acheson used in 1951 when he was actually looking forward to a process of change in the Alliance; the first enlargement of the Alliance to include Greece and Turkey. Dean Acheson told the Congress that the North Atlantic Treaty is far more than a defensive arrangement. He said, "It is an affirmation of the moral and spiritual values which we hold in common." He said the central idea of the treaty is not a static one. "It is conceived rather in the spirit of growth, of development, of progress and what we seek is to pursue the opportunity for a living heritage of freedom to continue to grow." That responsibility is now in our hands.

TRANSATLANTIC RELATIONS IN THE NEW CENTURY*

Senator Xavier de Villepin
President, Senate Commission on Foreign Affairs, Defense and Armed Forces
Paris, France

I am very happy that this seminar, focused on the perspectives of Euro-American relations in the 21st century, under the sponsorship of the National School of Administration and Indiana University, has been able to take place in the Senate. First because our High Assembly places a great importance on the quality of the future of transatlantic relations, and especially Franco-American relations. Next, because few subjects take on an importance comparable to this objective that is among the top priorities of French diplomacy: the development of a true global partnership in the next century between the U.S., whom the world needs the most, and an EU that is developing slowly but surely into one of the essential poles of the world of tomorrow.

A recent European study devoted to this subject came up with three scenarios. The first scenario called for a decline in transatlantic relations; the second scenario offered an imbalanced relationship, with the U.S. in a position of dominance; and the third scenario, predicted an equitable European/U.S. partnership characterized by a strong and balanced relationship.

Another expert suggested that the essential question to know is if the 21st century will be the second American century, or if it will see the emergence of a partnership between the U.S. and Western Europe, as we hope.

**translation by Daria M. Roche*

The experts are often mistaken and the facts take care of contradicting the most learned analyses, especially in the long term. It is clear, in any case, that we must do everything to prevent the first bleak scenario that would see the U.S. and Europe give exclusive priority to their domestic problems and move apart from one another. Parenthetically, in the French electoral campaigns, I am among those who are sorry that we do not speak enough about international issues and about Europe, for I believe that the world in which you and I live can be explained in large part by international events.

In any case, Europeans and Americans will have to deal with the same challenges in the future. We share the same values of peace, freedom, and world progress. We are exposed to the same risks and we have the same responsibilities to assume—whether it is a matter of crises that break out in the world, or of consequences of religious fanaticism, ethnic divisions, terrorism, the proliferation of weapons of mass destruction, nuclear security, clandestine immigration, or of health problems such as illicit drugs and AIDS. We face the same threats, and it is clear that it is only through joining our efforts that we will be able to attack these threats at their roots and do what we can to free the future generations from them.

In order to face these dangers, while preserving peace and economic prosperity, Europe must become a more and more credible and solid partner for the U.S. The U.S. will have to be able to lean on a strong Europe, and on a solid transatlantic relationship. I would like to give several examples.

First, on the economic level, the creation of a single currency must be the result of the integration of the European economies. I remind you that the commercial exchanges between Europeans represent more than one trillion dollars. The EURO is indispensable for assuring a stability of exchange rates. Europe and America will remain the two most powerful and the most open economic entities in the world. The relations between these two great poles are thus of capital importance, whatever the economic growth and development of Asia or of Latin America. These relations must remain based on free trade, in order to favor our ambition of creating open economic spaces and larger markets. We must resist the temptations of unilateralism and, even more so, of protectionism. We must avoid bilateral or regional discriminating accords, and resolve our differences when they aris—which is natural within the framework of the World Trade Organization.

I cannot say it better, I think, than by recalling the talk given by President Chirac in the U.S. in February 1996. He said, "For the first time in history, economic globalization is a reality. We are taking on the responsibility for it. It is creating in Europe, like in America, similar opportunities and challenges. Let us know how to organize it for the benefit of all." The constitution of regional groups must be compatible with these large economic rules.

I want to point out, in this respect, that if dynamism and vitality have always permeated and characterized America, and make it more than ever one of the great zones of prosperity and stability, the American states have also chosen the path of regional economic development. I am recalling the constitution of NAFTA and of MERCOSUR, without even speaking of the debatable and debated project for 2005 of a large zone of free trade from Alaska to "Tierra del Fuego." But it is clear that the EU represents today the most complete example of regional integration. I hold the conviction that European construction must remain, in the interest of all, our priority that cannot be ignored. Notwithstanding, the tangible proof of the success of the European project resides in its exceptional power of attraction. Twelve states, at least, are knocking today at the door of the EU, with an insistence that we know well. The EU's principle objective will be to not be the victim of its own success, and to know how to associate deepening and enlargement.

The regional groups with different ambitions that we represent, on both sides of the Atlantic, must not close up on themselves. They must enroll in a multilateral framework. They must hold a permanent dialogue on trade and investment but also on subjects as different as development assistance or the war against drugs. This is why France and Europe wish to develop an open economic relationship with the U.S. It also goes without saying, and in my mind this is fundamental, that the vitality of the transatlantic tie will also have to be maintained in the field of security and defense. The Atlantic Alliance is and must remain the manifestation of the transatlantic vitality and solidity, for it goes without saying that our objective is to cause a real European identity to emerge on the international scene, and that there will not be a political European Union without a Europe of defense. It is clear, in my eyes, that this European identity must find its place in the heart of the Atlantic Alliance. The President of the Republic has accomplished a decisive step in observing that the construction of the European pillar of the Alliance, to which President Kennedy alluded, had to be made within the Alliance.

All the members of the Alliance share the same willingness to maintain for tomorrow an efficient alliance that has triumphed over the communist challenge without fighting it. But the conflicts within the former Yugoslavia have demonstrated that, since the disappearance of the Soviet threat, the U.S. was no longer exercising a constant leadership in military policy affairs in Europe, and that the Europeans were not capable, with their means alone, of substituting for what has sometimes been qualified as an intermittent leadership.

The future of NATO forms a fundamental component of the new partnership between the U.S. and the EU. This renewed NATO, re-balanced, offers the only solution that is both viable and realistic in the notion of collective security in Europe. This reform that is taking place must allow the Europeans to secure their responsibilities completely, when the U.S. does not feel that it must intervene directly, as is its right. The concept of a "combined joint task force (CJTF)" must quickly become a fact and must allow the U.S. to adapt their participation in future crises. The emergence of a stronger European pillar must allow them to defend their interests in Europe at a lower cost and without risk of being rejected. France wishes to be able to take its own place in this enterprise of the renovation of the Alliance, as far as the European identity can be firmly and concretely established.

NATO's reform will facilitate its enlargement from the moment that we succeed in maintaining a positive relationship with Russia, and the events of these last days demonstrate this. In order to rest on a balanced transatlantic relationship, this reform must allow the expansion of its European component. I offer two brief remarks. First, is the necessity of preserving a strong transatlantic tie while progressing in the direction of a European defense. Next, to achieve this, it will be necessary to clarify the relationships between NATO, the EU, and the WEU. It is my conviction that the EU will only escape paralysis in the domain of security and defense if its decision mechanisms are rewritten.

Beyond these major records, of economy and security, Europeans and Americans share the same culture, are confronted by the same challenges and disorders. We will have to reinforce and solidify the transatlantic cooperation in many other areas. I will offer a few examples.

First, that of aid to devleoping countries, which will remain a major requirement in the next century. The demands of morale and of the defense of our values join with our common interests. The best security is solidarity. France and its European partners are convinced of this and commit enormous sums to aid developing countries each year—in fact, I must add, three times more than the U.S. does. On this problem of international aid, I do not think that we are totally on the same wavelength, and I am sorry about this. My conviction is that it is necessary to go further, and that Europeans and Americans must combine their efforts. Our political interest is at stake, our security, and even, in the end, our economic interest.

Europeans and Americans must better combine their efforts in the midst of the great multilateral organizations. This is the case first with the UN, which remains, whatever its imperfections, through its universality, the main wall against arbitrariness on the international scene. This is also the case with the World Trade Organization, which we created to succeed the GATT and guarantee multilateralism, by ordering world trade according to fair rules. Finally, this is the case of organizations that, like the World Bank or the International Association for Development, must dispose of means in order to pursue their struggle and their fight tirelessly against misery and for the development of zones for the most needy.

Americans and Europeans will also have to pursue their efforts in the domain of disarmament, beginning with the fight against proliferation of weapons of mass destruction.

I will conclude by making two complementary observations. The first is to say to our American friends that France places a special importance on the increasing of the dialogue and of the cooperation with the U.S., the leading and uncontestable world power. The Franco-American friendship, steeped in history and blood ties, has never failed. This exceptional relationship rests above all on a common vision of the world, which assures that it will last. Of course, disagreements come up from time to time. That is life. But France will remain, whatever its political situation, a faithful and solid ally of the U.S. Do not forget this. Allies that are at times awkward are also often the most solid. It is in this spirit that Jacques Chirac took his first bilateral trip outside of Europe to the U.S. in 1996. It is also in this spirit that we must analyze France's policy toward the Atlantic Alliance, in the framework of a complete reshaping of the defense policy of our country on the horizon of the next century.

My final remark will be to emphasize that on the base of this alliance, Europeans and Americans must build a global and more balanced partnership. Much contributes to making America, at the dawn of the 21st century, the sole superpower: its military strength, its economic efficacy, the humbling of our adversaries of yesterday, and the triumph of our common values of democracy and free economy. But it is my conviction, the U.S. will find tomorrow in the EU a more and more solid partner. We must not pass up this opportunity, which is perhaps historical, to build for tomorrow a viable partnership which, through its dynamism and the synergies that it will form, will allow the transatlantic relationship—which is already exceptional—to be more global and more efficient.

STRENGTHENING THE TRANSATLANTIC DIALOG*

Senator Paul Girod
Vice President, Senate
Paris, France

In this colloquium we have chosen to speak of the future and of the content of the relationships that link the Old World to the New, which seems to me very important in the era we are living in, and for the equilibrium of international relations of the next century. In fact, the rank of the European continent will depend a great deal on the energy and enthusiasm of this transatlantic dialogue. In a world that is characterized by the emergence of new and often unforeseen forces—whether they are Asian, Indian, South American, even Indonesian—the success and the economic density of this transatlantic dialogue will certainly be decisive for the future of the Atlantic pole in opposition to the Pacific pole. Let us remember how quickly the Mediterranean pole lost its influence when the Atlantic pole was formed. If we want the community spirit that exists between Europe and the U.S, to remain at the level of what occurred at the birth of the U.S. and in pursuit of the civilizing mission of Europe, it is in our interests to understand each other as much as possible.

It is in this context that I tried to re-boost this group of senatorial friendship between the French and the American Senates. Our vocation is to multiply our opportunities to meet, to reinforce the ties and the contacts in this respect. I would date the opportunity to reiterate our willingness to meet regularly with

**translation by Daria M. Roche*

our colleagues in the U.S. Congress, so that in addition to our intergovernmental relations we might also develop interparliamentary relations. We know what important roles the Congress, and especially the Senate—which is much more powerful than the French Senate—maintains in the U.S. and we cannot stop with intergovernmental relations, if you want my honest feeling.

On June 2, 1995, on his first official visit to Spain, Mr. Warren Christopher, the man responsible for American diplomacy, gave an important talk in which he wished the foundations of a new transatlantic dialogue for the 21st century would be found. Two years later Mr. Peter Tarnoff, who was Assistant Secretary of State, gave the same message during a pre-colloquium launching the ceremonies that we organized on behalf of the French Senate to thank the American Senate for its action at the time of the Marshall Plan, more than 50 years ago. I think that we need to put ourselves in the perspective on what was the strong and essential American contribution to the renaissance of the European economy after WWII, during which they also saved us from the threat of Nazism and its outrages.

The perspectives that Mr. Christopher had outlined were ambitious because, beyond the questions of security, to which I will return in a moment, he initiated the development of a transatlantic zone of free trade. He had thus evoked the creation of an entire regime of investments and more subtle definitions of rules to expand the access to the market, encouragement of investment in information technologies, the elimination of commercial barriers, and the opening up of the sky through air treaties. We have seen since then how far things have progressed. The long-term goal of this vast program was to lead to "the integration of North American and European economies in accordance with the principals of the World Commerce Organization."

This was a more than ambitious enterprise, and it has not remained dead because, as early as November 1995, more than 100 American and European CEOs, from companies such as Ford, Siemens, Péchiney, Xerox, Philips, Alcatel-Alsthom, and British Petroleum met in Seville, under the initiative of the American Secretary of State and some of the executives of the European Commission, to initiate this new economic dialogue. This dialogue among businessmen, who expressed the willingness to eliminate excessive regulation and to unify the norms, without going so far as to bring the inch closer to the meter, was taken over at the political level by the Euro-American summit in Madrid, December 3, 1995.

During this summit a declaration of intention mapping out the contours of a transatlantic economic space was settled upon. We are entirely conscious of the fact that this path is carrying the future and that it consists of a fundamental choice for the future of our economies. I would like to offer two remarks, one of which carries a bit of anxiety, and the other a bit of hope.

The remark which is full of anxiety consists of recalling the necessity for the Europeans to remain vigilant and circumspect in regard to agriculture, which concerns France more, perhaps, but which, all the same, is essential for this continent. I say this because the definition of a transatlantic economic space clearly risks finding itself incompatible with the Common Agriculture Policy.

My second remark concerns the dollar. We have just succeeded, after numerous periods of financial turbulence and a long phase of under-valuing of the American currency, in stabilizing the dollar at its current level. It is indispensable for the Americans to dispose of a certain guarantee that will disprove the proverb that states that the dollar will be their currency and will become our problem.

In these brief comments, I have left to evoke quickly the important diplomatic aspect linked to the policy of Atlantic security. Here, too, the stakes are high, because, since the agreement on June 3, 1996 on the renovation of the Atlantic Alliance, many new perspectives have come out. Europe is seeing its responsibilities in NATO reinforced, and the European defense identity has been affirmed. To this renovation is added the dying out of France's and Turkey's special statutes, which is in favor of the expansion of NATO to the countries of Central and Eastern Europe. The integration of Poland, the Czech Republic, and Hungary in 1999 probably mark the beginning of the founding of a new world in which reflections will never be the same as before, but in which vigilance must not decrease. For if we have moved away from a frighteningly dangerous world, but one which had certainties and clear organizations, we are entering a world in which certainties and organizations are diminishing but in which danger is far from being completely erased.

The transatlantic dialogue, in the ensemble of its dimensions, constitutes an essential framework for our two continents to decide on a common future. Earlier I recalled our common roots. Our ambition is to offer our inhabitants a better world, and to the entire planet the example of democracy which is both mature, relaxed, sure of itself, and open to all of the preoccupations of the world's citizens.

Section II: The Next Genration of U.S./EU World Trade Policy

INTRODUCTION, SECTION II

Charles F. Bonser

In the second section of this book, we move to the trade front. The rapid globalization of the world economy has produced many benefits to both North America and Europe, but it has also led to increased tensions and disputes between the old trading partners. These have been exacerbated by the Asian financial and economic problems that began in 1997, by the anemic economic growth in the 1990s in much of Western Europe, and by the Europeans' seeming inability to do much about it.

International economic interests are now demanding a more liberal global trade regime, more open economies, and as evidenced by the European Union and NAFTA, more closely integrated regional economies. The question now is whether ways can be found to resolve the problems between the trading partners, and can the U.S. and the EU work together in a new trade round to update and liberalize the General Agreement on Tariffs and trade (GATT) framework, while also working together to strengthen the world financial system so as to avoid other situations like the "Asian Flu" of the late 1990s?

In December 1999, a meeting of the principals of the World Trade Organization will be held in Seattle, Washington, to consider next steps, including whether or not to initiate a new General Agreement on Tariffs and trade (GATT) "millennium" round, and if so, when and with what framework and topics. Numerous issues remain to be dealt with that were postponed in the Uruguay GATT Round completed in 1995. These include further negotiations on agriculture, trade in services, and intellectual property rights (particularly biotechnology, "cultural exceptions," and entertainment media). The EU has also expressed an interest in a comprehensive round that would include issues such as trade and the environment (discussed in Section III of this book), and regionalism (e.g., is NAFTA in violation of GATT?). The U.S., to date, has been more supportive of a limited round that could be concluded in about three years.

Economic relations between the U.S. and the EU, of late, have been strained to say the least. The U.S. has been pressing the EU on such matters as their Common Agricultural Policy, and has also filed WTO complaints against the EU for their restrictions on the importation of bananas and beef treated with hormones. The WTO has decided these disputes in favor of the Americans, but as of this writing, the EU seems a long way from acquiescing to the decisions. As a result, the Americans applied for, and received the right from the WTO, to levy substantial tariffs on selected (so they would hurt the "right" countries) goods they export into the United States.

In August 1999, the EU published a report on "United States Barriers to Trade and Investment." They included a long list of U.S. policies which they believe interfere, many illegally, with an open trading system. These included, for example, extraterritorial actions such as the Helms-Burton Act that penalizes nations for conducting certain businesses in Cuba; tariff and custom barriers; trade defense instruments such as anti-dumping legislation; technical barriers to trade (e.g., FDA approval procedures, patent systems) at the state and federal levels; government procurement; and several other areas of complaint.

The reader will get the picture. Commercial relations between the U.S. and the EU leave something to be desired, and seem to be getting worse, much to the dismay of those who believe that our common interests by far outweigh these competitive irritations.

It was against this backdrop that the Paris conference cited in Section I was held. The papers presented in this section were originally offered at that conference, but have subsequently been edited and updated by the authors.

This section on trade leads off with a paper by Ambassador Jean-Daniel Tordjman on the future of world politics in commerce. Ambassador Tordjman points out that the past ten years have seen the discrediting of at least two political/economic ideologies that have been prominent for over 50 years. First, obviously, Marxism and the concept of planned economies, economically, politically, conceptually, and historically, have been put to rest. The second doctrine suffering a "great blow" over the past 20 or so years is the model of development based on import substitution. This model influenced developed countries such as France, and less developed nations like Brazil, Mexico, and India. "Today, with the general evolution of exchange . . . the system of international division of labor, and of world competition . . . has proven its effectiveness."

Mr. Tordjman recognizes the international negotiations over the past 25 years—in which he has been involved as a representative of France—that have resulted in such significant progress in opening up world markets for goods, services, and investments, and culminated with the completion of the Uruguay Round and the establishment of the World Trade Organization. He also points out the importance of the creation of regional groupings (e.g., the EU, NAFTA) which "have allowed for the different entities to be extremely integrated on the commercial level, . . . and which poses the question of the relationship between these entities."

Ambassador Tordjam then examines in more detail the development of the EU and Europe's commercial relationships with the U.S. and other parts of the world, concluding with the observation that France and the United States have a long tradition of both friendship and competition, based on fundamentally common values and interests. With leaders who are aware of these interest—"which is the case today"—we can survive the problems and normal rivalries from time to time."

The second paper—on the "Next Generation of World Trade Development—is by Geza Feketukuty, of the Monterrey Institute in California, and a person of long, high-level involvement in U.S. trade negotiations during his prior service with the Federal government.

Mr. Feketukuty observes that the North America and Europe have worked together for over 50 years to dismantle trade barriers, and *have reaped the benefits of extraordinary growth, prosperity, and peace. This has greatly influenced countries to the East and to the South to abandon their communist and socialist dogmas. For the first time in world history it now seems possible to unite all countries under truly global economic institutions, founded on principles of economic freedom.*

Globalization of production, which makes it possible to reap economic benefits from specialization in business inputs, promises to enhance the economic benefits derived from the reduction of barriers to expanded trade and investment flows. Concurrent with this globalization of markets and production has been a burst of technological creativity that promises to end the drudgery associated with production. All of these dramatic changes in technology and the global economy offer prospects for greater economic prosperity and a more peaceful world in coming years.

Yet, in spite of this extraordinary success, there has been a "deep political malaise in both North America and Europe on the issue of further economic integration." He suggests that the reasons behind this situation are result of the cause of the malady on both sides of the Atlantic is the same, namely a combination of adjustment fatigue and globalization. "These come from the impacts on labor in North America and Europe, where the globalization and automation of production has led to stagnating wages and unemployment. There have also been social impacts of this structural adjustment as governments have trimmed social programs as a result of increased global competition and the faster pace of technological change."

But, in his view, the answer to this situation is not to stall further integration but to develop public policies, particularly in America, such as adult education and manpower training programs to provide workers with skills necessary to participate in the modern economy. The Europeans need to work on removing regulatory obstacles to new business creation.

He also believes we need to pay attention to how the expansion of regional agreements like the EU and NAFTA affect the transatlantic relationship. While he discusses how regional agreements serve important functions, they also can become a problem for the world economy if they lead to the erection of trade barriers to outsiders, or if the building of the agreements become too burdensome and distracting as to cause member nations to neglect their trade relations with other countries.

Mr. Feketukuty also discusses some of the pros and cons of creating a free trade area between Europe and the United States. He takes note of the fact that: "It is somewhat curious that leaders in the Americas have committed themselves to eliminate tariffs by 2010, leaders in the Pacific have committed themselves to eliminate tariffs by 2010 for developed countries and 2020 for developing countries, and leaders in the two most developed regions of the world have not developed any similar visions with respect to each other."

After considering these issues in much greater detail, he concludes with the observation: *There are both tremendous opportunities and risks for the world economy in the current environment. The question is whether world leaders can rise to the challenge, and provide the leadership necessary for forward looking solutions to the adjustment problems facing voters around the world. The opportunities generated by the end of the Cold War, by the globalization of production, and by the new information technologies are endless. At the same time, there are tremendous risks posed by the fragility of many economies and the lack of political consensus in the United States, Europe and Japan in support of outward-looking trade strategies. Ultimately it is up to the leaders of the major economic powers to discharge their responsibilities, and the next Economic Summit might well be the time for them to collectively make the necessary decisions.*

Senator Jean François Poncet is President of the French Senate Commission on Economic Affairs and Planning, and is one of the most senior and highly respected members of the French government. His presentation in this section covers several topics on the transatlantic relationship from the

standpoint of the European Union. He opens with the observation that the kinds of exchanges provided by this forum, and the New Transatlantic Agenda, are extremely important in many ways it is more necessary than ever "to develop exchanges between Europe and the US, (and) to develop these exchanges at the level of the elites who do not always understand each other and who, I believe, need to explore their reciprocal thoughts." But the relationships within NATO—between the US and Europ—have a tendency to fail to make progress.

The Senator poses three questions on this matter: Do the interests of Europe and the U.S. coincide? He answers in the affirmative, but then wonders, if this is so, why do we so often have conflict? Finally, what can we do to improve the relationship?

He then examines these issues in some detail and remarks: *It seems to me that the first reason is the demand of an America with an undivided leadership, in any case that is how it appears to Europeans. It is the conviction, which we sometimes find naive, that in Washington they see things more clearly, they know better what needs to be done, and the best way is to decide alone and then try and impose on Europe the decisions that have been made. It is evident that this claim, supposing it is just, and, naturally, I grant the American auditors to disagree with this, clashes with certain European objectives. . . . It is not that this leadership is disputed in principle, but the manner in which it translates at times, the interests that it expresses and the differences which can come about in a certain number of situations in the world, all explain that there is a problem here.*

Turning to trade relations, Senator Poncet remarks: "There is a second general cause of problems that is not about to disappear, that is in the order of things, but that creates tensions, as you know. It is obviously the economic, commercial, and industrial rivalry between Europe and the U.S. that has materialized much more clearly since the end of the Cold War. "

On the matter of regional trading organizations, the Senator observes: "The U.S., inspired by the European example, established NAFTA in North America and APEC in Asia, resulting in blocs that have a tendency to form, beyond the oppositions that can exist between countries. We can wonder if the world economy is going toward free trade or, on the contrary, if it is going toward a structure consisting of regional groups. Consequently there are diverging interests, rivalries that go together with the convergences that I was talking about earlier (free trade, the protection of investments, the protection of intellectual property).

A third problem cited is "the U.S. attitude toward European construction, whose origins owe a lot, almost everything, to the US. It is certain that the Marshall Plan was accompanied by a very strong encouragement on the part of the U.S. for Europe to unite.". . . But as Europe created its own "consistency," it developed its own policies that brought it to resist what America would have wanted to see Europe do. [Consequently], little by little there was the feeling that the US was remaining favorable to European integration, but with the reservation that it not bother them in any way. It is very clear that European integration is itching powder for the US."

Senator Poncet's last section is a discussion of ways in which we can improve the transatlantic relationship. He also considers the role of the EU in the future, vis-à-vis the United States.

The final papers in this Section are by Ambassador John Weekes, Permanent Representative of Canada to International organizations in Geneva, Switzerland; and Yves Boyer, deputy director of the Foundation for Strategic Research, France.

Ambassador Weekes focuses his paper on economic policy convergence. He argues, "there is no longer the same difference of view between nations as to how economic life ought to be organized. The market has definitely come to the fore. The World Trade Organization (WTO) and is now moving towards potential universality."

He believes the next generation of world trade policy is already in view. "On average, every country in the world is exporting 22 percent of everything it produces in good and services. For some countries like Canada, the export ratio is now 40 percent. For non-oil exporting developing countries, interestingly, the export percentage of total output is approximately 30 percent. We now see a world in which we're suddenly forced to come together much more closely."

Ambassador Weekes reviews the progress made in the Uruguay Round of GATT, and the processes of the World Trade Organization. He observes: *An even bigger move has developed towards new agreements that are treating the international trade issues of tomorrow, but also which have very domestic oriented implications. Topics such as financial services, investment and competition policy, and trade and the environment are very much in the forefront of activity. We are already committed to new negotiations in agriculture and across the range of services issues to begin around the end of the decade.*

After discussing several related issues, including regional agreements, he observes: *I think it is somewhat paradoxical that we can look at some of the problems for which we have been trying to make progress with more limited initiatives, but sometimes it is easier to do things if you have a more ambitious bigger agenda. It allows the leaders to move in and help the negotiators overcome the difficulties. It mobilizes support for the positive side of what can be achieved, rather than only having those who look at it from a negative perspective entering the fray. I suspect that 1999 may well be the year to gather forces for that kind of major effort.*

Yves Boyer takes a global view of European Geo-Strategy and the transatlantic partnership. He begins by asserting that "the excessive weight that the United States pull in European affairs is becoming one of the major problems in the future of we Europeans." There are, he offers, different ways of approaching the organization and cohesion that Europe needs to hold its own geo-politically. Some think of Europe as a "supermarket"—the triumph of economic liberalism. Another vision is of a Europe that would resemble the Swiss Federation. The third vision ("rather French") is one that "unites a certain number of countries who share a single ambition: that of affirming and defending a European model. Of defending the interests of that Europe, from a monetary viewpoint (and this is the whole debate about the EURO); from a commercial perspective; and from a diplomatic and, if that fails, a military perspective."

His paper then explores some of the issues and challenges that will affect the outcome of this debate. These include the demographics of Europe, vis-à-vis its neighbors; the "relative weakening of the European economic and research capabilities, and the increase within Europe of an anti-European sentiment (e.g., consider the very low turnout for 1999 European parliamentary elections). Europe is also facing such challenges as border control and an increase in organized crime, terrorism, and migration from the south and east.

In examining these matters, he does end on the more optimistic note that, "I am convinced that finally the European countries are capable of mobilization and creativity. It is still necessary for the relationship between the State, the leaders, the elite and the citizens to function, and it seems to me that in a certain number of European countries this relationship is in a state of crisis. Nevertheless, European construction is developing."

Commentary

As in the previous section, there was a lively debate at the Paris conference where these papers were originally given. To offer some flavor of that discussion, a few quotes are included below.

Question

Our own president, Mr. Clinton, is going to be looking for what we call fast track authority in order to pursue the kind of agenda in the next round of trade liberalization that Mr. Feketekuty has mentioned. The kinds of populist disappointment, anger about the dislocations that the Bloomington case (RCA relocation) represents is dramatized on both sides of the Atlantic. . . . Can you be more specific in either case of why it is one should be optimistic about the capacity of the Executives in both countries to overcome increasing skepticism on the part of the public and the labor force?

Tordjman Answer

The process of adjustment is not finished. In Europe as well as in America they (corporations) will continue to choose the best places to produce, to develop, to trade and so on. But, we are not to be too pessimistic because the level of competition of America and Europe is still very strong. The problem for us is that the other nations are also advancing full speed and adopting our technology; having available the same type of financing. The end question is in the value of our people because that will make the difference. If they have the right level of education. If they are flexible and mobile enough. If they be adapted to a changing environment we will continue to win.

Feketukuty Answer

I think Jean-Daniel's answer is really superb. Let me just say it's been my own experience, that in the United States it's a question of political leadership. I've seen other situations where we have had a very negative environment. Where the president went up front, determined that this is going to be important, he mobilized the political forces, he had the business community out there, he got the message out and people responded. But without political leadership it can't happen.

But the fact is that we don't have much choice. The downside is very real. I remember what happened when Mitterand first came in and embarked on a very sharp shift in policy. It lasted 12 months until it became so apparent that there was no choice—that France had to basically also participate in the outward-looking process. The downside can become very clear very fast. In terms of currency crises, people just start putting their money elsewhere. It starts putting constraints on your policy. Things start collapsing. So you have to get into virtual cycles and then you have to have leadership to explain to the public. I think that is one of the big challenges for leadership: how do you explain it and why is it necessary.

Question for Geza Feketukuty

You mentioned several times the concept of competition policy, which for me is not striking or astonishing. With regard to this topic in the Atlantic Free Trade Area you discussed, what is exactly your vision of the debate with respect to competition policy?

Feketukuty Answer

This is a topic in which people other than the existing competition officials need to get into a dialogue. In particular, people with a trade dimension. There has been a stylized development on both sides of the Atlantic. We're both very happy with our rules on competition but also there is a difficulty of looking beyond the existing set of rules and rule making in the competition area to look at how the world trading system is working—what role can competition play and how can the various elements of competition relate to each other. How do government policy, business practices and trade negotiations all come together in defining the competition milieu. I think what we need is a new way of looking at this issue in which not only legal technicians in competition policy but people with a sense of the commercial realities and people involved in trade negotiations all get together and say "we've go to sort some of these issues out in a broader context."

Participant Comments

• *We are at the moment in a stage of reflection on the next international trade initiatives. But, during these periods of rest, it is inevitable that there will be forces at work to unravel the gains of liberalization. I do not think they ever really succeed because the consequences of going backwards are really worse for people's economic livelihoods than the consequences of going forward. But they must be dealt with because they reflect apprehension and fears of society at large about where we are going. Until these fears are dealt with, governments will have to be careful. Otherwise they risk going too fast and fracturing public support and confidence.*

• *I do think that competition policy is an area that lends itself to multilateral discussions, but clearly we see different nations around the world at very different levels of evolution in their thinking on competition policy. We have to remember that trade itself and the rules of trade in many ways were based on exceptions to the principle of open competition. Tariffs are an exception to open competition. They are a discrimination in favor of your own domestic producers. Anti-dumping rules were a way of saying you cannot compete too much on price because if you do you are engaged in an unfair activity. A lot of what trade people have done over the years is try to define exceptions to competition. So I am not sure they are necessarily the best people to be talking about internationalization of competition rules.*

But on the other hand competition authorities differ vastly on this subject. Interestingly enough, probably the greatest convergence has been between the United States and the European Union where, after all, they have a cooperation agreement; consultation arrangement; and information sharing. Articles 85 and 86 bear a strong resemblance to the principles in the U.S. anti-trust law. But clearly they are also clouded by national interests and by the inability to necessarily internationalize the process of setting competition rules. I think we have to be very careful with this because I can see a multilateral exercise going nowhere. On the other hand, I think it is inevitable that we talk about it.

Question

How far should considerations of national security go in limiting free trade? Even Adam Smith made an exception here. How important, to be more specific, would it be to have an American defense industry, a European defense industry, and perhaps a Russian defense industry, for example?

Feketekuty Answer

Obviously, governments feel strongly that they have to be able to have a certain capacity in the defense area that is nationally based. But at the same time there are clearly limits even in the defense area to what extent economies of scale within individual countries permit them to build a full array of security equipment, security materials. If you look at NATO, it is a very complicated patchwork of agreements in arms trade. I know that there have been talks sometimes in the past creating sort of a gap for defense within the NATO structure. I had numerous conversations with people in the Pentagon about this. There was always somewhere a gap between their concept of what this would entail and my notion of what this would mean. But clearly there is a need for a level of cooperation even in this area. Exactly how you structure it I am not sure I have a clear answer. I should add that in the United States the U.S. Trade Representative's Office has virtually nothing to say about the trade in defense products.

Question

The problem with respect to your answers so far is that from the point of view of the (European) Commission—with respect to the small plane manufacturer of Seattle (Boeing)—is that there is not an issue in defense but in the market structure. So how can we reconcile market structure, efficiency and defense with people not being able to talk about defense in the USTR or in the competition agencies in the U.S.? Whereas these competition agencies in Europe can consider, they can speak about a corporation without taking into account prima facie its specific defense industry. Besides, the major part of the contest so far is not on the defense issue.

Participant Response

I think there is a great deal of truth to what you say that obviously this involves broader questions than just the organization of the market. On the other hand, that is not unique to this sector. If you think about a sector such as the information technology and communications sector, which has had a history of vast governmental involvement and unquestionably a spillover between governmental (military) application shall we say and consumer or civilian applications. I think it is true, even of something as mundane as agriculture where clearly that which is driven by the market and that which is driven by government policy is hard to discern. There is no place of more government intervention than in agriculture. One of our largest bureaucracies in the United States is the Agriculture Department. But I would also say that in terms of analyzing the competition effects of all of these, it should be based strictly on the effect on the marketplace. It should not be based on other considerations. The other considerations have to be resolved through governmental agreements. If you are going to examine a merger or an acquisition, you really have to look not on the effect on competitors but the effect on competition and on the marketplace.

Weekes' Comment

I would make the point in closing that I think what is very important to understand is this increasing interdependence of economies and the increasing extent to which each of our economies is integrated into the global marketplace. This does not mean that international cooperation is perfect. It does not mean that anybody has all the answers. But I think what it does mean is that we are condemned to continue collectively to try to work toward the solutions. That to go backward would mean economic regression and dislocation that none of us are prepared to accept.

Participant Comment

If we look at what are the real consequences of this cumulative globalization, one conclusion is that we are witnessing the diminishing relevance of national governments to the regulation of commerce. If we do not struggle to find an international framework and a modus operandi for addressing these problems—whether the issue is technical standards, competition policy, or the environment—we risk the possibility that governments will simply engage in increasing tension and conflict with one another to the detriment of the economic well-being of their citizens. . . .

. . . In this globalization process there are winners and there are losers. In the final analysis, the losers cannot outnumber the winners. They have to be brought into the adjustment process and ultimately made to see how it is going to enable them to live better lives.

Editor's Comment

As has been alluded to in this section, trade and other tensions between the U.S. and the EU have interfered with the rational resolution of trade issues. It was therefore gratifying to see that, at the Bonn Summit in June 1999, President Clinton, German Chancellor and (then) EU Council president, Gerhard Schroeder, and Jacques Santer, acting president of the EU Commission, launched a series of initiatives to try to improve relations between the U.S. and the EU. President Clinton stated: "We discussed the need to have unresolved trade disputes not define our relationship at a time when we are working together so well on so many fronts." Recognizing that trade disputes will naturally occur, they agreed to set up an "early warning system" that can arise from policy, legislative and regulatory decisions, before they become damaging. This system will involve both government and industry representatives, who would be responsible for notifying government senior officials of trade conflicts that could worsen. The leaders also endorsed a draft framework agreement on mutual recognition in the area of services, with engineering and insurance as the first areas for negotiations.

THE FUTURE OF WORLD POLITICS OF COMMERCE*

Ambassador Jean-Daniel Tordjman
Ambassador at Large, Special Representative of France for International Investments
Paris, France

I will just say a few words of introduction on the current status of the debate between the French and the Americans. It was said earlier that we share the same values of liberty and democracy, we face the same threats, and, we are also both responsible for the prosperity of the world economy. And in these issues, if we clash often, we also have many common interests. As for these common interests, I am going to try and develop two ideas.

First, the essential idea is that for 50 years we have caused considerable progress to take place in the evolution of world commerce, and things of commercial nature, in and of themselves, have been widely exploited and facilitated by the regional and international evolution of negotiations.

The second idea is that today, in a world in which everything is much more mobile (capital, men, ideas, technology), the central question lies in knowing where world enterprise is going to place its investment. Because everything depends on this, the production value of American enterprise in Europe, for example, greatly exceeds the number of American exports from the United States. Thus we have an evolution of the center of interest, from the question concerning commerce to the much more strategic and elaborate question of knowing where investments are being placed.

**translation by Daria M. Roche*

At the level of economic doctrine, things are cut and dried. I am not speaking about Marxism or of planned economy. We know the history of this system and we have seen how it has evolved. Today the failure of Marxism is not only economic and political, it is historical and conceptual. The manner of development that had been proposed had seduced many people throughout the world, through its global vision and elements within it which are still pertinent, such as the fact that a certain number of ideologies react in relation to the ideas and the basic economic foundations. Now we have seen that, as a manner of development, the results are in, and Marxism is out.

The second doctrine that has suffered a great blow over the past 20 or 30 years, is the model of development with which the Swedish economist Gunar Myrdal is associated and which is called the "philosophy of import substitution." This has had an influence on many countries, such as Brazil and India. It has influenced countries as developed as France where there have been numerous attempts at approaching the economic system by import substitution. Essentially, the idea is not to develop world commerce. The idea is to find the weaknesses in the balance of trade and to try to cure them, via industrial politics that specifically focus on the sectors in need of development.

In relation to the international division of work, which is the basis of philosophies considered here as Anglo-Saxon (Adam Smith), the main philosophy of Ricardo is an entirely different approach: it is not to play on the strengths of the winners, but to prop up the losers. We have seen that this has not worked and that the developed countries are those that have specialized in their strong points and that have been able to succeed outside.

Today, with the general evolution of exchange, I would say that the system of international division of labor, of world competition has proven its effectiveness, because we are in a period of great prosperity in the world economy. There would be many things to say about the countries that have used the system to their advantage. They took as their basis a politics of massive investments in certain sectors; of freezing the internal economy in order to halt imports; and of subventions and support of exports through all means, including currencies that remain undervalued for a certain time.

Between the time when foreign countries could invest and buy back a firm and when one achieves great prosperity, the value of the currency increases and the borders are open to international investment (which is currently the case in Japan). But the domestic costs have become too high to allow firms to buy distribution networks. For example, companies like Ford hesitate to put in a billion dollars in order to try and buy a distribution network from the Japanese. Therefore, I would say that it is not the doctrine of the IMF, of cold hard capitalism which has taken it, it is, up to a certain point, the Japanese doctrine of strong expansion which the different countries have considered. But the global result is that on the conceptual plan of world commerce, the doctrine of the international division of labor has won.

So all of this took place through a cycle of negotiations in which some of us have participated for 25 years. We met in Brussels, in Geneva, in Washington, all proceeding in the direction of the lowering of customs rights, of the suppression of quantitative obstacles. and of the treatment of non-tariff obstacles in trade. It is a discussion that culminated with the Uruguay Round and the creation of the World Trade Organization.

Thus, we have a field of action based on a pertinent and logical evolution of thought that is translated by an entire series of worldwide negotiations which are going to continue now in the WTO, the OECD, etc., and which is a great line of evolution.

There has been a second related issue about which I will speak briefly. This is the parallel necessity to create large regional groupings that advance faster than global evolution, and which have allowed for the creation of different entities extremely integrated on the commercial level, and sometimes more, and which pose the question today of the relationship between these different entities.

The most striking example is that of Europe, which began with six countries based on the concept of the Common Market. In 1985, we went from the Common Market to a slightly more advanced notion—the Single European Market. The difference lies in the suppression of the former Article 115 in the Treaty of Rome. This allowed any country into the Common Market, if the goods came in and if that country wished to maintain an import control system, to have the right to do so. Now this is impossible with the Single European Market. As soon as a product enters Germany, or Greece, it circulates everywhere in Europe; that is the difference. And, now we are crossing a new frontier of the utmost importance—the progression into a single European currency. This is going to create a historical difference in relation to the preceding time period. This is going to create a great and useful challenge for the dollar. For the first time, we are going to see a "shift" of dozens and, in my opinion, of hundreds of billions of dollars toward the EURO.

This is a phenomenon of great importance that has been entirely underestimated. This phenomenon is going to cause enormous movements in capital and investments, one without precedent. Today there is one single world currency, and it is the dollar. The people of Hong Kong, the people of Latin America, do not invest in deutsche Marks. Few people invest in Yen. There is a single world currency and it is the dollar. The depth of the market, the liquid assets, and the general foundations are sufficient. With the single European currency, we have an economy that is superior in its scope to the American economy. We have approximately 8500 billion dollars of gross national product in Europe, compared to a little over 7000 billion in the United States, and we have this revolution of a Frenchman being able to buy a car with the same currency in Belgium or in Germany. You have a new movement of interest for Europe, which is going to be an extremely significant.

The new European Monetary System (EMU) is a major political and monetary event. It will be the end of a great uncertainty in Europe and the true beginning of a new era. It will present difficulties because one cannot have a single currency and significant economic variations without economic flexibility—that is to say, according to the Americans, the capacity to react quickly to basic developments. In that respect we may have difficulties, but I think that this has been foreseen by the two leading countries of Europe—France and Germany. Together these two countries represent 46 percent of the European economy and we are linked through a common historical vision of avoiding in the future what we have experienced in the past—three fratricidal wars.

A recent exhibition in Paris on the Franks teaches us something that has never been taught to the French previously—that the Franks come from the right bank of the Rhine, a region today known as Germany. For a century our grandparents and great-grandparents learned that our ancestors were the Gauls and not the Franks, and they were taught that the Gauls were certainly not Germanic and that the Franks came from Franconie, and perhaps a little more to the East. This means that what was at the basis of all of the past battles between the French and the Germans was false, that in reality we are extremely close.

When Chancellor Helmut Kohl spoke about the reasons for creating the Economic and Monetary Union, he referred to it as a matter of war and peace. We are not just talking here about interest rates, this is not only a financial issue, it is a political issue. And if Chancellor Kohl did not express himself clearly enough, read what Chancellor Schmidt has written. Mr. Schmidt does not beat around the bush; he speaks very clearly. He says what all of the German chancellors and political leaders of Germany say: that if Germany is all alone it gets too strong, and if it gets too strong it does foolish things and it risks being opposed by the other European countries. That is what the German chancellors say and that is the main reason why Germany wants and will create a political union. Its first step is the Economic and Monetary Union.

For we French it is a crucial point, because peace and security are much more important than 2 percent or 3 percent growth. That explains the permanent Franco-German alliance, no matter who the political leaders in each country are, because it stems from the historical tendencies of our two countries to move toward our increased prosperity. This is a model of development that is more and more integrated and which is approved of by almost all of the European countries, with the exception of our British friends, who follow another train of thinking. This is a model of integration that lies inside the current world economic level.

The Americans have engaged in an equally important effort with Canada and Mexico and, for many reasons, they want to spread this system throughout the North and South American continents. It is a very important effort with very important economies. But sometimes it seems to me that NAFTA is a dirty word in Washington. Why? Because the degree of economic development in Mexico is not exactly the same as that of the United States, on the political level or on the monetary level. Americans, and especially many of my friends in Washington, reason in terms of intellectual fashion. Ten years ago, it was the Single European Market. It was Europe. Seven or eight ears ago, it was NAFTA.

Of course our American friends think, "land of opportunities." The true criterion is the risk/reward relationship: the relationship between risk and the return on investments. If you concentrate solely on opportunities, you can make very serious errors, and we French speak from experience, for we, too, lost our shirts (as you did in Mexico) by investing in Russia and China before WWI. We would have been better off investing in the United States. This helps explain the reticence of the French in respect to pension funds today.

Thus, I said to my friends in the U.S., "There is a fashion today in Washington about emerging markets. But when a fashion becomes a passion, you can lose your shirts." And this same lesson is valuable for China. If you go into American business committees today, everyone is going to talk to you about China. We, too, are taking positions there. France has 6 percent of the world export market and we have only 2 percent in Asia. We must improve that, but we will do it with great caution. I asked my friends from Sumitomo what their criterion for investments in China was. They responded that their criterion for investment in China is a capital return in two years. If you do not have capital return in two years, do not invest. That is the essential point.

Given the creation of regional trading organizations such as NAFTA, APEC, MERCOSUR, ASEAN, and the European economic space, entire groups of trading zones are moving in the direction of free trade. The big question now is, how do these different groups interact. On that point we are forced to make progress.

I was in Mexico recently and one of the messages I reported to my colleagues, who were involved in these negotiations, is that it is urgent for us to form a bond between the European Union and Mexico. Why? Because, due to NAFTA, the Americans and the Canadians have a tariff advantage which, in many cases, is around 18 percent. The French exporters are pulverized by an 18 percent difference. Our interest, due to NAFTA, is to have an agreement with Mexico, and we are going to do it. And in the same manner, Europe is going to develop its relations with MERCOSUR and with ASEAN. The French president's recent travels to Latin America and to Asia have incited a great interest, to say the least, in the United States. I asked my American friends if they were in favor of the

European Union's efforts, to develop a commercial agreement with MERCOSUR and, of course, they could not say no. They cannot say no. But I would argue that it is entirely in our, and in the United States' interest, to go in that direction. In commercial matters, the Monroe Doctrine of 1823 is a little dated.

Europe will develop its relationships: this means that there is a very large agenda with another series of problems that we are going to debate, perhaps in terms of intellectual property, in terms of services, and in terms of agriculture. But essentially, the commercial matters between us are going in the right direction.

The true debate is about the problem of world investment, which has been essentially multiplied by six since 1985. I am speaking of direct world stock investment abroad, not pocketbook investments or currency investments. Exchange investments are 1400 billion dollars a day, but it fluctuates, it comes and goes. Pocketbook investments are also extremely important, but they, too, can change quickly. When you buy factories, the level of investment does not change immediately. It is therefore impressive to note that the world stock was at 650 billion dollars in 1985, and it is at 3000 billion dollars today.

That is the fundamental phenomenon, because after having exported, one must sell, and in order to sell, one must have distribution networks and one must produce. France is a good example of a considerable development in this area. For ten years we have been going at full speed in this sector. This is true for French firms abroad that have invested massive amounts of money during the last ten years because they had profitable returns, and because these returns were made possible by our government's good reaction to the petroleum counter-shock in 1985. This was in contrast to the petroleum crisis of 1973–1979, during which the governments at the time made a huge error by trying to maintain the standard of living of the French by making cuts in business. The result was that we were dragged through the dredges for ten years. Then French businesses had to go into debt, cut their investments, and had to cut their research. In 1985, we reacted in an intelligent manner, letting surplus profits go into business and not into the personal consumption. One does not practice good politics simply by having good intentions, but rather by understanding what is happening and reacting to it consequently.

Since 1985, French businesses have developed considerably in the world, mainly in Europe and America, and we have (and I myself participated in and assisted in this movement in my role as plenipotentiary secretary in Washington) assisted massive investments, whether we refer to Michelin, to Péchiney, to Saint-Gobin, to Air Liquide, to Schneider, to Total, to Elf, or to many others. That was criticized at times in France, but the result is that today French firms represent almost two-and-a-half million jobs in the world. It is not relocation, it is an absolutely indispensable expansion of French businesses. And in this sector, the United States, of course, is the world leader. But we are in fifth place among long-term world investors behind the Japanese, the English, and the Germans.

As far as investments in France are concerned, there is a parallel development of the increase of international presence in France. Why? It is because the successive French governments have understood that it was worthwhile to develop international activities in our country and to increase the presence of international firms in France. It is a source of technology, it is a source of new forms of management, it is a source of money, and it is a source of jobs. We have made so many errors in the past with the Japanese, and also a few with the Americans, that it is time to change and that is what we have done for the past several years, and with spectacular results.

Today, the most attractive country in the world is, of course, the United States of America, which has perhaps 650 billion dollars of direct investments within itself, and the size of the economy is massive. Behind them, at the moment, number two is the United Kingdom and France. We were fifth only four or five years ago, behind Canada and Germany. Today we are third in the world with a huge presence of 36 percent of investments coming from the United States. There are English journal articles pointing out that France is now challenging the United Kingdom, as the second country in the world in investments.

That is a revolution. I took on my duties in 1992, and when I visited the *Financial Times* of London, I told them that part of our objectives would be to have a major article in the *Financial Times* saying that France was among the two or three interesting countries in terms of world investments. Their response was, "No advertising section." Now I think that our British friends are taking us a little more seriously. So that is a subject of the utmost importance for the next several years. The cards are going to be reshuffled constantly for the multinationals in the world.

The world changes and it changes quickly, under the impact of three major revolutions: that of technologies, that of management, and that of markets. In the matter of technologies, we must remember that we invented the transistor 50 years ago. Today we put 5 million transistors on one memory chip, and we put 1000 chips on a diskette, and we have systems which manage several billions of operations a second. This technology has transformed the entire world industry. If we look at the telecommunications system, 20 years ago 12 telephone lines ran on one copper wire; today, 70 million telephone lines are run on one. All of this goes at great speed—with a capital "S." We must remain at the forefront of the world economic ensemble.

Thus, to conclude this very brief tour, I would say that on the commercial level we have points of dispute with the U.S. which are due to our common interests for certain sectors: services, telecommunications, and agriculture. It is especially important for our American friends to realize that France, with a population of only 58 million, is constantly the second country in world exports of agricultural food products. Five percent of our population works in agriculture. Why? It is because there is a great interest in French products.

I was recently at a conference of English bankers in London where I gave a "speech," and someone asked, "Are you worried about the new millenium?" I said, "Well, I am not at all worried. I do not see why I should be worried, because there are no risks." They told me, "No, no, no, we are not talking about that: Have you bought your cases of Champagne for the year 2000?" So I responded, "Uh, no . . . I had not thought about that." And they said, "As for us, from January 1, 1999 until the last day of the year 2000, we are having Champagne every day." And after that I looked at what our Champagne vintners were offering as "Special vintage 2000, limited to 2000 bottles." Look at the prices. The magnums are selling for between 6000 and 12,000 francs per bottle . . . $1000 to $2000 a bottle. And there are people who are going to pay $1000 to drink their two liters of Champagne. And that occurs when they tell us that the French are no good at marketing. I can tell you that you have an immediate response: we are the only ones who sell millions of bottles of red wine at $20 and up per bottle.

Thus, that explains our major trade surpluses—a structural competitiveness. I will end on that. I say to my American friends, "Do not worry. No matter what the results of the polls are, France is a rich country structurally, with an extremely powerful agriculture. We are the number one country in the world for tourism, with 61 million tourists and 140 billion francs of revenue from tourism. We have a luxury commerce that has its roots in history and which stems from the fact that we had flamboyant kings, and so an entire industry of luxury has developed. We will continue this advantage with high technology, present in all domains. In the most advanced domains of defense, we are very often the principal competitor of the United States. We are therefore concerned when, as clients and as partisans of an open and competitive economy, we see the two top American firms, Boeing and McDonnell-Douglas, together controlling 68 percent of the world market.

But, in conclusion, there are many questions yet to be asked. I support a dialogue on the interest of the United States and France to work in common toward their common prosperity and for their joint success. France and the United States are probably two of the only countries in the world who have not been at war against one another. The United States has been at war with the United Kingdom, Germany, Japan, Russia, China, Italy, and with many more countries . . . but never with France. And that is something that comes out at the military and political level on both sides and translates into a very strong alliance. An alliance that is fundamentally based on common values and interests, and which can allow itself to make explicit the problems and the normal commercial rivalries from time to time, if we have leaders who are aware of the interests. This is the case today and will still be the case tomorrow.

THE NEXT GENERATION OF WORLD TRADE POLICY DEVELOPMENT

Geza Feketekuty
Director, Center for Trade and Commercial Diplomacy
Monterey Institute of International Studies
Monterey, California

Over the past 50 years, Europe and North America have worked together to dismantle trade and investment barriers, and have reaped the benefits of extraordinary economic growth, prosperity, and peace. The ultimate testament to the success of these policies has come from the countries to the East and to the South. These countries have decided to abandon their communist and socialist dogmas, and their opposition to open, market-oriented economic policies. This has brought about an end to both the Cold War with the East and the Cold Peace with the South. For the first time in world history it now seems possible to unite the countries of the Earth under truly global economic institutions, founded on principles of economic freedom. And while democracy has not triumphed everywhere, it is more widespread today than ever before.

At the same time that more countries than ever are seeking to integrate themselves into the world market economy, the globalization of production promises to enhance the economic benefits derived from the reduction of barriers to expanded trade and investment flows. Globalization of production makes it possible to reap economic benefits from specialization in business inputs—the services, components, technology, professional, and managerial talent that businesses use to produce goods and services. This new trade in components, services, intellectual property, and professional talent promises to boost the economic dividend from trade and investment liberalization.

In the past few years we have also seen an extraordinary burst of technological creativity, which is transforming the way we produce goods and services. This technological revolution holds out the promise for eliminating much of the drudgery associated with production, offering more workers than ever the possibility of holding jobs that challenge human creativity, knowledge, and intelligence. These are jobs that require high levels of skill, but also hold out the promise of higher incomes.

Together, the integration of the developing and formerly communist countries into the global market economy, the globalization of production, the automation of routine manufacturing and services job, and the creative application of technology to the development of new goods and services, holds out prospects for greater economic prosperity and a more peaceful world in coming years.

You would think that people on both sides of the Atlantic would be dancing in the streets to celebrate both what has been accomplished and the promise of even greater prosperity and job satisfaction in the future.

Yet, exactly the opposite is the case. There is a deep political malaise that seems to afflict the body politic in both North America and Europe on the issue of further international economic integration. New proposals for trade and investment liberalization appear to lack broad political support, the drive to expand the EU to the East is moving slowly, and the expansion of NAFTA to the South appears stalled. I believe the cause of the malady on both sides of the Atlantic is the same, namely a combination of adjustment fatigue and globalization phobia.

The global trends that hold out so much promise for increased economic prosperity in the future—the integration of developing and formerly communist countries into world markets, the globalization and automation of production, and the shortening product life cycles—are creating major structural adjustment problems in labor markets. In North America these labor adjustment problems have resulted in a decline in the real wages of unskilled workers, and wage stagnation for workers in the middle. In Europe, labor laws have prevented a decline in wages in response to the structural changes, and instead have led to higher levels of unemployment.

The social impact of the structural adjustment has been magnified as a result of budgetary pressures, which have forced governments to trim generous social welfare programs such as pensions, unemployment benefits, and health care benefits. Cuts in these programs, in the face of the increased global competition and faster pace of technological change, are raising anxiety levels among all workers about reduced job security. This in turn leads to globalization phobia, a concern that unfair competition from low wage pollution havens with exploitative labor conditions will threaten the quality of life in North America and Europe.

The structural adjustment problems in both the American and European labor markets are real, and pose major challenges to the respective governments. In the United States, the major challenge is to improve adult education and manpower training programs to give more workers the skills needed for technology-intensive production processes and for the production of technology intensive products. In Europe, the challenge is to remove many of the regulatory obstacles to the establishment of new businesses.

The structural adjustment problems and policy challenges in Europe and North America are real enough, but they pale in comparison to the problems and challenges facing Eastern Europe, China, and major parts of the developing world. It is inconsistent for North America and Europe to preach the virtues of market adjustment and trade liberalization to the countries in the East and in the South, and not face up to the challenges posed by structural changes in their own economies.

The question we ought to address today is what the countries in North America and Europe can and should do to move forward on trade and investment, and how they can build public support for such initiatives in the face of the current political climate on trade.

Both Europe and North America have committed themselves to a near term expansion of free trade areas in their regions—an expansion of the European Union in Central Europe in the case of Europe, and the expansion of NAFTA into South America and the establishment of a wider Free Trade Area of the Americas in the case of North America. On both sides of the Atlantic internal political difficulties have slowed the process and raised questions on the timing and the pace of the expansion.

The question that needs to be posed here is how the expansion of the respective regional agreements will affect the transatlantic relationship. Some analysts have expressed the fear that a continuing focus on regional integration agreements, particularly by Europe and North America, will have the effect of undermining the global system. This could become a real concern if the United States and Europe become so preoccupied with domestic political resistance to regional expansion that they neglect their own bilateral relationship or the continued expansion and strengthening of the global, multilateral trading system.

In my view, the development of a regional structure within the global system is in itself a desirable development, because not all questions in world trade are most effectively dealt with at the global level. Some questions are best resolved at a regional level among neighboring states. Other questions are better addressed initially by smaller groupings of countries with a more homogeneous set of interests before they are tackled at the global level. Regional solutions provide room for experimentation and models that might be followed later in global agreements on an issue. Regional agreements in this sense fit into the application of the subsidiarity principle to the management of the world economy.

Regional agreements also provide the basis for maintaining a forward momentum in the liberalization process when progress toward further liberalization on a global basis is blocked because some important countries are not ready at the global level, or because the larger number of countries involved creates the need for an extended period of consensus-building. Economists have spent a great deal of time worrying whether the trade creation effects outweigh the trade diverting effects of regional agreements. Experience has shown, however, that the major economic gains from trade liberalization come not from the static efficiency gains derived from increased economies of scale, but from the dynamic efficiency gains derived from increased competition. Increased competition creates economic benefits by stimulating producers to seek out more efficient production methods, or new products that will appeal to consumers.

Regional agreements in the post–Cold War world also serve important geopolitical objectives in establishing stable political relationships among nations in various regions of the world, and in securing progress in domestic political and economic reforms. In Latin America as well as in Central Europe, the expansion of regional free trade agreements provides the basis for embedding democratic political reforms and market-oriented economic reforms in international agreements that are more difficult to undo, and create an economic cost for national policies considered inconsistent with international norms in areas such as human rights.

Regional agreements can become a problem to the global economy if they lead to the erection of new barriers against outsiders, or if the task of building the regional agreement becomes so burdensome to the member countries that they neglect their trade relations with other countries.

Seen in this light, the regional integration efforts in Europe and the Americas are not in themselves a bad thing for the transatlantic relationship, provided it does not lead to the erection of new barriers to transatlantic trade, and provided the countries in Europe and North America do not become so preoccupied with their regional efforts that they neglect the transatlantic trade relationship. During the years of the Cold War the security alliance against the Communist threat provided a strong glue, which prevented the two sides of the Atlantic from drifting too far apart on trade matters. In the absence of the Cold War and the security ties it provided, the challenge of preventing the two continents from drifting apart has become significantly greater.

IS IT TIME FOR A "TRANSATLANTIC FREE TRADE AREA"?

This brings us to the question of whether it would be desirable and feasible to consider the negotiation of what has been called by some a "Trans-Atlantic Free Trade Area," or TAFTA. The negotiation of such an agreement could help assure that regional integration efforts in Europe and the Americas did not result in a widening of the economic gap across the Atlantic, either through neglect or the advertent erection of new barriers.

The idea of a TAFTA was explored informally on both sides of the Atlantic a few years ago. It was set aside in 1995 at the Madrid Summit for the less ambitious and fuzzier concept of a "New Transatlantic Marketplace," which was to be created by "progressively reducing or eliminating barriers that hinder the flow of goods, services, and capital between us." To implement this vision, the leaders agreed to a "Joint U.S.- EU Action Plan," which called for efforts to deal with mutual problems in areas such as customs, standards, and regulatory issues. It also called for a joint study of the costs and benefits of removing tariffs across the Atlantic. So far, the results of these efforts appear to be fairly anemic to outside observers.

Three major difficulties or obstacles have been identified to an effort to negotiate free trade across the Atlantic. The first is the adverse impact of a TAFTA on the World Trade Organization and global trading system. The second is the great difficulty of liberalizing barriers to agricultural trade. And the third is the political realism of talking about any kind of free trade in the context of the current political malaise. Let me address each of these in turn.

The major objection to a TAFTA has been that the negotiation of a free trade agreement involving the United States and the European Union would deprive the World Trade Organization of the leadership provided by its two principal members, and send the signal to the rest of the world that the United States and Europe were abandoning the liberalization of global trade on a nondiscriminatory basis. The question of whether the negotiation of a trade agreement across the Atlantic will harm the global system will very much depend on how such an agreement relates to global trade liberalization and rule-making efforts. That, in turn, depends on the leadership the U.S. and the EU are willing to provide for future negotiations in the WTO.

It is somewhat curious that leaders in the Americas have committed themselves to eliminate tariffs by 2010, leaders in the Pacific have committed themselves to eliminate tariffs by 2010 for developed countries and 2020 for developing countries, and leaders in the two most developed regions of the world have not developed any similar visions with respect to each other. The establishment of a similar vision for trade across the Atlantic could do much to provide a greater coherence to the global movement for the elimination of tariffs.

A decision to establish a transatlantic vision to eliminate tariffs by a certain date to parallel the vision established by leaders in the Pacific and in the Americas would require a decision on whether tariffs would be eliminated on a preferential or on a nonpreferential, MFN basis. This is, of course, the crux of the matter, with respect to concerns about the potential impact of a TAFTA on the global system. The elimination of tariffs by North America and Europe on a nonpreferential basis vis-à-vis outsiders would hardly raise any concerns by the rest of the world, but would be very difficult to adopt politically because of a concern about free riders. It could also reduce the global movement to free trade by reducing the incentive of countries in other regions of the world to reduce their own tariff barriers. On the other hand, the negotiation of preferential tariff cuts could be seen by the rest of the world as North America and Europe turning their back on the multilateral trading system. A solution to this dilemma would be to leave a decision on whether tariffs would be eliminated on a preferential or MFN basis to the future, and link it to the willingness of other regions of the world to participate in a parallel global effort in the World Trade Organization.

This brings me to the rule-making issues. Paradoxically, tariff liberalization is seen as a far more sensitive issue than rule-making, even though rules on standards and regulatory issues are likely to prove far more important to trade flows in the future than tariffs. Increasingly, the barriers to trade that are the most disruptive of trade are barriers embedded in standards and regulations, and in private restrictive business practices. At the same time, new opposition to trade liberalization efforts has emerged from nongovernmental groups concerned with the achievement of social objectives in areas such as health, the environment and labor standards. This has led to a new trade agenda focusing on issues such as regulatory policies in infrastructure services, competition policy, investment rules and laws of corporate governance, bribery and corruption, environment, and labor standards. If the transatlantic negotiations are seen as a stepping stone to global cooperation on some difficult issues, there is likely to be far less opposition to bilateral negotiation between the transatlantic partners.

There are both tremendous opportunities and risks for the world economy in the current environment. The question is whether world leaders can rise to the challenge, and provide the leadership necessary for forward looking solutions to the adjustment problems facing voters around the world. The opportunities generated by the end of the Cold War, by the globalization of production, and by the new information technologies are endless. At the same time, there are tremendous risks posed by the fragility of many economies and the lack of political consensus in the United States, Europe, and Japan in support of outward-looking trade strategies. Ultimately, it is up to the leaders of the major economic powers to discharge their responsibilities. The Economic Summit scheduled for Seattle at the turn of the century might well be the time for them to collectively make the necessary decisions.

OBJECTIVES AND PRIORITIES OF THE EU IN TRANSATLANTIC RELATIONS*

Senator Jean François Poncet
President, Senate Commission on Economic Affairs and Planning
Paris, France

Thank you, my dear President, for this welcome and bravo to ENA and to the School of Public and Environmental Affairs of Indiana University. I think that these contacts are useful. I think that it is in many ways more necessary than ever to develop exchanges between Europe and the U.S., to develop these exchanges at the level of the elites who do not always understand each other and who, I believe, need to explore their reciprocal thoughts.

I am stricken, and this is my beginning observation, to notice that in 1997 in Paris, NATO and Russia, through what we have perhaps pompously baptized a foundational accord, have laid down the bases of an entirely new relationship. Certainly this relationship is burying the Cold War (in a certain way it was already buried) but, beyond this, it is laying down the basis of a new relationship between Russia, Western Europe, and the U.S. It is laying down this basis around NATO which is being extended, justified, comforted in its existence, and which is extending its boundaries to the ex-USSR.

This is an important innovation; a historical step forward has been accomplished, and, in relation to this evolution in the relationship between what we called East and West, we are surprised to admit that on the contrary, the relationships within NATO—between the U.S. and Europe—have a tendency to

---

**translation by Daria M. Roche*

fail to make progress. It is not that we are not paying attention to it. We have talked about this a lot. I am not saying that we have not progressed, but it seems to me that regarding the alliance that ties the U.S. and Europe, on both sides, everyone is in agreement on the necessity of adapting it to an environment that has changed significantly—not only because the relations with Russia have changed, but because the worldwide context has completely changed. And yet we are not making much progress.

Thus, there is a paradox, and it seems that this paradox marks the basis of our debate. I would like to consider it in terms of three questions to which I am going to give you my own answers. I do not claim that they are France's answers, nor the answers of Europe.

The first question is that of knowing if U.S. interests and European interests coincide. I believe that we must begin from this question. Are we pursuing the same objectives? My response to this question is a firm yes. I answer yes, and I am going to tell you why, but that leads me to a second question. If our interests converge, then why do we often have conflicts between Americans and Europeans, and, perhaps more so, between Paris and Washington? This leads to a third question: what can we do to improve these relations, to redefine them and project them into the future?

I am going to look at each of these questions, if you like, just as the Director of studies of the School of National Administration during my time at the school taught me to do.

It appears to me that there are not a lot of doubts that the values that the U.S. and Europe defend, the challenges they encounter, and the objectives they pursue in the world coincide. It seems to me that we hardly need to emphasize this. The values, we know them on both sides of the Atlantic: Democracy, the Rights of Man, Liberty. How many times has this been said? How many times have we emphasized that we draw from the same roots, whether they be Christianity or Greco-Roman heritage?

The challenges that we must raise are also much the same, whether we think of crime, drugs, or insecurity. There was a time when we thought that these problems were much more American problems than European ones. This time has passed. It is the same with ethnic problems. I remember a time when the African-American problem was considered by Europeans with a willingly critical eye. When we look at the problems that France faces today with a strong minority of North Africans, no one can look at this with the same critical eye on the problems of the U.S. When we think about the problems of the political society, mediatization, the crisis of representative democracy . . . when we think about the family, about single parent families which have become today on both sides of the Atlantic, not the norm, but something that is, alas, more than commonplace . . . when we think about globalization, new competitions that interpellate a certain number of our economic sectors—it is true that faced with globalization the Americans have an attitude of flexibility and adaptation which incites both our admiration and our jealousy . . . fundamentally, the problems that we come across are the same.

It is very logical, very normal that, defending the same values, confronted with the same challenges, we develop the same objectives. I will list them very quickly, and this follows from what I have said.

The defense and the diffusion of democracy and of the rights of man in the world are the common objective of the U.S. and Europe. There was a time when Europe was less mobilized, less militant than the U.S. If you think, for example, of the situation at the beginning of the 20th century after WWI, with President Wilson on one side and his European interlocutors on the other, it is clear that the Europe of Versailles was not exactly what Wilson would have liked. But I think that this time has passed. It was in France that the new formula, "duty to intervene," was invented a few years ago. Was this a formula for the future? Was it a formula that describes French diplomacy? I am allowing myself to doubt it. This formula, I think, simply indicates that, from now on, the democratic militantism exists on both sides of the Atlantic and implies, on both sides of the Atlantic, the same eclipses. When China is concerned, there is less zeal than when other countries that carry less weight on the world scene are concerned. Nevertheless, I get the impression that, from this point of view, there is a clear connection.

In the same manner, when it is a matter of the defense and the diffusion of the market economy, of individual initiative in the functioning of our economies, we are equally attached to the free distribution of products and free access to primary materials, to the protection of investments, to the protection of industrial property, to the multilateral rules in world commerce, on both sides of the Atlantic. So of course there is an old debate that comes up again periodically, that consists of knowing if the U.S. are more free-traders than Europe. That is what the U.S. thinks. This is not what Europe thinks.

There are nuances in this debate that you recognize well. For the U.S., Europe was quickly christened "The Fortress Europe," and we find in this justification when we look in the Common Politics, when we think of the subsidies that the states and the European governments have been accused of giving their industries. But I would say that Europe has as much of this as the U.S., whose bilateralism in commercial negotiation matters often tends to eclipse the multilateral zeal. It is Europe, more than the U.S., who pushed for the establishment of the World Trade Organization and procedures of restricting arbitration, to which Europe complies more willingly than the U.S., because the former doesn't have the same means of bilateral pressure as the U.S. It is not that they lack the desire, but it is often the means and the structures that are lacking.

This said, in reality, the interests are the same in free trade. Let us not forget that Europe is first in world exports, and that no one has more interest in free trade than Europe. France does not always understand because it has an old protectionist side that comes out at the first opportunity, but as soon as it is reminded that one job out of four in France depends on exports, the protectionist fervor diminishes. I would like to add that when the U.S. uses the means of pressure which they possess, more than Europe, against Japan or against China, they are serving their own interests, but at the same time they are trying to open the markets to everyone, and so are the Europeans. Thus, it is in our interests to see these pressures develop and succeed. As a result, it seems to me that in this second axis (the diffusion of a market economy founded on individual initiative), there, too, is a common objective.

A third convergence: on both sides of the Atlantic we are powers of status quo. The world order suits us. We must admit that we have done a lot to create it, and it cannot be said that it serves our interests, but the fact is that we are, globally speaking, satisfied powers. And this satisfaction distinguishes us from powers like China, Iraq, Iran, or, more recently, Serbia. We stand not only for peace, but for the resolving of existing differences through negotiation or international arbitration, but not through force. We have the same interests: that does not mean that we pursue the same interests in the Middle East. We have the same interest in the establishment of peace between Israel and the Arab world. We have the same interest in seeing Saudi Arabia stabilized. There are reciprocal irritations, but when we come up against an obstacle, there is not one Frenchman who would not prefer to see Saudi Arabia overseen by Americans than by an Islamist stronghold.

Well, we could go on with the list. Europe and the U.S. are against the proliferation of nuclear weapons, against the diffusion of chemical weapons, against drug traffickers, and in favor of protecting the environment.

I have made a quick enumeration of the convergences, but I hope that it was convincing. Having made this enumeration I find myself against the observation that we are going from one difficulty to another and that the clashes between Europe and the U.S. are a resurging matter in our relations. I cannot say that since the end of the Cold War harmony has prevailed in comparison to the previous era. It seems to me that the opposite is true. How can we have so many converging and fundamental interests, and how can we observe that, at the same time, we have a hard time getting along?

Well, and here I am coming to the studies of the ENA (National School of Administration), this is the dialectic gymnastics at the heart of all French-style lectures. As a result, having stated my thesis, I am now going to state the antithesis and analyze the reasons for these clashes.

It seems to me that the first reason is the demand of an America with an undivided leadership, in any case that is how it appears to Europeans. It is the conviction, which we sometimes find naive, that in Washington they see things more clearly, they know better what needs to be done, and the best way is to decide alone and then try and impose on Europe the decisions that have been made. It is evident that this claim, supposing it is just, and, naturally, I grant the American auditors to disagree with this, clashes with certain European objectives.

First, it clashes with an objective of principle. I think that the Europeans are ready to accept American leadership. Partners, junior partners, yes! Servants, no! Even more so in that, to achieve their goals the U.S. does not always hesitate to play on the European divisions, which understandably annoys the Europeans. I am thinking for example of President Bush's discourse after the fall of the Berlin Wall when he went to Germany. As you know, he put into circulation an expression which has been used many times since then: "partnership and leadership." For the rest of Europe, this gave the impression that President Bush was unaware of the EU and the anxiousness to put forth a Europe that naturally excluded an individual relationship between the U.S. and any one European country.

This claim for leadership clashes with another objective. It is the feeling that we have in Europe that the positions that the U.S. takes on the international scene are very often the expression of an interior political equilibrium, I would say, of domestic political preoccupations, rather than of an objective analysis of the situation that must be confronted. This is a recurring sentiment. We could cite many examples. Before the presidential elections, when President Clinton was in a great hurry to take the American forces out of Bosnia, it was obviously because Congress was on his back. In 1996, when the U.S. gave a visa to the president of Taiwan and welcomed him, everything indicated that the president would rather have wished not to do so, but Congress did not give him a choice. And you know what happened as a result: the crisis in the Formosa Strait and many difficulties that they have since tried to resolve or reduce.

Today when we consider this capital element of the international situation, that is our relations with China or the U.S. relations with China, there is obviously a great rift between the president and Congress. I was in America not long ago, and I heard Henry Kissinger define this problem. He was worried, incidentally, although he was a Republican, of what the Republican majority of Congress wanted to impose as the policy. So there are obviously not many reasons to ask Europe to line up with the uncertainties, the highs and the lows of American domestic policy. This is certainly not the path to international wisdom.

And then, we must recognize that there are differing interests. I was speaking of the fundamental convergences, but there are also, on a daily basis, differences of judgement. There are naturally differences in the Israeli-Arab conflict. The predominant feeling in Europe is that American policy is in a large part dictated by the Jewish lobby in the U.S., which is very strong and in relation to which European policies, and notably French policies, like to take some distance—not to ignore the interests of the State of Israel, but in order to have a more balanced policy, which we feel has better chances at bringing about an accord than a policy that seems too partial. And I do not need to recall Cuba—the Helms-Burton Amendment—the differences that can be found where Iran and Iraq are concerned. I do not claim, moreover, that the European positions are the right ones, especially concerning Iran. The European critical dialogue seems to me to be inspired more by commercial preoccupations than by a realistic vision of the situation in Iran. But when it is a matter of Boutros Ghali, for example, and his replacement, it is certain that in France, but also in Europe, there were doubts that were manifested by a veritable European unanimity in the United Nations. And, moreover, the manner in which America executed Mr. Boutros Ghali incited a lot of criticism in the United States itself. Consequently, there are differences.

So it is the demand of the American leadership that is the first consideration. It is not that this leadership is disputed in principle, but the manner in which it translates at times, the interests that it expresses and the differences which can come about in a certain number of situations in the world, all indicate that there is a problem here.

There is a second general cause of problems that is not about to disappear, that is in the order of things, but that creates tensions, as you know. It is obviously the economic, commercial, and industrial rivalry between Europe and the U.S. Which has materialized much more clearly since the end of the Cold War. The Cold War had not erased these problems, but I would say that they take on a more muffled aspect because of the need for alliance in front of the Soviet threat that stood before the Atlantic partners. Since then, it has often been stressed, economic interests have been much more freely expressed, and the president of the U.S. weighed directly in the scales many times to snatch up contracts, notably after the Gulf War in the Middle East. The European countries have not been ashamed to do the same thing, relative to their means, which are very limited. Consequently, there are clashes which result and which are entirely in the nature of things.

The Europeans have the feeling that the U.S., whose influence on the IMF or on the World Bank is considerable, have a tendency to influence these organizations in a sense that conforms to their interests.

The U.S., inspired by the European example, established NAFTA in North America and APEC in Asia, resulting in blocs that have a tendency to form, beyond the oppositions that can exist between countries. We can wonder if the world economy is going toward free trade or, on the contrary, if it is going toward a structure consisting of regional groups.

Consequently, there are diverging interests, rivalries that go together with the convergences that I was talking about earlier (free trade, the protection of investments, the protection of intellectual property). There are in some domains or, at least this is the European sentiment, strategies of annihilation by certain branches of the American economy toward their European competitors. I am thinking of aviation, for example. We have the feeling that if Boeing could make Airbus disappear, it would not be refused. We have the feeling that in the domain of the military industry, the American industries do not see the usefulness of a European obstinance to make their own military arsenals. Consequently, I believe there we have something that is as permanent as the convergences of interests that I was mentioning.

There remains a third problem that we must mention with a question mark. It is the U.S. attitude toward European construction, whose origins owe a lot, almost everything, to the U.S. It is certain that the Marshall Plan was accompanied by a very strong encouragement on the part of the U.S. for Europe to unite. It is for that reason that the OEEC, the ancestor to the OECD, was established. One must not have a memory if they do not remember the support given by the U.S. to the idea of a European army. It is not the U.S. that killed it, it is France. It is one of the great aberrations of the contemporary history of our country, and I do not know if we are not close to committing others. The fact remains that we can allow no one to forget these memories, and this U.S. role.

But it is certain that as Europe was building consistency, it developed its own policies that brought it to resist what America would have wanted to see Europe do—naturally, I am thinking of the European agricultural policy: think of the chicken war led by General de Gaulle against the U.S. Think, too, of the dollar and of the gold standard. In short, little by little there was the feeling that the U.S. was remaining favorable to European integration, but with the reservation that it not bother them in any way. It is very clear that European integration is itching powder for the U.S.

Today we are asking ourselves, perhaps a little late in Europe, about the real feeling of the U.S. toward the European single currency project. Especially since it is certain that it will lead to a sharing of the financial power in the world. Nothing causes us to say that the American government is hostile to the single currency. It is when we read the American press that we wonder. It jumps on all the opportunities and reasons to lay a cloud of doubt on our chances of succeeding. Perhaps the American press is seeing the truth, I do not know, and I would not like to give my talk a biased angle. The fact remains that there is an interrogation there which, whether right or wrong, exists in the minds of the Europeans, and I think that I have to list the three big chapters that seem to me to explain the clashes that, despite the convergences, we are running into (that is, the demand of leadership, the economic and commercial rivalries, European construction).

Since I am still following the thread of French-style presentations, now it is time for me to attempt a synthesis and try to say how we can hope to make transatlantic relations healthier. I think that the answer is that we must both clarify them and balance them.

I think that the answer is that we must clarify them through a better understanding of the preoccupations and the orientations of both sides. I think that there are three things that the Europeans must understand. It seems to me, incidentally, that they have more or less understood, but probably not all of them.

The first thing and, to use President Reagan's well-chosen expression, I think the Europeans have all understood this, "America is coming back." Not only it is the only superpower remaining, and, in all probability, it will remain so during the first quarter of the 21st century, but, additionally, it has taken up this tradition of dynamism, of initiatives, of innovations again, that at a certain time we had the feeling that it was losing. At the beginning of the 80s, the idea spread that Japan had dethroned the U.S. in the areas of computers and electronics, and that this change was irreversible. We have seen American capitalism make a spectacular recovery, and we have the feeling today that it is the U.S. that is giving lessons on economic behavior to the planet, and especially to Europe. There is no electoral meeting today—and I speak of this because I have just returned from one—that does not rely on the American example, either in the hopes that we can imitate it, or in the hope that we do not move in that direction. But the American example is in all of our minds. So I think that the Europeans have understood this first truth, America is coming back.

Second, I think they have understood, or they must come to understand, that isolationism is dead, at least that is my belief. Not as a current of thought, it is still expressed: in the last primaries, we saw a certain number of candidates on the far right develop isolationist theses, but they are minorities; they are condemned, in my mind. What is happening in the U.S., that we must understand, is that America is embracing globalization. Globalization is from now on the master word list in the U.S. I am a member of one or two consultative councils, administrative councils of large American companies, and I am stating that "internationalize" has become the master word of all the American companies. Consequently, we are turning our backs on isolationism which, in my mind, is of the past.

The third truth that the Europeans must understand, I think that they have also more or less understood, is obviously that Europe has become retrograde in American priorities. And I think that this evolution is irreversible, simply because other parts of the world have become as important for the U.S., more important than Europe. This is true of Latin America, it is naturally true of Mexico, and it is evidently true of Asia. This is not only true of the U.S., it is also true for us. Everyone has finally noticed China, but China is not the only one. Tomorrow it will be India. And, of course, for a long time now, Southeast Asia. Consequently, priorities have changed.

In my opinion these are the three observations from which we must begin (the return of the U.S., the globalization of American perspectives and a relativization of what Europe can present). This brings up the question: "How must we Europeans appreciate still today what Europe represents in the American priorities and preoccupations?" And it is obviously from here that we must begin. I am not sure, incidentally, that the U.S. has totally decided on its position yet. This is a problem that is at the heart of many thoughts and debates. I am not speaking and I am not thinking of a preoccupation which is obviously of major significance in the U.S., that is, the Soviet nuclear arsenal, which is a problem for us all; I would say that it is both a dramatic and a circumscribed problem. I would like to get into more general areas.

It seems to me that on both sides of the Atlantic, and notably in the U.S., there is a diffuse feeling of political solidarity. There is also something that we must not forget; that is, the considerable importance of the economic solidarities and ties. On the level of investments, and even on the plan of trade, Europe is a heavyweight, even more so today than Asia. But obviously the dynamic is on the Asian side, and the time is coming for Asia to bypass Europe firmly in terms of American economic interests. There are very close relations there. And here again, to evoke my own American experience, which is certainly not on a weekly, but on a monthly basis, I observe that American businesses continue to shop in Europe to buy back competitors, they continue to develop in Europe. Meanwhile Japan has, in a large part, reconverted almost entirely in Asia. This is not as true in the U.S. as in Japan.

Next, it seems to me that Europe is a strategic platform for the U.S., notably in regard to the Middle East. I know that today there exists airborne forces, but we have seen what happened at the time of the Gulf War, and don't you believe that we are safe from serious incidents in the Middle East. It seems to me that a major interest of NATO for the U.S. is to serve as a permanent aircraft carrier from where operations can be conducted, if necessary, into the Middle East tomorrow. And beyond that, it seems to me that the U.S. clearly needs a partner within the world, and there are only two possible partners: one is Japan, with its own particular problems, and the other, with which the relation is simple, direct and spontaneous, is Europe. It seems to me that, due to civilization, economics, and military issues, which are all political, Europe is an interesting and permanent partner for the U.S. for the future.

It remains to be seen what Europe must do in order to make this partnership take on the consistence that Europeans wish to give it. It seems to me that there are very precise responses. The first condition that the Europeans must fulfill, and this is not the easiest, is union. It is clear that Europe will not be the partner it can be with the U.S. unless it begins to speak more and more with a single voice. It is essential that Europe be sufficiently united, I would say, to resist the U.S. when it (Europe) believes it necessary, and at the same time, to constitute a true partner in negotiations with the U.S., which laments the following two problems. The first is that Europe is always divided. Consequently, it is very difficult to know what Europe thinks. One often makes reference to an observation made by Henry Kissinger, who, invited by the Commission of Foreign Affairs of the National Assembly (presided by Mr. Giscard d'Estaing), while many criticisms were being made about the U.S. to him, he said, "Bring me a telephone," and then, when someone brought him a telephone, he said, "Would you please give me the telephone number for Europe?"

So this is evidently a task that the Europeans must overcome, knowing that division is not the only problem. Sometimes the Europeans end up taking a common position, but they had so much difficulty in reaching agreement that afterwards it is extraordinarily difficult to negotiate—because in moving from the position that they have defined, they run the risk of becoming divided once again—and, consequently, the U.S. is faced with an inflexible European partner. Either inflexible or entirely divided. This is obviously what Europe must correct in carrying the Union further, so that it has a union that allows itself simultaneously to define a common position and then to call it into question in a negotiation. This is to say that Europe must progress more toward a federal type of structure. That is what is in question. And, alas, I do not claim that we will make revolutionary progress in this path.

Second, Europe must learn to accept the regional responsibilities that are incumbent upon it. Obviously, in saying that, I am thinking of the events of Yugoslavia and of Bosnia, in which Europe should not have needed the help of the U.S. In any case, that is my conviction. And yet, everyone can see that, neither on the realm of a common viewpoint, nor in the realm of military capabilities was Europe up to the task which confronted it. But I think that there is something that the Europeans must understand there; the U.S. will take an interest in the problems of Europe from the moment it has the feeling that its vital interests are in jeopardy. Not as long as they have the feeling that it is only a question of regional problems that logically come from within Europe.

There remains the third point. And it is here that I will end. I think that the Europeans must begin to ask themselves what their behavior on the international scene will be once they have made sufficient progress toward the Union. What sort of international animal will the EU be? This is a reflection that has barely begun, and in relation to which I would like to make a few provocative comments. I think that Europe has all the possibilities to be, what it already is, incidentally, but which the Single Currency will surely make it, that is to say, an economic superpower. Will it also be a political superpower?

Personally I do not think so. I do not think so for two or three reasons. The first is a reason concerning structure. A political superpower is not defined only by the importance of a population, the importance of an industrial plant, the sum total of its scientific and technical capacities. Europe has the means to be a political superpower about on the same level as the U.S. But the Europe we are building will be a federation of states, and not a federation of peoples. It will give, as you know, a very big space to subsidiarity, that is to say that we will have, of course, in the heart of what I would dare to call the European Federation, states much more independent and autonomous than the American states ever were, even at the time of confederation.

Consequently, this weak structure, inevitably heavy and bureaucratic, will not be in a postion to react to stimuli, to challenges of the international conjuncture of the moment with the speed and the capacities that the U.S. possess. We have on the European scale, a very minimal budget. This budget is made up of between 1.7 percent and 2 percent, but no more, of the gross domestic product of Europe. And there is very little chance that Europeans will reach an agreement to increase it. Their tendency would be rather to reduce it. It is not with such means that one gives Europe a military force that could compare with that of the U.S.

So, having defined the contours of what will be/could be the European power, there remains to deduce what could be its international comportment. My feeling is that the inclination will be to play the game of multilateralism in the domain of economics and the game of the UN in the domain of politics. I think that we are going to witness a reversal of the historical positions of the U.S. and of Europe. Europe was, it has often been said, the territory of real politik, the balance of the forces (Metternich), and that is how things turned out in 1918. The U.S., on the contrary, was known for idealism, a diplomacy founded on the principles that are the founding principles of American democracy.

I am not sure that we are not seeing these positions turn around: America, because of its role as the only world superpower, led to arbiter according to the necessities of the moment and according to the available means, and Europe becoming, with more sincerity, the apostle and the support system of the UN, of environment, of the preoccupations which have traditionally been those of the U.S. Which does not mean that the U.S. is going to abandon them, nor that Europe will give up on the use of force. But it seems to me that his strange animal that Europe will become, unique in the world, will have something very interesting, because you know that Europe has been, basically, the political laboratory of the contemporary world.

Europe is the one that invented individual liberty in the 18th century. The French Revolution played a considerable role, very quickly backed up by American independence, incidentally. Europe is the one that invented the National State, to its misfortune. And it seems to me that Europe is currently inventing a new, yet very necessary, international reality; that is the combination of the maintaining of national identities with the development of a supranational structure. And that is what is making this quite strange animal that the European federation will become, if it succeeds—for I assign to this success, as you may have observed, limits that I believe we will have a lot of trouble escaping, at least, in a foreseeable future.

Obviously, this leads me to a conclusion. That is that there is a natural complementarity between the U.S. and Europe, because we will be international animals that are simultaneously solidified and different. It is for us to understand it and to bring out the consequences in the redefinition and the consolidation of the Atlantic Alliance.

DOMESTIC AND INTERNATIONAL ECONOMIC POLICY CONVERGENCE

Ambassador John Weekes
Permanent Representative of Canada to the United Nations and Other International Organizations at Geneva, Switzerland

It's clear that we are living in a world that is dramatically different from the world of ten years ago. There's no longer the same difference of view between nations as to how economic life ought to be organized. The market has definitely come to the fore. The World Trade Organization (WTO) is now moving toward potential universality. It already has 130 members and there are 30 or more countries trying to accede to the organization. But, although there's a greater unity in terms of some of the fundamental objectives of how things should be organized there are still some very important differences of interests between different countries.

The next generation of world trade policy development is already visible. In fact, I would argue as well that there is much less separation between domestic and international economic policy than previously. I'll expand on this theme, but believe one of the factors propelling us forward, creating difficult policy differences, is that countries everywhere are becoming more and more dependent on the global marketplace.

It is quite dramatic to look at the relevant statistical changes that have occurred over the last 25 years. WTO statistics show that in 1996, the nations of the world as a whole exported more than 22 percent of their domestic product. That means, on average, every country in the world is exporting 22 percent of everything it produces in good and services. For some countries like Canada, the export ratio is now 40 percent. For non-oil exporting developing countries, interestingly, the export percentage of total output is approximately 30 percent. We now see a world in which we're suddenly forced to come together much more closely.

I will briefly review, in very broad terms, the results of the Uruguay Round. But it is worth noting that there have been interesting changes in the subject matter from that which was negotiated in the old GATT. In the old GATT, we basically dealt with border measures and quantitative restrictions. In the Uruguay Round, we saw an agreement on services for the first time covered in a comprehensive way in international trade. We also dealt with intellectual property rights issues. Both of these matters are issues of serious domestic as well as international economic policy. We found that out in the Canada-U.S. trade policy context.

The reform of international trade in agriculture was a very important part of the Uruguay Round. Here much of the result dealt with disciplines on domestic agricultural policies. We also began to see investment issues addressed in the Uruguay round—particularly in the context of services, but also in the context of what was called "trade related investment measures" (TRIMs) and things like performance requirements.

Another matter that becomes very intrusive into the domestic economy is an agreement on what kind of domestic subsidies might be acceptable to the international community. Of course, the automatic dispute resolution process of the new GATT, managed by the WTO, is a major step toward globalization with important domestic policy considerations (e.g., the interface between international trade and domestic environmental policy.)

Product standards, which first came out of the Tokyo GATT round, and the first agreement on technical barriers to trade, is one of the most critical issues on the international trade negotiating agenda.

We have clearly moved, in the Uruguay Round, beyond the old issues that were seen as being appropriate for international trade negotiation, and the pattern has continued since the WTO has been established—for example, the agreement to eliminate duties on information technology products. This is an agreement which covers approximately 10 percent of world trade in goods—a very big deal—and the elimination of duties for participating countries that cover 94 percent of the trade in those products (a number which is continuing to expand as more countries join into the agreement.)

Another very big agreement in the WTO is the completion of the agreement on basic telecommunication services. In this agreement we found 69 countries committing themselves to specific undertakings in the agreement. Not only that, the agreement also provides undertakings by countries on regulatory principles to ensure the openness of the markets. This is important because it represents the first practical example of developing an international discipline in a world trade organization that actually covers competition policy.

Thus, as we move forward from the end of the Uruguay Round into what people thought might be a lull in negotiating activity, an even bigger move has developed toward new agreements that are treating the international trade issues of tomorrow, but also which have very domestic-oriented implications. Topics such as financial services, investment and competition policy, and trade and the environment are very much in the forefront of activity. We are already committed to new negotiations in agriculture and across the range of services issues to begin around the end of the decade.

There is a very ambitious work program in the WTO on other issues as well, including such topics as technical barriers to trade, or product standards. We are also looking at the agreement on sanitary and phyto-sanitary regulations, which will raise again a number of the practical problems in the U.S./European relationship.

I might add there are issues which have also involved the Canadian government. We have a work program on trade and the environment. As national economies become more dependent on trade, it is clear that governments are going to have to spend more time considering how to address issues that relate to that substantial part of their economy that lies outside their national borders. This is sort of the reverse, if you will, of people saying that trade agreements are threatening our sovereignty. You can turn this around and say maybe that's not the right way of looking at it. How do governments ensure the livelihood of their citizens when perhaps between 20 to 40 percent of everything that is produced in the country is being exported? How do you ensure that the workers in those areas, who are often better paid than the workers in some of the less export-oriented industries, continue to prosper in a global environment? I think it's pretty clear that we're going to need even more effective ways of managing international economic matters and more comprehensive rules then we have seen to date.

REGIONAL AGREEMENTS

It's clear that it is not only in the WTO that such negotiations are taking place. We have an extraordinarily ambitious regional agreement agenda. In this decade alone, the WTO Committee on Regional Trade Agreements (which I chair) has been notified of some 75 regional free trade agreements. We have been busy trying to examine these agreements to determine whether they are compatible with WTO disciplines.

I do think we have to be somewhat careful and not inadvertently create some system friction in some of the things we undertake on a regional basis. Here I'd come back again to technical barriers to trade, which is one of the issues that the regional committee in the WTO has taken up. Not because we have any particular problem in mind, but because we'd like to have a better look—"we" being the members of the organization—at what the multilateral rules are, and what people are now doing regionally with world-wide results. Do we really want a world in which we have bilateral or plurilateral recognition agreements and different standards of equivalence? Is this a world in which we're going to be able to bring everything back together again with countries where we can make sure that the parts fit together on a global basis?

I think that technical barriers to trade over the next ten years are going to be far more important issues in the international trade negotiating environment and in the practical life of businessmen than tariffs. They may well be already, but certainly I think we're at a point where the relative importance of tariffs is declining and the relative importance of some other matters with a much more domestic interaction is becoming important.

Finally, I'd like to say a bit about vision. I would agree with Geza Feketekuty that if you're going to make further progress, you need a sense of vision; you need some timeframes. It is interesting to note that in some of these regional initiatives we already have vision. Nobody said we should eliminate duties on a global basis in the WTO. At least we have not agreed to that. But there is certainly a lot regional initiative driving us in that direction. One of the arguments that is raised about global free trade is the practicality of it; how would you do it? How could you get 160 countries in the WTO to agree to eliminate their duties? However, if you look at what we have done in information technology products, and you actually sit down and figure out how many countries would you need to get to agree in order to have "practical" global free trade, it is very doable. I suspect the number is around 45—close to a quarter of the WTO's membership—and you would have well in excess of 90 percent of world trade free of duties.

From a practical basis, if we are talking really about eliminating duties in APEC, in the Asia Pacific area including China, in the Americas, in Europe, and possibly across the transatlantic, I think you could ask yourself: who would it be that would be left out of this kind of process, and would any country that had already entered into those very ambitious regional undertakings really have anything to fear by completing the process of doing it on a global basis? I think the answer is that there really wouldn't be anything to fear. But we would be leaving out important parts of the world from this process of globalization, and opportunity created through the elimination of duties. I think we need to think about how we approach this subject over the coming years.

This is not something where we need to decide today. I think we should let matters evolve and see what happens. At the end of 1999 there will be a major ministerial meeting in the World Trade Organization. We are already committed to launching negotiations at that time in services and agriculture, and I suspect that we will also do so on some of the other issues that I have mentioned here. I think it is somewhat paradoxical that we can look at some of the problems for which we have trying to make progress with more limited initiatives, but sometimes it is easier to do things if you have a more ambitious bigger agenda. It allows the leaders to move in and help the negotiators overcome the difficulties. It mobilizes support for the positive side of what can be achieved, rather than only having those who look at it from a negative perspective entering the fray. I suspect that 1999 may well be the year to gather forces for that kind of major effort.

THE EUROPEAN GEO-STRATEGIC PLAN AND THE AMERICAN PARTNERSHIP

Yves Boyer
Deputy Director, Foundation for Strategic Research
Paris, France

The title of the intervention that I have been asked to make suggests, in my opinion, at least two things. First, it suggests an effort to turn firmly toward the future, and the future I will put forward will occur based on very concrete elements which predetermine, it seems to me, the geo-strategic plan which the Europeans will have to use and, at the same time, the means that they will have to use in order to be able to react to events whose outcome remains to be seen.

The second thing that the title of this session suggests is a kind of small rite: it displays its attachment to the Americo-European partnership, even if we can measure the limits here and there and feel—at least on this side of the Atlantic—the excessive weight that the United States pulls in European affairs. And, in fact, if it appears that the relationship between the U.S. and the EU must be coddled and maintained, for it displays a common attachment to common values that we are ready to defend together; it seems to me that the EU will not be able to cross certain qualitative boundaries of integration during its development without asking itself about its relationship with the U.S. In other words, it seems to me that the excessive weight that the United States pulls in European affairs is becoming one of the major problems in the future of we Europeans. So when I say excessive weight of Washington, it is an excessive weight that is concerned

**translation by Daria M. Roche*

with the obviously very important capabilities of this country, but it is especially because, in a certain manner, there is a certain number of lacuna with the Europeans, who lack the cohesion and the willingness to get organized.

So precisely in regard to Europe, that is, concerning essentially the EU, there are different ways to approach the subject. There is an optimistic manner, which states that everything is fine, that finally the EU is making progress. Look at Amsterdam; we are going to make a certain number of decisions and, finally, despite several crises, everything is making progress and the EU is fitting in nicely with this new Atlantic community.

Personally, I will use a rather different tone that contains, on the contrary, a moderately pessimistic viewpoint of the situation concerning the ambitions and Europe's means of facing problems of security, in order to face the different challenges with which Europe will surely be confronted in 10, 20, or 30 years from now.

First of all, I think there are a certain number of points to cover, and the first is, I believe, that of knowing of what we are speaking when we talk of the EU and of the process of European integration. Of what are we speaking when we speak of European construction? It seems to me that there are three possible visions. There is a vision of Europe as a "supermarket." It is a vision that we attribute to the English, at least to the conservatives. It is a vision of Europe which gives ultra-liberalism a good deal, and it is the triumph of economic liberalism.

There is another vision of the EU. I do not want to say that it is a German vision of Europe, but in France we tend to associate Germany with this vision. It is that of a kind of large Switzerland. That is to say, it is a group of countries which possesses a high standard of living and a strong and stable currency. It contains a relative level of economic prosperity. It tries not to interfere with the exterior, and if it does, it does so only with extreme caution. This is the vision of a certain number of our partners, and we can say that, if we consider the analogy with the Swiss: yes, it works, but where is the ambition?

There exists a third vision that we can characterize as being a rather French one, although there are still some debates going on in France on this subject. It is the vision of a European power—that is, a Europe that unites a certain number of countries who share a single ambition: that of affirming and defending a European model. And, moreover, it consists of defending the interests of that Europe, from a monetary viewpoint (and this is the whole debate about the EURO), from a commercial perspectiv, and from a diplomatic (and, if that fails, a military) perspective.

We see today that these three visions mark the debates on the evolution of the structures of this EU. Indeed, the idea of flexibility, that we call in France the idea of "coopération renforcée" (strengthened cooperation), is an idea that advanced with Paris. It is more or less well considered by our partners, but it indicates, I believe, a willingness to move toward the European power.

As for the debates concerning the EU, that is, what is the position, for example, of the European national parliaments? What is the form of representation of the States in the Commission? Behind these questions we see the three different visions of Europe, but for now none of these visions has risen over the others. Thus, there is a matter of concern, a kind of dissatisfaction, I would say, for the everyday citizen. What is the nature of the Europe that we are creating, the EU that we are creating? What is the meaning of this Union? And I believe that on that point we have not brought about a decent response to these questions, which prompts the worries that we currently face in Europe.

So, to this question on the nature and the meaning of the EU is added, it seems to me, a certain number of significant weakness which weigh on Europe and which create a troublesome lifelessness, a kind of burn-out of European dynamism. These weaknesses are certainly going to have an effect on the EU's capacity of influence on the international scene. Thus, I would like to consider three elements of weakness.

The first seems to me to be of a revolutionary nature. It is the problem of demography. I do not want to exploit the statistics, but, nevertheless, I would like to give a few which I find extremely disturbing. Today Europe—in the sense of the large Europe without Russia—has about 500 million inhabitants. This number is going to remain in the 20 to 30 years to come. What do we see elsewhere? We see, for example, Africa, which has 700 million inhabitants today and which will have 1.7 billion inhabitants in 30 years, according to the predictions (of the United Nations, etc.). I remind you that Europe will remain at 500 million. In Asia, the same phenomenon occurs, even more so.

If we look closer to our borders, if we look at the Mediterranean basin, there, too, we find important statistics. Take Spain, France, Italy, and Greece, four members of the Union, and take the countries south of the Mediterranean, from Syria to Morocco. In 1950 there were 125 million inhabitants in the north; in the south there were a little less than 50 million inhabitants. Thus, a ratio of at least 1:2. Today, we have more or less 160 million inhabitants in the north, 140 million in the south. In 20 years, in 2020 to be exact, there will be 166 million in the north and 237 million in the south. So we can see that there are truly revolutionary demographic progressions, which show that the south is becoming more and more populated, that its population is younger and younger, and that it is, in general, at least in reference to the south lying beyond our borders, becoming more and more poor. And we have a north, that is, the EU, which is becoming less and less populated, which is becoming richer and richer, and which is growing more and more older. And in this, I will stop the statistical comparisons; I would like to cite the example of Germany.

Today the unified Germany has a population of about 80 million. In 30 years, there will be 70 million inhabitants and in 30 years there will be in a unified Germany approximately 600,000 more deceased than births per year. That is, each year a city like Frankfurt will disappear. So, not only is there a demographic decline, but there is also an aging of the population. Today one-fifth of the German population is less than 20 years old, and one-fifth of the German population is more than 60 years old. In 30 years, about 16 percent of the population will be less than 20 and 38% of the German population will be over 60. So we see all that this implies, not only in terms of the distribution of the budget, because we must foresee considerable expenses for the social budgets, health, etc. And all of this will occur, of course, but it will occur to the detriment of a certain number of other priorities, like defense, for example.

Thus, this is a demographic weakness which I find extremely troubling, if not dramatic.

We can add a certain economic lifelessness to this demographic weakness. On that point I am not going to get into the numbers either, but I am going to remind you that if the EU remains the principle commercial power in the world, it is more and more closely followed by the Asian countries. And these Asian countries have witnessed an extraordinary growth. What is especially troubling for the future is that in Asia we see more and more often that the civil budgets of Research and Development are increasing in considerable proportions and are going to bypass, by a wide margin, the European budgets for Research and Development. In time that will undoubtedly result in a much higher capacity for imagination and innovation in Asia than in Europe.

In conclusion, on the weaknesses of this EU, I will add the following element, which is not quantitative. What I would like to add is that it seems to me that, because of the economic crisis, because of unemployment and the social fracturing, Europe is no longer perceived as the only solution. It is an important phenomenon which, at least in some countries, is evident in the fact that when the Maastricht Referendum was proposed, it was passed with a very, very slim majority. If we look at the presidential elections of 1995, during the first round a little more than 40 percent of the voters supported parties that displayed an open hostility toward Maastricht and to the idea of moving down the path toward the EU. This anti-European sentiment exists almost everywhere in Europe. It is fairly strong in France, and we can assume that the persistence of the unemployment rate, and the absence of projects that the EU represents, could result in an increase in the power of these forces that are hostile to the European project. In France it is true, and I emphasize this fact with some of our partners.

To summarize, the uncertainties on the nature of the European project—the demographic decline with its troublesome consequences, the relative weakening of the European economic and research capabilities, the increase (at least in a certain number of European countries) of an anti-EU sentiment—all of that paints a pretty dark picture. So if we look a little bit at the threats this EU could come up against, we can see that the current structures (NATO, etc.) do not appear to be adapted, or are poorly adapted, to face the challenges ahead of us.

I do not want to dwell on this, but what are these challenges? They include, for example, organized crime. With liberalization, with the opening up of the borders, we are seeing the expansion across the entire planet of a certain number of Mafioso networks, which are coming out of their traditional zones of action in order to open their illicit trafficking in Europe. We have seen, for example, the Cali coalition, the Columbian coalition, which created an import-export company of agricultural products in Prague. The same coalition created a Poland-Columbia partner company in Krakow, which seems a little bizarre. And it is obviously a shield, or shields, to cover up their trafficking of illegal substances. These are minor points, but in any case we can see the action these Mafias are taking in Central Europe, in Western Europe, and more and more in the EU. I should say that these organizations are trafficking drugs, etc., but they could traffic more dangerous substances in the future (nuclear or chemical weapons, etc.).

Another problem is that of terrorism. Terrorism caused approximately 11,000 deaths and injuries across the planet between 1990 and 1996, if we look at the State Department's numbers. These are not high figures, but at the same time they are very high, and I think that it is a phenomenon that is with us, that will continue to increase, and against which we need to take several measures.

Another equally important problem, which is linked to Lawrence Korb's view of the enemy as being "chaos," is the problem of migrations—of the displacement of refugees which can be seen as the development of chaos in certain areas. I want to remind you that today there are approximately 20 million refugees and 25–30 million displaced persons. So when I say that these refugee movements, these movements of population can cause chaos, we have seen clear examples of this in West Africa. Everything around Sierra Leone, Liberia, and Nigeria is an area of population movement and refugees, etc., and, strictly speaking, chaos is settling in.

Faced with these pathologies of our international society, pathologies that exist and that risk worsening in the future, it is in Europe's best interest to reduce the magnitude of these crises which could occur as a result of these disturbances. First of all for economic reasons. Europe, as I said, is one of the principal centers of world commerce, and it is evident that world commerce handles crises or chaos poorly, as we know.

Other considerations are those of a political nature. The crises and chaos that could occur in certain areas might become contagious, causing conflict and crises to move into other areas, especially into Europe. There are also moral considerations, of course. European public opinion cannot remain separated from events which it would find intolerable.

So, given these considerations, how do we respond? What do we do? And with what means? Here again, if we take our military means, it seems to me that we are a little bit in a position of relative crisis. The president of the Republic said that we are in a kind of strategic pause, which allows us to reduce the budget and to let down our guard a bit. This is true for France and for the European countries. And we must note that between 1990 and 1995, if we take the military numbers of the principal European powers, we used up the equivalent of the entire English army—the land troops and the air and marine troops, and, in terms of the budget, we used up the equivalent of Italy's defense budget. So a noticeably lowered potential that, in my opinion, is not accompanied by innovative measures. That is, we are becoming conscious of the fact that it is necessary to develop reconnaissance means, the means of gathering information. But, and I may be too critical here, I do not believe that our countries have sufficiently reoriented the budgets in favor of priorities such as intelligence, which is essential for evaluating crises. Lawrence Korb argues that Europeans should develop these projection forces, and in that category we immediately bump into budgetary obstacles, and then we bump into other obstacles of a more political nature.

There is another European weakness: there was a debate in the U.S. on what they call the "revolution in military affairs," which is beginning to heat up the debate in the U.S., even modifying the nature of investments in military equipment. In Europe, however, and I'm speaking of France, Great Britain, and Germany, which represent 85 percent of the EU's military spending, it seems to me that we are well below having reached an interesting and profitable debate on the revolution of military affairs. There, too, lies a kind of lifelessness in Europe which I find particularly disturbing.

Just a word of conclusion. I have been fairly dark in my presentation, but I would like to finish on a more positive note. I am convinced that finally the European countries are capable of mobilization and creativity. It is still necessary for the relationship between the state, the leaders, the elite, and the citizens to function, and it seems to me that in a certain number of European countries this relationship is in a state of crisis. Nevertheless, European construction is developing. Earlier I said that there is a problem concerning the nature of this European construction. But I would like to recall what Jacques Delors said about European construction: that for 40 years, from the Treaty of Rome to the Single Currency Act, we have experienced nearly ten years of crises. In five years, that is when there were advances; that is when there was an intense period of creativity, and, thanks to these five years, we have finally succeeded in reaching a threshold of integration, which is not as bad as all that.

SECTION III:
GLOBALIZATION AND THE ENVIRONMENT

INTRODUCTION, SECTION III

Charles F. Bonser

The New Transatlantic Agenda created by President Clinton and the leadership of the European Union in 1996 also highlights, as a key concern for the Atlantic alliance, the improvement of national and regional environmental quality. Therefore, in the final section of this book the authors focus on what might be referred to as a major externality of the global economic expansion of the post–Cold War period. This is the interaction between the environmental problems associated with an expanding and more affluent world population, and the economic institutions that have developed to serve this population. Some of the questions pursued in this final section are:

- Does a more liberal trade regime threaten national environmental sovereignty? Do national environmental rules and regulations pose unreasonable barriers to trade? What are the issues and challenges to achieve both trade and environmental goals?

- How might the standardization of manufacturing processes prove helpful or harmful to local, national, regional, and global environments? Should voluntary environmental management systems begin to replace command and control measures for environmental protection?

- Why are U.S. and EU-member governments seldom "in synch" on trade and environmental issues? To enhance cooperation between the U.S. and the EU, how might Atlantic partners anticipate and overcome obstacles bearing on trade and environmental policy?

- Many advocates of sustainable development urge that sustainable societies can be realized only at local levels of organization, with modes of production kept small to protect the environment and to give average citizens more power over economic decisions. Can globalizing economic forces be reconciled with the demands of sustainable development?

- Do post-industrial nations' strict environmental rules compel pollution-prone industries to relocate to countries where environmental rules are weak?

- How might the transatlantic partners encourage multinational companies (MNCs) to dedicate more private initiative to serve the public interest in environmental improvement?

The papers presented in this section were originally offered at a late 1998 follow-up colloquium to the Paris SPEA/ENA conference referred to in Sections I and II. Both are part of the Transatlantic Consortium for Public Policy Analysis and Education project described in the foreword to this book.

The first paper—a keynote at the colloquium—is by Nigel Roome, Professor of Environmental Management at Erasmus University, The Netherlands. Professor Roome attempts to weave together contrasting and complementary aspects of globalization and the environment.

His primary argument is that sustainable development is "the first concerted response to the process of globalization, or global change, experienced in the past 50 years. And the question of whether and how we resist, seek to control, or try to mitigate the effects of change remains unclear." One of the main issues Roome deals with in his paper is how governance, in both the public and private sectors, is evolving as a result of globalization, and how this is likely to affect the goal of sustainable development. He concludes by considering a projection of the state of the world of the next century, with alternative scenarios describing a sustainable world. He also offers some ideas about how the U.S. and Europe can use their transatlantic agenda to better deal with this globalization/environment interface.

The second keynote paper, by Professor Jeffrey Dunoff of the Temple University School of Law, looks at the "limits of law" in the globalization/environment interface. He makes three different arguments. First he shows how environmental issues challenge and perhaps undermine our conventional understandings of the trade system. Second, he identifies a paradox these issues pose for WTO dispute resolution and suggests a strategy for resolving this paradox. Third, he discusses why efforts within the NTA (New Transatlantic Agenda) and TEP (Transatlantic Economic Partnership) may be more successful at addressing trade-environmental issues.

Next he identifies three models of why we have a trade regime—the "efficiency model" (based on traditional exploitation of comparative advantage), the "collective action" model (based on game theory, where gains come from detecting and correcting defections from trade agreements), and the "embedded liberalism model" (based on creating open multilateral trade systems, while preserving the states right to intervene in domestic economies.) He then goes on to show how trade and environment issues challenge each of these three models.

Dunoff then moves to a discussion of the difficulties that trade and environment issues pose to the World Trade Organization, and suggests that the WTO may wish to consider an approach often used by judges in our legal systems—simply "ducking" some major issues. He finishes by wondering whether there might be other more flexible forums—such as the NTA and the TEP—that might better address some of the trade/environment issues.

Kilian Delbrück, of the Federal Ministry of Environment in Germany, has considerable experience in the trade/environment policy debate and negotiations, and his paper reviews key problem areas now under consideration in the World Trade Organization with regard to these issues. Delbrück points out that the GATT agreement is not only a fundamental globalization and liberalization agreement, but it also has the function of developing a rule-based system for dealing with disputes. It is, in essence, a court. He describes the legal basis for the GATT rulings, and then discusses three of the important issues handled by the WTO dispute process in recent years: the Shrimp-Turtle case; the Tuna-Dolphin case (which are import issues in the U.S.), and the U.S. Beef-Hormone complaint against the European Union (which is an exporting issue.)

He concludes with the observation that "the status quo, as it is described by the panels (convened to resolve disputes) is not satisfactory." Furthermore, it is "not conceivable to have any future major liberalization agreement without including the environment." In addition, the developing countries will have to play a much stronger role than ever before in the negotiations. He then discusses some of the key issues which he believes will have to be dealt with in the next round of trade negotiations, which will likely be initiated early in 2000.

The next three papers focus on the topic of voluntary environmental management systems (EMS). The papers are by Eberhard Bohne, professor at

the Speyer School of Administration, Germany; Marc Aviam, from the Ministry of the Environment, France; and Randy Dougherty, Vice President, NSF International, Ann Arbor, Michigan. The issue at hand is the usefulness of this type of approach as an augmentation of the more traditional command and control systems of regulation. The three papers provide different perspectives on the role and success of the use of environmental management systems in the three countries.

Randy Dougherty discusses the "real world" of environmental management systems registrations and the progress that is being made by this approach. He believes that EMS, as delivered by ISO 14001 (of the International Standards Organization) will be successful, and that organizations like his own—NSF International—can persuade business to shift toward a self-regulation model.

Marc Aviam reviews the experience of France with voluntary environmental commitments beginning in 1971. He presents a model of voluntary arrangements that range from commitments developed by individual firms to collective commitments mediated and shaped by governmental-voluntary associations. He believes some of these—for example, the French Enterprise Environment Plan—might serve as a stepping stone to EMAS (the European alternative to ISO 14001) or ISO 14001 certification. At the moment, French firms seem to favor neither of the international approaches.

Aviam also discusses three key issues: Who chooses voluntary commitments and why? Are these commitments only "cosmetic"? Can regulation and voluntary commitments function in a complementary way?

Eberhard Bohne addresses three issues: (1) Which are the main differences between the EU's "Eco-Management and Audit Scheme (EMAS) and the ISO 14001 in terms of concept and implementation? (2) Which conditions justify regulatory relief for certified or registered companies? (3) Is there a need for regional environmental management standards such as EMAS?

In Europe, some see ISO 14001 as an attempt to weaken environmental management systems already in place. For example, EMAS requires improvements in a firm's environmental performance, while ISO 14001 requires improvement in the management system, which may or may not improve performance.

The three papers, although taking different approaches, have unifying themes. These can be postulated as:

- Voluntary environmental management systems can play a significant role in managing the environment in the future.

- Each voluntary system has both strengths and weaknesses.
- We will likely see in the future a variety of environmental management systems.
- Government can play an important role in promoting voluntary environmental management systems, but should not abandon its regulatory role to the private sector.

All three papers seem to agree that voluntary management systems, in partnership with a strong regulatory process, can move us in the direction of a "new era" of environmental management and help us do a better job of handling the problems associated with the interface between trade and the environment.

In the first of three related papers on the effectiveness of environmental policy, Professor Arthur Ringeling, and his associate Monique Hozee, of Erasmus University in The Netherlands, look at the implementation by member states of EU environmental policy directives. In the second, Professors Tom Lyon and John Maxwell, of Indiana University's Kelley School of Business, consider the role of multinational companies as instruments of environmental improvement. Finally, Stefania Borghini, of the Fondazione Eni Enrico Mattei, in Italy, describes a study conducted by her organization of European companies perception of environmental issues.

Professors Ringeling and Hozee state that their goal is to examine how the relation between the characteristics of the policy instruments and the specific institutional setting of the implementation of policy in the EU member states influences the EU's environmental goals.

The authors focus on the implementation phase of the EU directives concerning the regulation of packaging waste. Their hypothesis is that the separation between EU policy and member state implementation restricts the policy's effectiveness. "In other words, the effectiveness of environmental policy depends on the fit between the characteristics of the environmental instruments on the one hand, and the 'setting' in which actors take decisions with environmental consequences on the other." The goal of their research project, therefore, is to examine the relationship between the policy instruments and the specific institutional setting in the member state.

The research design used involved two clusters of countries representing Southern European countries and Northern European countries. The countries chosen were Greece and Spain in the South, and Germany, The Netherlands, and Belgium in the north. The policy sector chosen was the packaging industry.

Their finding was that EU policy did harmonize the national policies on packaging to some extent. Where there were differences, they could be explained by attempts to reach agreement with the private sector in a specific country. In general, therefore, they concluded that "the so-called implementation deficit is less a deficit than easily assumed. . . . The packaging policies of the member states were harmonized more than before the EU took action." The authors do observe that the EU has serious monitoring problems, due to a lack of manpower and competencies.

Professors Lyon and Maxwell are interested in how multinational companies (MNCs) can be encouraged to devote more initiative to serving the public good. They begin with looking at three types of voluntary company programs. The first is unilateral programs that are initiated by the companies themselves, for example, ISO 14001. The second is voluntary programs where the government is the prime mover, with companies being encouraged to participate. An example here is the European EMAS described above. The third is negotiated agreements in which both the government and the companies "bring something to the table." Examples here are the German CO_2 reduction program and, in the U.S., the EPA-negotiated program under the name of "Project Excell."

The authors first examine the motivations of the companies who get involved in these alternative style programs. They then consider the effect on the public of these approaches, and whether welfare might be reduced by corporate voluntary actions. They also discuss ways in which the programs might be made more effective (e.g., government monitoring and oversight).

With regard to multinational companies specifically, they suggest that there is some evidence that firms operating in multiple countries "tend to be better environmental performers." In addition, the negotiated agreement seems to offer the most promise for dealing with these types of organizations, since a small company, on its own, may have difficulty influencing the large multinational firm's behavior.

Stefania Borghini's study queried companies on which environmental problems they considered most important. The answer almost uniformly was the generation of solid waste and energy consumption. They then looked at how these companies tried to implement strategies to deal with these problems, and she discusses their findings.

The next group of papers focuses on the issue of "Pollution Havens." The first paper is by Mathew Auer, professor in the Indiana University School of Public and Environmental Affairs (SPEA). He examines some of the evidence on pollution havens and associated industrial flight. Professor Roy Shin, also

a SPEA professor, presents a pollution case study of the chemical industry in the U.S. and DuPont's decision to locate its titanium dioxide plant in Korea in the late 1980s. The third commentary, by Wolfgang Haas, of the Ministry of Economics in Germany, is in the form of an intervention about the German situation.

Mathew Auer first recognizes some of the difficulties in actually determining whether on not a particular investment can be primarily attributed to an environmental situation. He argues that there is not much evidence that "environmental regulations have much influence on the location of industrial plant. . . . If you look at the data over the past 25 years, you don't see a big rise in the share of dirty industries moving to the LDCs (less developed countries)."

Auer categorizes as "dirty industries," those industries for which pollution abatement costs range from 12 percent to 25 percent of production costs. These include petroleum refining, chemicals, non-ferrous metals, primary metals, and the pulp and paper industry. There is "scarce evidence" that the LDCs are trying to attract these kinds of industries away from the developed countries. While there has been a small shift in world trade in these goods coming from Southeast Asia, Mexico, and India, he points out that other reasons, such as labor costs, and economic expansion of those countries account for most of the shift.

He concludes that the LDCs may, over time, be gaining a comparative advantage in these "dirty" goods. But environmental regulations don't go very far in explaining the change.

Roy Shin's study explored the question of industrial flight by examining the DuPont case in Korea. The principle conclusion of the case study was consistent with Mathew Auer's findings. Namely, that "strict environmental regulations in less sensitive countries are unlikely to result in widespread loss of investment in industrial production." In DuPont's case specifically, Korea "presents a favorable business climate because of its domestic markets, infrastructure, and the fact that the government offered financial incentives for general manufacturing in Korea."

In fact, as Shin points out, the DuPont project was initially rejected by Korea's EPA, and it took four years of difficult negotiations before DuPont proceeded with the investment. He then reviews some of the reasons DuPont pressed ahead with its investment, and draws lessons and policy implications of the case.

Wolfgang Haas looks more particularly at the question of whether strict environmental standards have been a factor in Germany's record, over the past few years, of running a negative balance of business investments.

There has been a debate in Germany for several years about the level of business taxation compared to international competition. In April 1999, Germany introduced a special tax on energy consumption. One of the purposes of the tax is to contribute to sustainable development. This, of course, has further fueled (no pun intended) the arguments.

Haas' view is that, in order to reduce the risks of industrial dislocation, we must make better use of international cooperation, under such UN frameworks as Agenda 21 (Rio Process), the Montreal Protocol, and the Basel Convention on hazardous waste.

The final two papers in Section III, by Montserrat Cuchillo, of the University Pompeu Fabra in Spain, and Hilary French, Director of Research at the Worldwatch Institute in Washington, D.C., discuss the difficulties between the U.S. and Europe in achieving environmental cooperation.

Professor Cuchillo suggests the fundamental differences between trade and environmental objectives make it difficult to find a common ground between the U.S. and the EU for the protection of the environment. This is further complicated by the pull between national and EU policies and approaches (see Ringeling arguments above.) She argues that, invariably, the trade objective will dominate, but "it is important to take into account the fact that freedom of trade incorporates the cost of environmental protection." Professor Cuchillo believes that the U.S./EU Transatlantic Agenda can help this situation.

Hilary French first discusses the chronology (beginning in 1993 with the Tuna-Dolphin case) of the relationship between the U.S. and the European Union on trade and the environment issues. "It has been a changing story, and one that has important implications for where we are going to move in the future." In the first stage—which led to the creation of the Trade and Environment Committee (CTE) of the World Trade Organization—the Americans had a view of themselves as "the good guys." The Europeans, on the other hand, were perceived as creating problems for the U.S.' effort to integrate trade and the environment. Meanwhile, the Europeans were concerned about American "unilateralism" that interfered with trade.

In the stage we are now entering, the Europeans have also come under fire for environmental laws that affect trade, and the U.S. has challenged some of them on grounds of unfair trade barriers (e.g., the Beef-Hormone issue). She discusses a number of other important issues, such as bio-diversity and the Shrimp-Turtle case where the rules of multilateral environmental agreements and those of GATT and the WTO are in conflict.

French believes the WTO Committee on Trade and the Environment has "done essentially nothing to move the debate forward." This has led to proposals for a dialog to be launched on these issues to accelerate progress. "The transatlantic economic partnership ideas discussed by Jeffery Dunoff (in this volume) . . . hold a lot of promise for breaking this logjam." She does caution, however, that the developing countries cannot be left out of the discussion. "We need to move on the transatlantic partnership issue, but we need to keep this broader international context in mind."

Editor's Comment

During the past decade both world trade policy and world environmental policy have made advances. The multilateral trading system made very important strides with the conclusion and adoption of the Uruguay Round of the GATT. The establishment of the World Trade Organization, and its new ability to take serious measures to settle trade disputes, may be the most important step in the history of the GATT. The Rio Conference put sustainability on the agenda, and it was put into the WTO goals at the Marrakech meeting, in 1995, when the CTE was created.

At the same time, the multilateral environmental agreements (MEAs) of the 1990s have also been extremely important. There are now over 200 MEAs that have to be reconciled with GATT. Some 104 countries have ratified the Basel Convention on the Control of Movements of Hazardous Wastes and their disposal. Other key agreements reached include the Montreal Protocol on Substances that Deplete the Ozone layer and the various UN negotiations, including the Framework Convention on Climate Change. There has also been excellent progress in complementing environmental regulation with voluntary environmental management systems. But one of the main problems now is that the environmental side of the equation does not have a dispute resolution mechanism comparable to the World Trade Organization. One result is that we use systems—like the WTO process—to resolve conflicts for which it was not designed, and, as Montserrat Cuchillo points out, the trade side of a trade/ environment dispute can usually be counted on to carry the day.

Some of the main issues that came up during discussions in the colloquium included:

- Should the WTO implement environmental standards into GATT, or should they be agreed by MEAs?

- Can the dispute resolution process in the WTO reconcile environmental conflicts?

- The GATT approach is quite different from the environmentalist's approach. GATT looks at the product per se, while the environmental approach focuses on how a product is produced and its lifecycle.

- WTO member states have widely different views on the importance and relevance of environmental considerations, and they are too often willing to act unilaterally.

The key trade/environment issues expected to need attention in the new trade negotiations include:

- To what extent do MEAs relate to the narrow trade considerations being discussed within the WTO/GATT framework?
- Ecolabeling
- Cooperation with the UNEP, as there are several international organizations in which environment is on the agenda and decisions taken in one organization have an impact of all.
- Transparency in the WTO and its actions.
- The perception by the LDCs that environmental considerations in trade negotiations is an element of "Green protectionism" or a factor in trade distortion.
- The conflicts between sovereignty and global harmonization.
- It is now no longer acceptable to have any general agreement without including environmental factors.

As we move toward the next round of GATT negotiations, which will likely be initiated early in 2000, the leaders of our governments need to take steps to move us beyond the GATT Committee on Trade and the Environment. The OECD countries, and particularly the European Union and the United States, need to put past differences and petty competitive behavior behind them and see that this happens. And as several authors indicate, the developing world countries also need to brought into the conversation at an early date. We need to find a way of bringing together, peacefully, environmental concerns with world trade liberalization, if we are to avoid a "train wreck" between the two policy concerns.

GLOBALIZATION AND SUSTAINABLE DEVELOPMENT— TOWARD A TRANSATLANTIC AGENDA

Nigel Roome
Professor of Environmental Management, Erasmus University Rotterdam, The Netherlands

INTRODUCTION

Globalization is an issue of increasing significance to society as we enter the new millennium. While the precise nature and implications of globalization remain unclear (Clark 1997), the concept is imbued with multiple meanings, it is open to multiple interpretations, and is the subject of intense debate (Gladwin 1998). When globalization is considered in relation to the equally elusive, contested and normative notion of sustainable development (Lélé & Norgaard 1996) we might be forgiven for wanting to hide away from global change in some "imagined rural idyll." A vernacular cottage removed from the infrastructure of telephone, television, and Internet, without convenient access to an international airport hub or a local expressway spur, far removed from the complexity of choice presented by the world products available at the hypermarket, the electrical goods displayed in the superstore, or the choice of international equity funds at, say, <http://asiancapital.com>. However, the reality is that the pressures of globalization and the demand for sustainable development are ubiquitous. There is no place left in which to hide from their effects.

The core argument of this paper is that sustainable development is one of the earliest international responses to the pressures of globalization—or global change—that have arisen during the past 50 years. Despite these efforts, global change continues in new and different forms. Indeed, global change should be viewed as a continuing series of waves of change that are increasingly interconnected and turbulent. They create outcomes that are uncertain and ambiguous, and providing the ground for sites of dispute and conflict within society. Even the issues of whether we should resist, control or mitigate change and its effects remain unclear. What is certain is that we need to address these competing perspectives and conflicts within society and to adapt the frameworks and institutions we have traditionally used for governance to better fit the characteristics of global change.

A particular issue of global change is the way it is shifting the balance of power in society toward the private (economic) sector. This focuses debate on the need to adjust private sector models of governance to bring them in line with the realities that go with this redistribution of power. This paper examines these issues, offering some preliminary recommendations for a transatlantic response to global change and sustainable development.

The paper begins by defining sustainable development and its relationship to globalization. It describes the main waves of global change and considers the characteristics that underscore a globally connected and turbulent, meta-world.[1] This analysis provides the context from which to develop some projections about the future state of the world and to anticipate how the demands presented by this future world will impact all levels of society (local, national, regional, and global) and all sectors (public, private, non-governmental, and community), but particularly business. The paper concludes by considering this image of the future against a range of recent scenarios developed to help describe a more sustainable world. It closes by offering a prognosis of our likely success in coping with the anticipated changes.

DEFINING SUSTAINABLE DEVELOPMENT

Sustainable development, as set out in the World Commission on Environment and Development (Brundtland 1987), Agenda 21 (Agenda 21, 1992), its side agreements, and the protocols signed since the Earth Summit, assumes five distinct forms. At one and the same time it is a response, a goal, an agenda for action, a process, and an approach to the governance of global change. Each of these is considered in turn.

Response

Sustainable development is often regarded as a response to the "problems of development" and the global political imperative of bridging economic interests, environmental concerns, and social needs. It also seeks to span the interests of developed, industrialized countries and the concerns of the developing world. The problems of development that provoked the call for sustainable development are well-rehearsed (IUCN 1981). However, these problems continue today (UN 1997a; UNEP 1997). They arise in three main dimensions. In developed economies there are the environmental consequences of industrialization. "Problems of affluence" accompany the resource and energy demands of these industrial economies. These are a consequence of the high levels of material transformation and throughput, which generate economic wealth but also bring potentially toxic and hazardous products, toxic and non-toxic by-products, and large volumes of waste. Increasing disposable incomes accompanying industrialization lead to changes in living patterns and lifestyles, which place pressure on land and ecological resources through the demand for homes, and industrial and urban space. Rising real incomes also provoke higher levels of material throughput to feed consumer demand.

Rapidly industrializing countries and those countries that have undergone recent transition from central planning to market-based systems have experienced their own set of environmental and social problems. These "problems of transition" include the environmental burdens created by relatively unsophisticated or un-enforced systems of environmental regulation, land zoning, and resource planning. The exclusive focus on production in central planned economies has left a serious legacy of environmental damage that remains to be dealt with. Problems of affluence and transition are often treated as economic externalities, which arise from the failure of markets to account for the environmental costs of human activities.

The environmental, social, and economic issues of underdevelopment invoke other problems especially when they occur in association with rapidly increasing levels of population. The "problems of poverty and population" center on the access that the poorest of the poor have to basic resources in the less developed countries and regions. These groups experience a lack of security over supplies of food, potable water, and fuel required to meet their needs. This is an issue of the distribution of resources rather than resource allocation and externalities. The causes and impacts of poverty are complex. For instance, poverty can be exacerbated by the move to allocate scarce land away from traditional, subsistence agriculture into cash-based agricultural economic systems even when these are designed to contribute to the inflow of foreign exchange earnings which is needed to ease the burden of a country's international debt. In a similar way, industrial logging, designed to yield foreign exchange earnings and support development, has contributed to insecurity in the supply of agricultural produce or potable water, and, heightened the risks of soil erosion and flooding through the disruption of the natural properties of the watersheds. Increasingly, environmental and resource problems of this kind are linked to ethnic, religious and tribal, and national conflicts.

The problems of "affluence," "transition" and "poverty" are important dimensions of change linked to the overall process of development. They arise in many locations around the globe. Their global significance is determined by a number of characteristics. Some problems arise locally but can be traced to a common root which is more universal (such as inappropriate industrial practices or badly directed development aid). For some issues their cumulative effects have global impact (such as global warming linked to carbon emissions), for others their management requires a global (supra-national) level of responsibility (such as controls on the trans-border movement of hazardous wastes).

Even so, global change is seen here as a tyranny of small deçisions. Change arises as the aggregate of many individual choices and actions; few, if any of these are designed to generate the social and environmental concerns they provoke. Under these circumstances, redirecting global change is difficult, small choices are not easy to control. However, choice is driven by a set of pervasive ideas or myths that are perpetuated in society. Such myths arise in every age. They underscore the social givens. They are rarely subject to social or political critique until they are replaced by other myths. The myths that have influenced the history of recent global development are mainly economic in orientation. For example, they include the idea that human development is measured by the growth in GDP, or that unfettered, "free" markets are synonymous with perfect markets, or that allocative efficiency is a supreme human goal. The power of these myths derives from their widespread acceptance and the position they assume in the credo and language of discourse of institutions.

During this century, we have experienced a number of powerful myths. These include the myth of state intervention to maintain national employment and capital formation—the myth of Keynesianism—that guided thinking and action by governments in much of the industrial world from the early 1930s through to the early 1980s. Many held to the mythology of state industries, as part of a mixed economy, a myth that was ended by the equally powerful myth of privatization. Sustainable development can be viewed as a concerted response to the social and environmental consequences of development that have arisen during the last 50 years under the influence of such myths—economic and otherwise.

Goal

Sustainable development assumes the status as a goal when it is accepted as a normative intent of policy- and decisionmakers. The notion of sustainable development as goal, is contained in the suggestion by the Brundtland Commission report (Brundtland 1987) that sustainable development is a particular form of development, which meets the needs of the present generation without jeopardizing the opportunities available to future generations to meet their needs.

The operationalization of sustainable development is no different from the operationalization of any goal. Realizing goals requires a comparison to be made between criteria that determine success in goals and changes that occur over time and/or space. Sustainable development spans three different domains—economic, social, and environmental. It requires criteria and measures of change in each of these domains. While the importance of these domains to sustainable development is widely accepted in a conceptual sense, their application in operational decisions is problematic, as the means to evaluate change in each domain is frequently contested. On the one side, we have the "econocrats," who contend that change can be measured according to the metric of money. On the other side are the advocates of political or social choice models, who maintain that the value of change to interests should be assessed and weighted through institutional processes. The second approach has been adopted as the basis for the Sustainable Development Indicators advanced by the United Nations Commission on Sustainable Development. They identify the need for economic, social, and environmental indicators as well as new institutional indicators which signal a strengthening of the process of decision-making.

A further problem in operationalizing sustainable development is the importance attached to the interests of future generations. How do we specify what is important for future generations? Environmental limits change as natural systems change and as our understanding of those systems develops. Moreover, societal needs change with our experiences, values, and as we adopt new myths. Although sustainable development implies operating within environmental limits and social norms, both limits and norms are subject to change overtime. Consequently, the criteria used to judge progress toward sustainable development should be dynamic.

Agenda

Sustainable development has achieved the status of an agenda for action, despite the problems in operationalizing the concept and in specifying whether we are making progress toward it or not. Agenda 21, the Biodiversity Convention, the Kyoto Convention on Global Climate Change, and the many local Agenda 21s provide a series of action points, targets, and time scales designed to move society progressively toward more sustainable forms of development. These international agreements provide the means to slow down, or arrest, currently unsustainable levels of global resource use or mitigate the pressures on environmental and social systems. This agenda changes with achievements and altered circumstances. It does not seek to define what a sustainable society would look like and it is not constructed as a grand design but as an action plan that is time and context dependent.

Process

Sustainable development, then, is a specific form of development. It is a process in the same way that development is a process. The perception of the need for society to address the issue of sustainable development implies that recent development has not been sustainable. We therefore have to re-evaluate our experience(s) of development and re-learn how we approach development (Roome 1998). This emphasizes learning and reflective evaluation, not only on the myths that frame past thinking but also the actions and processes that contribute to development. Learning and reflection are process-based human activities.

Sustainable development is also a process because it is concerned with re-directing development from an unsustainable path to one that is more sustainable. Whether this re-orientation is a response to human concerns and environmental changes, or whether it is driven by a goal or as an agenda, it involves a process of change.

We can use these ideas to develop some statements about what sustainable development is and what it is not. First, sustainable development implies moving beyond present myths, including our dominant social paradigm(s) which have generated problems that sustainable development now seeks to resolve. Second, sustainable development does not involve a commitment to sustain organizations or institutions. Organizations as structures and institutions as rules are valuable only as long as they remain relevant to our construction of the process of development. Organizations and institutions generally have a time-limited relevance. While they guide and frame human action and choice they have value only in relation to what they represent or bring about. Third, sustainable development is not synonymous with sustained economic growth, rather it involves forms of economic activity which take place within environmental limits and which take cognizance of, and respect, a broad set of social and environmental needs and values. Finally, sustainable development is not the same as environmental management, environmental protection, ecologically sustainable development, or the accommodation of environmental values in existing economic myths or paradigms. Sustainable development is a wider and deeper concept that provides a paradigm or myth within which development, and the activities that contribute to development, should fit.

Governance

In earlier work I suggest that sustainable development is by definition a contested and ambiguous concept that must be played out through a series of negotiated social and industrial experiments. Central to the process of sustainable development is a need to expose and reconcile the contested and ambiguous issues that contribute to views of development which are then reflected in choices about sustainable development (Roome 1998). In this way sustainable development represents a reforming process where the only real constants are the principles or values that govern human choices and actions and the mechanisms of decision-making. It is a reflective process in which we constantly consider our experience of change and our notions of progress.

Principles that govern sustainable development relate to the three domains that define the concept: economic/administrative, social, and environmental. Values systems that might reasonably apply in each domain are set out in Table 1. This table describes the values that need to permeate all structures of governance—whether in government, business, the voluntary sector, or the community, if we are to bring about sustainable development. These values place responsibility on individuals both to represent their own positions, to take cognizance of the positions of others, and, to assess the impacts of their actions on others and the planet. The adoption of these values radically alters the responsibilities of business. For example, if they were adopted as the basis for business decisions it would be necessary to modify the Acts of Incorporation that apply in most jurisdictions around the globe. Their acceptance would impose responsibility on managers of companies to maximize shareholder value within the constraints imposed by other social and environmental principles of the model. Adopting these values would also lead to a new framework for governance affecting government, the voluntary sector, and the community.

The contention that sustainable development involves a new approach to governance is consistent with the argument that it is a response, a goal, an agenda, and a process. It also fits with the idea that sustainable development is a new paradigm, a new guiding myth more appropriate to our environmental condition and the needs of the present and the future.

SUSTAINABLE DEVELOPMENT AND GLOBALIZATION

Sustainable development has been described as an approach to governance provoked by problems of global development. It is regarded as the first concerted international response to the issue of global change. However, global change is not restricted to the social and environmental issues provoked by development. Global change arises from more recent trends in financial and economic markets and from our increasingly global society and culture. It also arises out of the complex interaction between all three waves of change—development, economic and financial, and social and cultural. Each of these waves of change is now examined.

Table 1. Domains and Value Systems for Sustainable Development

Domains	*Values*	*Description*
Economic/ Administrative	Utilitarian	The value of resources, products, and services is derived from the value assigned by those who produce and use them
	Efficiency	Resources, products, and services should be allocated in ways that minimize input for a given output
	Effectiveness	Organizations should seek to achieve their goals with the minimum use of resources
Social	Fairness/justness	The rules that govern human interactions should be fair and just. E.g., following Rawls (1971), rules should be derived without knowing what position the rulemakers will have in a society
	Inclusiveness	Choice and action that affects others should involve the values, perspectives, or voices of others
	Futurity	Choice and action should involve evaluation of the implications that will arise in the long- as well as the short-term
Environmental	Stewardship	We should act in ways that are consistent with protecting the value of environmental assets and endowments
	Precaution	Proponents of innovation should be responsible for assessing the implications of innovation on environmental assets and endowments
	Appropriateness—acting within environmental limits	Choice and action should take place within the carrying capacity of the environment at all levels from local to global

ECONOMIC AND FINANCIAL GLOBALIZATION

There are many indicators of the trend toward global financial and economic markets. The rapid increase in world trade as a proportion of global GDP indicates the growing attention to export-oriented economic activity. In the period from 1987 to 1996 world trade rose over 100 from US$2.39 trillion to US$5.25 trillion. World trade now represents over 20 percent of world gross product (IMF 1997:116–7). In 1987, 27 percent of this trade originated in developing countries and 73 percent in industrialized nations. By 1996 the proportion of trade originating from developing nations had risen to about 32 percent by 1996 (ibid.). The role of business in shifting export-led production from developed to developing countries is linked to the substantial movement of foreign direct investment (FDI), as firms invest outside their home countries in new plant and fixed capital. In 1990 FDI was US 232 billion, it hit a trough of US$71 billion at the end of the recession in 1992, and rose again to US$350 billion by 1996 (UNCTAD 1994; UNCTAD 1996; UNCTAD 1997a).

The mobility of private sector investment capital is outstripped by the fluidity of global foreign exchange and financial trading. In the period 1987 to 1996, trading in international securities and derivatives, based on futures and options in interest rates, currency, and stock market indices, rose from US$1 trillion to US$10 trillion per year (WTO 1997: 10–11). In 1996 trading in securities and derivatives of this kind stood at almost twice the annual value of world trade in goods and services.

Internationally, business is aware of the global market place, engaging robustly in markets outside traditional domestic frontiers. The move to a global span of production, marketing, and sales takes many forms. But a concentration of capital through the growth in the economic power and influence of multinational corporations (MNCs) have accompanied it. For example, Gladwin (1998) identifies that the 200 largest MNCs accounted for 28 percent of world economic activity in 1995 rising from 7 percent in 1971.

The drivers of these changes are connected to a range of technological and political forces. The advent of advanced communication and information technology has brought with it the capacity to continuously monitor global changes in equity and foreign exchange movements. Computing power, coupled to the Internet, brings the possibility of real-time trading on the worlds major equity markets to the desktops of many, not simply those who are in the trading desks of large banks and financial institutions.

These technological advances have been matched by political moves to liberalize trade and foreign investment under the influence of GATT and the World Trade Organization (WTO), to deregulate industries and industrial sectors, and to privatize previously state managed assets—particularly energy, water, and transport. This is maintained by the continued belief in the virtue of open, global markets. Business managers and political decision-makers alike are caught in the myth of the value of global markets and open financial systems.

Even so, the secretary-general of the United Nations Conference for Trade and Development, Rubens Ricupero, recently warned that this act of faith is fragile when he says: "There is a real threat of a political backlash that may wipe out several of the benefits of recent economic reforms. . . . The 1920s and 1930s provide a stark . . . reminder of just how quickly *faith* [my italics] in markets and openness can be overwhelmed by political events" (UNCTAD 1997b: vi). This faith is based on the view that the advantages of global market opportunities outweigh the disadvantages and on an assessment that there is an unstoppable tide driving toward more open, global markets.

An indication of the recent conflict around this act of faith is found in the calls from leaders in the tiger economies, bruised by the 1997 and 1998 East Asian financial turbulence, for a more protected financial and economic regime (*Financial Times* 1998). And the announcement on October 30, 1998 by the G7 leaders of the introduction of a package of financial aid for countries subject to international currency fluctuations and facing lack of confidence in world financial markets is another such indication. Historically, we have gone through periods where commitments to more open trading systems have flourished or floundered.

The response of business to the force of the global market has involved the world's largest economic actors in the formation of new structures through mergers and acquisitions, as they seek scale economies and global reach. This is not a phenomenon that affects just MNCs. Smaller companies counter economic concentration by establishing their own looser strategic alliances, as a way to expand their international market opportunities while trying to protect their established market positions. These changes impact all companies searching out market opportunities for their products and services, from small to multinational. They bring with them new structures for enterprises and new forms of competition.

SOCIAL AND CULTURAL GLOBALIZATION

There are other global trends affecting our social and cultural fabric beyond these developments in international trade and finance. The global village, envisioned by Marshall McLuhan as an outcome of the advance of the global communication network, is not simply about communication. It applies to many aspects of global society and change in our culture(s). Here the image of the village is something of a delusion. It might be more appropriate to regard globalization of society and culture as the advent of a series of "global clubs" and "global ghettos."

Members of "global clubs" have elite status derived from their wealth and the demand for their distinctive knowledge and skills. Wealth and skills enable the elite to move across the boundaries of nations that constrain many. However, the elite are not a homogeneous group. They include international personalities and members of the bureaucracies and organizations that embody globalism such as the World Bank, the World Trade Organization, the United Nations, the CEOs and international managers of MNCs, and a growing international intelligentsia. The "badges" of this club include homes in more than one country and multiple nationalities. They hold international rather than national perspectives. The products and services consumed by club members distinguish them as "global elite," "global middle class," and "global teens." They are among the world's wealthiest citizens. But ,irrespective of which sub-group they belong to, they have a tendency toward the consumption of goods and services with global brand identity—Rayban, Montblanc, Gucci, and Rolex as well as Walkmans, Nike, Levi, even McDonalds. Frequently these products carry premium prices. Their consumption is the aspiration of many. As the 1998 Human Development report says, these designer products and services are "available to a few, visible to many" (UNDP 1998: 62).

There are temporary members of the elite. For example, the international long-haul tourists and business travelers: elite for a week or more. The growth in this market is considerable. World travel arrivals from abroad rose from 285 million in 1980, to 518 million in 1993, and on to 595 million in 1996. Total air miles flown have risen more dramatically, from 980 billion kilometers in 1992 to 1 377 billion kilometers in 1996 (World Tourism Organization 1998).

Others aspire to mimic the elite by appropriating the products they associate with membership. Brands have emerged as icons that transcend national boundaries and identities assuming an international status and meaning—itself a phenomenon of an internationalized economy. These icons span a curious mix of products, but they all combine an image conferred by their luxury, exclusiveness, or design with the potential to appeal to a massed global market place. This is not so much mass accessibility as mass aspiration. Curiously, the production and distribution of counterfeit icons is the market's way to close the gap between aspiration and accessibility. Deception is added to mimicry.

At the opposite end of the spectrum of a globalizing culture and society are the members of the global ghettos. These form around economic migrants and political refugees who seek sanctuary from economic, political, and environmental plight, by moving between countries or continents. The figures for the total world stock of migrants rose from 75 million in 1965 to 120 million in 1996. While this represents only about 2.3 percent of world population, the stock of migrants is not evenly distributed around the globe. In 1996 it represented 8.6 percent of the population of North America, 6 percent of the European Union, 4.5 percent of the developed countries as a whole, and 1.6 percent of the population of the less development regions. At the same time, the total world stock of refugees rose from 8.2 million in 1981 through 14.9 million in 1990. And, as repatriation took place in the 1990s, the figure reduced to 13.2 million by 1996 (UN 1997b: 16). The stock of refugees has risen as a consequence of conflict, for example, in Vietnam, Ethiopia, the ex-Yugoslavia, or Kurdistan. These are mass movements, which often involve refugees aiming for "focused" destinations. Here the first migrants establish footholds in distinct neighborhoods and the economic hierarchy of cities to which others from their original communities are drawn.

Refugees and economic migrants, whether going from Mexico to the United States, North Africa to the European Union, or Bosnia to Canada, are all involved in the search for an "identity" in the new spaces in which they live. There are common issues for all these communities as they seek to build their new identities. They draw on their cultural traditions, yet are molded by the cultures in which they now find themselves. A 1998 report to the United Nations on international migration policies states how second-generation migrants in particular "are divided between two cultures, alienated from the civil and political life of the country in which they were born and uncertain where their future lies." It goes on to say "In many countries an entire generation of youth has been growing up with hyphenated identities, in countries that do not even have this concept in their cultural framework" (UN 1998: 63). Often members of these communities are highly networked with family members in other international destinations around the globe: the Sikh in Calgary, with cousins in Birmingham (England), Dortmund (Germany), and Abu Dhabi as well as the Punjab; the Croatian with an extended family dispersed between Paris, London, Toronto, and New York. This phenomenon, the simultaneous global dispersal and local concentration of cultural groups, is not new. It is characteristic of the spread of the Jewish community for over 2000 years. What is recent is the extent to which many different communities are replicating this phenomenon in cities around the globe. Under this pressure, these "focal cities" are emerging as multi-cultural, multi-racial, multi-ethnic, multi-religious mixes.

In the ghettoized city-society there are a range of tensions. New migrants vie with indigenous economic and social groups for economic opportunities and accommodation. They form their own spatial clusters, which follow successive waves of new residents. Indigenous economic and social classes often choose to avoid competing directly with new entrants by exercising their right to establish economically and socially in other areas. As newcomer communities move in and more established communities move out, so a process of spatial, economic, and cultural stratification across the city, its suburbs, and surrounding areas takes place.

What we see then are contradictory forces. At a macro scale, cities are becoming more heterogeneous and multi-cultural yet, at the scale of the neighborhood, cities are more economically stratified and more homogeneous within each level of stratification. This duality—heterogeneity and homogeneity—creates the ground for social fragmentation. It provides, at one and the same time, a basis for new multi-cultural societies and the potential for social groups in conflict. It also provides individuals with a basis for multiple levels of identity—for example, the engineer, born in Pakistan, Muslim by religion, trained in Lahore, then Imperial College, London, and finally MIT, Massachusetts, now a resident of Washington D.C., a U.S. citizen, a baseball fan, and consumer of halal meat. Such a complexity of identity can enrich. It provides great opportunity for those able to transcend notions of tribality and ethnicity. But it can also lead to a loss of self-identity, to alienation, to the fracture of social ties and structure, as individuals are no longer able to identify clearly around the varied dimensions of their fragmenting character.

Within this fragmenting society, individuals are distanced further and further from their cultural and environmental roots, despite the tendency to cluster into areas with other members of same community. They have to cope with the strong cultural and economic forces of the societies in which they now live—in particular, the powerful and seductive images of economic identity and belonging that lured many to the developed economies of North America, Europe, and Asia. For some, the search for "identity" may take them to discover, or rediscover, fundamentalist beliefs of a religious or ethnic nature. For others, identity is found in associating with their new cultural setting through the possession of products and brands that replace lost cultural and social identity with a new economic or consumptive identity. Members of the ghetto may have the highest aspirations for the icons of the global elite.

This suggests that global social and cultural transformations are interwoven with and reproduce some of the economic and environmental changes previously discussed. For example, global media and mass communication through television, telephones, Internet, and transport propel brand images into the popular domain on a global scale. The way these icons provide a basis for aspirations and belonging has already been discussed. Echoing this point, Juliet Schor (1998), in her recent book on the overspent American, identifies how the income needed to fulfill the aspirations of those seeking the "American dream" has risen from US$50,000 in 1986 to US$104,000 in 1994. She suggests "an inflation of aspirations" as Americans are continuously exposed to lifestyle images of the elite through media and advertising. But the real issue is that these images, and the aspirations that go with them, spill over into other societies. They are not localized but globalized. Moreover, they contribute to the interaction of the waves of global change. In this way the recent "fight and flight" events that have pushed migrants from Bosnia, Indonesia, or Rwanda combine with the pull of aspirations seen on television screens. The rural to urban migration of the last 150 year of industrialization now has a stronger and stronger cross-border, north-south dimension.

INTERCONNECTION, COMPLEXITY, TURBULENCE, AND THE RATE OF CHANGE

This discussion suggests that the three waves of recent global change—environmental, economic, and social/cultural—are all expressions of the trend toward extended spatial and temporal connections. Moreover, these waves increasingly overlap to create greater uncertainty about the future.

In terms of interconnection, each wave of change exhibits similar properties. Change arises over extended spatial and temporal horizons. Change occurring at many different local levels is traceable back to more universal causes/effects or combinations of factors. Often what appears as a local event is then found to aggregate into an issue of global importance. The properties of development that generated the call for sustainable development are to be found in the other forms of global change.

The characteristics of global change also include complexity, turbulence, and the pace of change. In the case of complexity, the relationships involved in systems of global change are complex and non-linear. The important point about complexity is that there are no fundamental cause-and-effect relationships. There is a mutual causality of relationships, which means that even fairly trivial factors can combine to generate substantial changes in whole systems. Complex systems, therefore, are at the interface of order and chaos. These systems are difficult to model and can appear erratic and unpredictable as they flip from one state to another. For example, it is possible to state with confidence that a grain-growing prairie in Midwest America or East Africa has the potential to become a dust bowl, but it is not possible to predict at what point in time, or under what combinations of circumstances, this will occur. In economic systems it is possible to anticipate that bull stock markets will reverse. But it is not possible to predict when and under what combination of circumstances this will arise.

Turbulence, following Emery & Trist (1965), arises in fields when organizations in that field pursue their own self-interest without any reference to a more universal set of values that enable collective action to be taken to dampen change. In this sense, interconnected waves of environmental, economic, and social/cultural change, are expected to contribute to more and more turbulence, as actors pursue their own agendas without reference to common organizing principles or common sets of beliefs. Beyond these properties of the overall system, the interconnection of economic, social, and environmental actors creates a social dilemma around legitimacy. No one actor or group of actors can command legitimacy across all three domains. No one actor can set the organizing principles that apply to all three domains. For example, while Agenda 21 provides a response to pre-1990 environmental and social change, its authority is not universally accepted. Although the G7 countries recently agreed on measures to help stabilize future economic and financial turbulence this took little cognizance of the impacts of these measures on sustainable development. We still have no real global response to the governance of social and cultural globalization. Little attention has been given to the interaction between the different waves of change or their effect on the existing agenda for sustainable development. We have not addressed the overall pattern of production and consumption or the combined effects of environmental, economic. and social/cultural globalization on that pattern. As a result, we confront a future that is highly contested and stalked by many partisan actors and advocates (Gladwin 1998), none of whom has the span of knowledge or commands the authority across domains to assume a position of credibility and leadership. In the absence of institutions that command respect and authority at local, regional, or global levels, we face a future that is at best uncertain, at worse, socially divisive and catastrophic.

The pace at which global change is taking place is also beginning to outstrip our capacity for timely responses. Responses are outdated before they are fully implemented. For example, Agenda 21 is a reaction to the environmental and social aspects of development experienced in the 1970s and 1980s. Yet it did not anticipate the significant impacts of recent waves of change. As it is being implemented so are these other forms of change eclipsing it.

These characteristics define the advent of a "meta-world"—a world of interconnected, turbulent change that challenges and undermines our existing notions of governance. Meta-problems, such as poverty, human health, and environmental quality are not new. What is new is that these problems are increasingly recognized as a set of collided issues arising globally as well as locally. Responses to one aspect of a meta-problem spill over to affect responses to other problems.

TRANSITION TO A META-WORLD

Moving from this description and analysis of recent global change, what do these perspectives imply for the future, say the next five decades? Table 2 attempts to describe the transition we are currently going through as society moves from an industrial world to the world of the future.

Table 2 describes a present world, where chemical science, materials technology, and engineering provide the basis for industrial and chemical production. This has required hierarchical forms of organization and structure. This world has experience of the division between rich and poor. In contrast, the future will emphasize information, biological sciences, systems, and networked forms of organization. This will be an increasingly populated world, with more and more of that population concerned about their lifestyle and the search for new identities. The table sets out four distinguishing dimensions of these worlds—past/present and future. Problem definition refers to the way that central issues are defined. Symbolic issues are the concerns that describe our collective human condition. Root definitions specify the dominant way society analyzes these problems and, responses and outcomes, specify how we frame our response.

The problem definition for the past/present world is focused on economic growth and the environmental burden of industrialization. This involves both the economic "externalities" of industrial activity and the problem of security of basic access by the poor to water, food, fuel, literacy, and safety. Consequently, the symbols of this world are different for rich and poor. For the rich the symbols

Table 2. Transition from an Industrial to a Systems World[2]

The past—a scientific, technological world; a chemical and industrial world; a world of rich and poor	**Transition**	**The future—an information world; a biological, systems, highly networked world; a densely populated world with a concern for "lifesyle"**
1. Consequences of economic growth 2. Chemical and industrial externalities 3. Security of primary needs—food, water, fuel, health, safety, and literacy	**Problem Definition**	Increasing manipulation of primary systems, information rich yet knowledge poor, growth of population, lifestyle issues, and migration. Competition over systems
1. Dioxins, CFCs, greenhouse gases, material extraction, processing and waste, chemical agriculture 2. Desertification, soil erosion, deforestation, over-fishing, failed harvests 3. War and conflict 4. Literacy	**Symbolic Issues**	1. Biological systems and genome 2. Water systems 3. Carbon cycle 4. Nutrition systems 5. Energy systems 6. Communication systems 7. Population systems 8. Distributive systems 9. Household service systems 10. Financial and trading systems
Who impacts what and whom? 1. Local spillovers and global impacts 2. The forgotten and the un-represented between	**Root Definition**	**Who owns and controls which system?** 1. Who owns primary systems, the genome, information, and knowledge? 2. Competition and conflict over use and access to systems business, nations and communities
Accommodative integration 1. Environmental management, Product stewardship, Dematerialization 2. Aid and technology transfer	**Responses, Outcomes**	**Rivalry and conflict—what this will look like is not clear** 1. A new socioeconomic and political order 2. Definition of property rights and responsibilities

are dioxins, CFCs, greenhouse gases, the environmental consequences of material extraction, and processing, use, and waste. For the poor the symbols are different. They are represented by environmental issues, such as desertification, deforestation, soil erosion, the loss of fisheries, and bad harvests, and by social and political issues such as war, famine, and literacy.

The root definition used to understand these problems draws on the dominant language of this era, the language of economics. Problems are seen in terms of "who impacts what and whom." This is the language of economic "externalities" and their internalization. It raises questions about who represents and understands the poor and underprivileged. The responses to these problems are shaped through a process of accommodative integration whereby responses are identified and driven by the unreconstructed myths of our economic and social systems. Myths that helped generate the problems in the first place. For industry, the process of integration is brought about through the application of concepts such as product stewardship, the use of a raft of tools and techniques that contribute to environmental management, the dematerialization of products, and the slow move from products to services. The problems of the poor are accommodated through development assistance and aid and the transfer of technology.

The meta-world of the future has a different set of circumstances and characteristics that emerge from global change. The problems for this world center on the manipulation of primary systems, aggravated by the growth of population, mass migration, and the demands of lifestyle. These problems are made worse by excessive information and technical knowledge while there is a serious shortage of "systemic knowledge" and people who are capable of integrating environmental, economic, and social issues. The security of primary needs, previously only a concern of the poor, is translated into a wider concern for global society. However, the nature of the problem of security is changing. No longer is the focus of security on the resources that provide for needs of the poor. Instead the concern will be the integrity of basic systems, such as water, nutrition, energy, and the carbon cycle, and the services provided by those systems to almost everyone.

Pressures on these systems from human demands linked to lifestyles and the pressure of population pressures will cause corporations to link their strategic survival to their ability to secure access to services derived from the systems that most strongly relate to their business activities. One way for corporations to maintain access to these systems services is through acquisition. The idea that corporations might acquire and enclose natural and other systems as a way to secure their services becomes a real possibility. Some corporations will have the economic power to pursue their strategies. But this enclosure is unlikely to go uncontested. Enclosure will probably involve a hyper-competitive period where companies compete for ownership of systems. Competition is likely to arise between companies in the same business sector as well as between companies in different sectors which share interest in systems. For example, water systems, especially watersheds, provide service to both the water and beverage industries. They also contribute to the food and nutrition industry through their significance to agricultural production. As a result, the root definition moves from the previous focus on externalities—"who impacts whom"—to a concern about systems ownership and governance—"who owns and controls systems." Ten important systems for the future are set out in Table 2 and discussed below.

Consideration of these systems is used to anticipate some unfolding aspects of the strategies of the private sector. In the case of biological systems, biotechnology companies (for example, Monsanto) are already devising new genetic technologies and lines of business that will impact the integrity of the human and biological genome. Biotechnology companies will seek to control aspects of indigenous knowledge and human and other genetic material, by searching for and patenting this material and its DNA code. Genetic manipulation will be found increasingly embedded in the products of food producers as the dividing line between ethical pharmaceuticals and nutrition blurs through the common interest in genetic modification. For example, genetic manipulation to produce insulin, for medical use, is not far removed from the genetic manipulation needed to boost the vitamin C content of kiwi fruit.

These developments have implications for the structure of sectors, as they compete for parts of the biological genome. They also have implications for the way companies compete for the human knowledge and skills required to support their work on genetic engineering. This will cause some food and nutrition companies to merge or enter into technology development alliances with pharmaceutical businesses. A number of trends are anticipated around corporate interests in food and nutrition systems and water systems. Looking at these systems from the business viewpoint, companies such as Nestle, Unilever, and Kraft Food, will progressively redefine themselves as nutrition providers rather than food companies. Nutrition will come to involve fisheries and agriculture-based products and will follow the whole supply network from food production, to food processing, and distribution. Value for these companies will be obtained through vertical integration of the supply chain. But in order to provide consumers with assurance over the provenance and integrity of food products they will have to exercise rigorous control down the supply chain over issues such as food hygiene (BSE-free meat), food integrity (organic, pesticide-free), and specific market demands (GMO-free soya). Companies may assume direct ownership of the food and nutrition system or exercise contractual control over other actors on whom they rely. Some companies will develop guidelines on acceptable practices in the food and nutrition system as shown by Unilever's support for sustainable fisheries codes, as a way to ensure the continued supply of fisheries resources.

The overall context for water systems is determined by the growing demands on the world's supplies of potable water. Beverage companies, such as Coca-Cola, will increasingly find themselves in competition with privatized water companies and other interests as they seek to gain access to water system(s) that provide a key ingredient of their products. The ownership of watersheds and water systems as a way to guarantee supply will become easier as water companies are deregulated and privatized. However, this will create intense competition between water companies and beverage suppliers as they focus on an increasingly scarce resource.

In the energy sector, oil companies, such as Shell and BP-Amoco, have already begun to redefine themselves as energy supply companies rather than simply oil companies as they acquire competence and market shares in non-oil based energies. The next stage is to define themselves as energy systems service companies concerning themselves not only with energy supply but taking on a role in demand-side management. This will expand their core competence from oil exploration and sales to energy management and customer service.

Other corporations will begin to rethink their core managerial and technological competencies as a result of their focus on systems. The recently privatized water companies, power utilities, and gas companies may recognize that their capability is not in the management of a resource but the management of distributive networks, the provision of mass customer service and their assets based on knowledge about customers and customer data bases. Companies that recognize their core competence in distributive management will seek to expand their business through mergers and acquisitions across previously separate sectors—water, electricity, gas, and other mass consumption products distribution networks. This will create new and much larger corporate entities.

There is similar potential for companies involved in transport, information, and communications to combine as they move toward a shared orientation around communications, involving information technologies, computers, and communications media. For example, in the automobile sector, "smart cars" are propelling manufacturers to develop increasingly sophisticated on-board electronics, telemetry, and other tracking devices. As the information and computing content of the automobile increases, so is the importance of the physical transport function of the automobile reduced. What then is the core competence of the automobile company? It no longer rests on the design, manufacture. and distribution of automobiles or the application of core technologies such as the internal combustion engine. It is more likely to center on the design and presentation to market of highly compact communications platform services. Whether these platforms are in automobiles or modular offices is a matter of indifference. The structural implications for business rest on the potential for mergers and strategic alliances between companies like Ford and

British Telecom or Motorola, Chrysler/Benz, and AT&T. There is a similar synergy between companies that produce communications systems and those that provide household services, through the design and manufacture of domestic goods. The key here is the way that domestic goods are destined to become more "intelligent" as they incorporate computer chips and "smart" materials. There is a clear link between intelligent products, information technologies, and communications networks that permit people to interact with their homes at any time from any place. It will stimulate joint ventures and more formal alliances.

Lifestyle demands will continue to generate markets for "intelligent" products and services that offer "designer" attributes. The space for small to medium-sized enterprises will open up around the technological innovations that provide the basis for these products which larger corporations will then seek to acquire. Acquisitions will take place where innovations are linked to the development of new products and service and where technology improves the manipulation, management, and control of primary systems—nutrition, energy, and water. Small companies will find a place in providing for a range of local needs including the demands of "retro" householders for craft-made products.

In this meta-world, large corporations will become more high-tech and knowledge-based. They will become rivals over the ownership of systems, technological acquisitions, and human knowledge assets as well as markets. Competition and conflict will not only occur between businesses, it will arise between businesses, nations, and communities. Particular points of conflict will develop over access to systems' services and the responsibilities that go together with system ownership. These competitive pressures and strategic positions will prompt demands for a new social and political order and the redefinition of rights and responsibilities that go with property.

What is envisioned here is a move from our historic concerns around economics, markets, technological applications, and management to legal issues about the ownership of systems, the ethics of system manipulation, and questions about property rights and patents. This will include a range of concerns about national and territorial interests and governance issues in relation to social needs, property rights and responsibilities, and the capacity of markets to allocate the services provided by systems. A key role will continue to be played by information networks and by the media. These too will be subject to disputes about ownership and public policy/private sector control. None of these conflicts will be trivial. It is not clear what the outcome will be of attempts to redefine fundamental property rights. Neither is it clear what implication these changes will have in terms of a more or less sustainable society. The move toward the ownership of systems by corporations is in itself value-neutral. Whether the private ownership of systems encourages or undermines the move toward sustainable development will depend on the responsiveness of corporations to consumer and market interests in relation to social and environmental concerns. What I contend is that sustainable development can only be realized if companies recognize that their future survival in a meta-world is linked to the maintenance of the systems on which their economic performance depends. It is also linked to the maintenance of corporate legitimacy in relation to the responsible ownership of systems. However, three particular problems are envisioned.

This paper anticipates a period of hyper-competition, in which companies and others seek ownership and control of systems, followed by a period of consolidation in the form of systems management. However, the hyper-competitive period will generate turbulence as companies ruthlessly pursue their own self-interests. This turbulence will give rise to the call for forms of corporate governance that are better adapted to dealing with complex human and environmental systems. It is unclear how companies will deal with this turbulence and the potential it creates for rapid, irreversible systems change. Second, markets allocate services from systems on the basis of ability to pay rather than on needs. This has immediate implications for those social groups denied access to systems services because of their inability to pay. Ignoring needs, which exist beyond the market, is potentially damaging to the social fabric but is not part of the conventional governance model of the corporation. However, ignoring needs will undermine the legitimacy of the companies that own systems. How then do companies adjust to satisfy both market signals and social needs? Third, while the future described here is information-rich and requires a rapid expansion in technical knowledge, a "knowledge gap" will arise. The knowledge gap will arise from the systems that corporations own pitted against their capacity to understand and manage them wisely.

Where will this interdisciplinary knowledge about ecological and social systems come from? It is not presently available to any large extent in the education system, which would take at least a generation to reform. Neither are corporations presently endowed with this knowledge.

SCENARIOS AND PROGNOSIS

So far, this paper has moved from our current understanding of global change and sustainable development to envision the characteristics of an emerging meta-world. The paper identifies some of the dynamic interactions between changes in business and key issues in the economic, environmental, and social aspects of globalization. These are set out in Table 2. The paper raises questions about what our experience of sustainable development as a response to global change says to our emerging approach to the overall process of global change. The main concern of the paper is to address the societal implications of these changes with a particular focus on the implications for corporate strategy and governance over the next 50 years.

This final section moves beyond this analysis to develop a prognosis for this future. It relates these ideas in the paper to recent work on scenarios for sustainable development generated by the World Business Council for Sustainable Development (WBCSD 1998). Members of Shell International's scenario development team and member companies of WBCSD developed these scenarios for WBCSD. The global scenario project 2000–2050 identifies three possible scenarios for sustainable development. WBCSD refers to these as FROG, GEOpolity, and Jazz.

In the FROG scenario, human systems are unable to meet the demands of sustainable development. The imperative of most nations is economic growth. Sustainable development is recognized but as a secondary or lower-order consideration. Concern centers on local environmental quality, which gains global proportion as we become aware of how widespread these problems are. In addition, there are a series of looming environmental disasters. The slow accumulation of local effects and the unpredictability of disasters means that no long-term view or bigger picture of the need for new approaches to governance emerges until too late.

In the GEOpolity scenario, human systems and institutions are overwhelmed by a paralyzing loss of legitimacy. This applies first to the legitimacy of government activities and then business is found wanting in terms of its contribution and position in society. There is a poverty of leadership. This creates a vacuum, which is filled by new institutions and structures built around sustainable development ideas. These ideas are cemented in place through technocratic solutions that appear to offer the basis for social cohesion. Government reforms embrace a more active civil society, which is then involved in the creation of a mixed market with business under the guidance of a Global Ecosystem Organization.

The Jazz scenario has a more extemporary feel. Jazz describes a world of social and technological innovation, experimentation, and voluntary interconnections with the power to change global markets. It is an information-led world with a corresponding level of transparency driven by the age of "knowledge democracy" (Roome 1998: 14) that follows from wide access to information technology and cheap communication. This is a world of partnerships between many social actors—governments, NGOs, concerned consumers, and businesses. Their shared goal is to incorporate social and environmental values into market mechanisms.

None of these scenarios is more likely than any of the others. What the authors of these scenarios have sought to do is provide a basis for strategic assessments of the circumstances that future corporate plans and actions might encounter. They argue that Jazz has the highest potential to deliver a more sustainable society while GEOpolity is caught in the tension between competing myths and perspectives on development, the economy, and society. The question is, how do these scenarios for sustainable development fit with the ideas developed in this paper about an emerging meta-world, which is shaped by the moves in business toward systems ownership and systems organization as core to global business survival?

The analysis of the meta-world suggests that, rather than the three discrete scenarios suggested by WBCSD, it is likely that we will see emerge a world that has characteristics that cut across all three scenarios. The future will be fragmented in many dimensions and with that will come the potential for rivalry, tension, and also innovation. The paper also highlights the importance of the "knowledge gap" and need for new approaches to corporate governance as one of the arenas for innovation. Both the "knowledge gap" and the failure to development new forms of governance will mean that there is no satisfactory basis to resolve the social and private claims to property that arise from the new corporate ownership of natural systems. Put another way, current business thinking and practice are not capable of resolving the social and environmental conflicts that will arise from the pursuit of economic interests in a meta-world.

What the future calls for is a commitment by all social, economic, and political actors to experiment with new systems of governance. Part of that experiment will be the development of a new language for governance. This will have a number of features. It will oblige business leaders to develop more distant horizons and broader visions of change using techniques like scenario-building. It will demand the capacity to measure and integrate the economic, social, and environmental changes that are perceived by many different groups—not only government and community, but also business. This will not only involve technocratic choice but legitimacy for the process of decision-making, which only becomes possible when discourse and choice are more open and plural. This implies a broader, more inclusive approach to participation and consent within the governance structures of all sectors of society, particularly business (Roome 1998: 259–76).

New governance systems and education to resolve the "knowledge gap" will involve social innovation as well as technological creativity. This implies an open and creative approach to learning. It suggests a move away from notions of the professional and the manager, with their adherence to codes of practice and responsibility to the profession and the organization, toward a notion of decision-making as a facilitated, multi-party process informed by broadly accepted principles. It also implies the move toward the need for global and local resilience of systems—based on ideas such as restraint, diversity, locality, and appropriate responses to needs. Processes based on these characteristics are under development in relation management and governance of living resource systems, such as forests (Östland & Roome 1998). These new approaches can operate even where there are strong economic interests. They are based on processes that set sustainable levels of output based on the assessments of the carrying capacity of the environment and the determination of the social limits to resource use. These social limits are determined in relation to the whole range of human interests in a forest or fishery resource.

This approach stands in deep contradiction to the broad thrust of present-day business, management, and management education as it faces economic globalization. We have poverty in how we educate managers for the future. Currently they are educated around the myths and language of the present world rather than on the basis of the myths and language that will be needed if sustainable development and globalization are to be reconciled in the meta-world of tomorrow. The paper suggests that we should begin to replace the current language of economics with a language that reflects the value of systems services, systems maintenance, and the asset value of systems. This would need to recognize the plurality of perspectives and the multiplicity of identities that need to be heard and maintained as part of our global and local society. This is a distributive and restorative social and political economy that values sufficiency and human relationships as much as efficiency and material relationships.

POSTSCRIPT—A TRANSATLANTIC AGENDA

A footnote is necessary as this paper was presented in the context of a transatlantic agenda for globalization and sustainable development. How might the myths and new language for the future be more speedily realized through an agenda shared by the U.S. and EU? It is suggested that this kind of capacity-building needs to operate at different levels in a transatlantic agenda for governance. At the highest level there is a role for a U.S./EU Presidents' Council for Global Change. This would involve a standing group to exchange experiences of the full range of issues addressed as globalization in this paper. The purpose of this group would be to create a setting from which to identify innovative approaches to governance and to advise the presidents of the U.S. and EU on appropriate reforms in institutions and governance. The recent (U.S.) President's Council on Sustainable Development provides a model for this group.

The key need for new approaches to education sets the stage for a highly networked "Transatlantic University" based on academics, practitioners, and learners who want to commit to the development of the critical social, institutional, and educational skills demanded by global change. This would include business programs that support the needs of future managers who are able to deal with the issues of competition and consent in a meta-world.

The work of this Transatlantic University should connect to a leadership program. This would seek to attract "young leaders," identified at municipal level, and drawn from government, business, science and technology, NGOs, and community settings to develop the broad experiences and values required in the management of the multi-party processes that underpin a more sustainable form of society and enterprise.

Finally, it is recommended that a series of standing groups on the governance of "systems" are established with core membership drawn from the three initiatives set out above. These groups would be charged to bring forward specific suggestions for the governance of the systems identified in Table 2.

ENDNOTES

1. Chevalier (1966 and 1967) first discussed the concept of the meta-problem. Meta-problems occur when individual problems are seen to form part of a related problem set. The nature of these sets is that they demand comprehensive responses because any isolated response to a problem in the set generates issues that affect other problems in the set.

2. This table is adapted from a submission by the author as a member of the Natural Resources and Environment Expert Panel for European Commission Futures Project organized by the Institute for Prospective Technological Studies, Joint Research Centre of the European Commission. See <http://futures.jrc.es>.

REFERENCES

Agenda 21 (1992). *Earth Summit '92: The United Nations Conference on Environment and Development*. London: Regency Press Corporation.

Brundtland, G.-H. (1987). *Report of the World Commission on Environment and Development.* Oxford: Oxford University Press.

Chevalier, M. (1966). *A Wider Range of Perspectives in the Bureaucratic Structure. Working paper*. Ottawa: Commission on Bi-lingualism and Bi-culturalism.

—— (1967). *Stimulation of Needed Social Science Research for Canadian Water Resource Problems*. Ottawa: Privy Council Science Secretariat.

Clark, I. (1997). *Globalization and Fragmentation: International Relations in the Twentieth Century.* New York: W.W. Norton.

Financial Times (1998). "A Backlash Begins." September 4, p 11.

Emery, F. & Trist, E. (1965). "The Causal Texture of Organizational Environments." *Human Relations,* 18, 21–32.

Gladwin T. (1998). "Economic Globalization and Ecological Sustainability: The Search for Truth and Reconciliation." In Roome, N. (ed.). *Sustainability Strategies for Industry: The Future of Corporate Practice.* Washington. DC: Island Press.

IMF (1997). *International Financial Statistics Yearbook.* Washington, DC: IMF.

IUCN (1981). *World Conservation Strategy.* Gland: IUCN.

Lélé, S. & Norgaard, R. (1996)."Sustainability and the Scientist's Burden." *Conservation Biology*, 10, (2), 354–65.

Östlund, S. & Roome, N. (1998). "Sustainable Forestry Management as a Model for Sustainable Industry: A Case Study of the Swedish Approach." In Roome, N. (ed.). *Sustainability Strategies for Industry: The Future of Corporate Practice.* Washington. DC: Island Press.

Rawls, J. (1971). *A Theory of Justice*. Cambridge, MA: Harvard University Press.

Roome, N. (1998). *Sustainability Strategies for Industry: The Future of Corporate Practice.* Washington, DC: Island Press.

Schor, J. (1998). *The Overspent American*. New York: Basic Books.

UN (1997a). *Critical Trends: Global Change and Sustainable Development*. United Nations Department for Policy Coordination and Sustainable Development. New York: United Nations.

—— (1997b). *International Migration and Development Concise Report.* New York: United Nations.

—— (1998). *International Migration Policies*. New York: United Nations.

UNCTAD (1994). *UNCTAD Bulletin No. 26*. New York: United Nations Conference for Trade and Development.

—— (1996). *UNCTAD Bulletin No. 37.* New York: United Nations Conference for Trade and Development.

—— (1997a). *UNCTAD TAD/INF/2710 July*. New York: United Nations Conference for Trade and Development.

—— (1997b). Trade *and Development Report*. New York: United Nations Conference for Trade and Development.

UNEP (1997). *Global Environmental Outlook*. Oxford: Oxford University Press.

UNDP (1998). *Human Development Report*. New York: United Nations Development Program.

WBCSD (1998). *Exploring Sustainable Development: WBCSD Global Scenarios 2000–2050.* Geneva: WBCSD.

WTO (1997). *WTO Special Studies—Open Markets in Financial Services and the Role of the GATS*. Geneva: WTO Publications.

World Tourism Organization (1998). *Yearbook of Tourism Statistics Vol 1, 50th edition*. Madrid: World Tourism Organization.

GLOBALIZATION AND THE ENVIRONMENT: THE LIMITS OF THE LAW

Jeffrey L. Dunoff
Associate Professor of Law, Temple University
Philadelphia, PA

INTRODUCTION

I am deeply honored to have been asked to deliver the keynote address at this Institute for Development Studies Conference. It is indeed a privilege to address such a distinguished group on the topic of "Globalization and the Environment: Opportunities and Challenges for the New Transatlantic Agenda," and I am grateful to the Institute, the School of Public and Environmental Affairs, and the Ecole Nationale d'Administration for this opportunity.

This conference could not be more timely. We meet at a time of significant WTO activity on trade-environment issues. The Appellate Body is finalizing its report on the Shrimp-Turtle dispute and discussions are intensifying over an EU proposal for a high-level meeting of trade and environmental ministers next year.

There is also significant activity at the transatlantic level. Last May, the European Union and United States launched the Transatlantic Economic Partnership ("TEP"). As you know, two weeks ago the European Commission approved a draft Action Plan for the Partnership, which will be considered at the U.S./EU summit in December. Just last week, EU Trade Commissioner Sir Leon Brittan met with the United States Trade Representative and other U.S. officials to discuss the TEP and draft Action Plan. Environmental NGOs are today meeting with the United States Trade Representative to discuss the role NGOs will play at the December Summit.

But, although the Action Plan highlights trade-environment issues, and U.S. and European NGOs recently held a very constructive meeting in Paris, candor compels acknowledgment that progress on trade-environment issues has been halting at best. In this short paper, I'd like to discuss why progress has been so difficult, and identify one promising venue where progress might occur.

A wide range of issues falls within the trade-environment area. Our organizers have highlighted for us certain parts of the debate, such as whether the trade regime threatens environmental sovereignty, and whether domestic environmental laws impermissibly impede international trade. These questions are surely among the most difficult—and contentious—that confront the international community. While many have addressed trade-environment conflicts, I'd like to present a rather novel approach to thinking about these issues. In so doing, I hope to challenge some conventional wisdom and stimulate your thinking about these topics.

To do so, I will outline three different arguments. First, I will argue that trade-environment issues undermine conventional understandings of the trade system. Second, I will identify a paradox these issues pose for WTO dispute resolution, and detail a controversial strategy for resolving this paradox. Finally, I will discuss why efforts within the Transatlantic Economic Partnership hold particular promise for successfully addressing trade-environment issues.

THE CONVENTIONAL MODELS

How do the "trade and environment" issues—as well as other "trade and" issues such as trade and labor or trade and intellectual property—challenge conventional understandings of the trade regime? To answer this, it is first useful to review why we have a trade regime. What purpose does the GATT/WTO system serve? Trade scholars typically invoke one of three types of answers to these questions. The first is the familiar economic answer: the GATT helps private actors exploit comparative advantage and maximize gains from trade. It does so by sharply limiting government interference in market transactions. I call this the "efficiency model."

Game theorists provide a second answer. They suggest that trading nations face a "Prisoner's Dilemma." Each is tempted to pursue individually rational strategies that produce collectively suboptimal results. From a game-theoretic perspective, the trade regime helps nations solve this Dilemma and achieve collectively optimal results by credibly promising to detect and address defections from trade agreements. I call this the "collective action model."

A third answer, most closely associated with the writings of John Ruggie, suggests that the GATT incorporates two fundamental aims. First, it creates an open, multilateral trade system. But it also preserves the state's ability to intervene in domestic economies to maintain stability. Ruggie understands the GATT as a form of economic liberalism that is embedded in a larger commitment to broad interventionist policies. Adopting Ruggie's terminology, I call this the "embedded liberalism" model.[1]

In short, contemporary scholarship provides three answers to the question of why we have a trade regime: the efficiency model, the collective action model, and the embedded liberalism model.

Having identified these three understandings of the trade regime, we need address only one more topic before discussing how "trade and environment"—and other "trade and" issues—challenge these models; that is, the ways in which "trade and" issues differ from more conventional trade disputes. For now, I'll simply identify some of these differences, which I'll return to later in this paper. First, these issues, more so than other issues, bring the trade regime quite deeply into what has previously been considered the domestic domain. Second, while the trade regime has traditionally been one of negative integration, "trade and" issues often pose, at least implicitly, more difficult issues of positive integration. Third, many "trade and" issues involve difficult tradeoffs among incommensurable economic and noneconomic values. Finally, the "trade and" issues, including trade and environment issues, are deeply distributional in the sense that they pit the economic interests of one state or group of states against those of another.

THE CHALLENGE

How do these and other features of the "trade and" issues challenge the three models?

The Efficiency Model

Under this understanding of the trade system, we limit government interference so that markets can operate on their own. The model assumes that, left on their own, welfare-maximizing markets will flourish, but can be distorted by government action. But "trade and" issues suggest that markets don't simply operate on their own, and that we do not always desire to maximize economic wealth.

Writing in the 1930s and 1940s, the legal realists taught that domestic markets presuppose property, contract, and other background norms, all made and enforced by states. These norms are not "distortions" of the market—rather they are what enable markets to exist in the first place. That is to say, domestic markets do not simply exist on their own.[2] Much the same is true of international markets. Absent background norms, markets may never develop. And different norms would give rise to different types of markets. A current example in the environmental area is the Kyoto Protocol. To implement this treaty, nations just concluded a meeting in Ottawa and will meet next month in Buenos Aires to begin the process of, literally, creating a market in tradeable emission rights.

Or, shifting to the trade system, consider the intellectual property (IP) context. Before the TRIPS agreement,[3] many developed nation intellectual property-holders were reluctant to operate in countries with lax IP regimes, arguing that these weak laws "distorted" the market. TRIPS seeks to address these so-called distortions by requiring nations to protect various IP rights. Presumably, this will facilitate markets in many goods that did not previously exist. But this suggests that international markets do not simply form spontaneously or without government action. Paradoxically, the free international market, just like the free domestic market, requires state intervention. The efficiency model thus presupposes a distinction between "markets" and "government action," and an autonomy for markets, that "trade and" issues tend to undermine.

Similar arguments undercut the efficiency model's sharp distinction between government action that distorts trade and government inaction that permits "normal" trade. Suppose Country A enacts a rigorous and costly environmental standard. Domestic producers might argue that this standard threatens their international competitiveness and is therefore trade-distorting. To avoid this "distortion," Country A's government might pay for the equipment needed to meet the environmental standard. But this may prompt producers in Country B to challenge this act as a "subsidy" that is itself trade distorting. Of course, as a conceptual matter, the *failure* of the government in Country A to impose the standard in the first place might also be seen as a trade-distorting subsidy—particularly by foreign producers who have to comply with costly environmental rules enacted by their governments. The point is that both government action and inaction is potentially "trade-distorting," rendering problematic the efficiency model's attempt to sharply distinguish between them on economic grounds.[4]

More importantly, the "trade and" issues challenge the assumption that the goal is always to maximize economic welfare. Many environmental laws, in particular, reflect a collective decision not to maximize efficiency or economic welfare in certain contexts.[5] So when we have a conflict between, for example, a trade law and an environmental law, it often raises the question of whether the goal is to maximize economic welfare or some other value. The typical response offered by efficiency model advocates—that the environmental law is not wealth-maximizing—actually begs the question presented, which is whether, in any particular context, wealth maximization is the primary goal we seek.

So, by questioning the autonomy of markets and the goal of wealth maximization, the "trade and" issues pose serious challenges to the efficiency model.

The Collective Action Model

Recall that this model views nations as locked in a Prisoner's Dilemma, where individually rational trade policies produce collectively suboptimal results. The trade wars of the 1930s are a classic example. By facilitating collaboration, the GATT helps solve the Prisoner's Dilemma and achieve the collectively optimal results associated with liberalized trade. In this model, states are typically understood in classic realist terms, as unitary, rational actors, and as the key players in the international arena.

But "trade and" issues challenge the assumed links among collaboration, market liberalization, and optimal results. Opening the U.S. market to Venezuelan gasoline, for example, may enhance the welfare of Venezuelan producers, but may not produce optimal environmental results.

Other "trade and" issues illustrate how collaboration can even produce sub-optimal economic results. Again, the TRIPS Agreement provides a good example. This agreement sets out the minimum levels of protection for different IP rights. There is significant dispute as to whether this form of partial harmonization is welfare-maximizing. But even if it is, the collective action model is silent on the most important political issue raised: how should the gains from the agreement be distributed? In other words, these issues demonstrate that, in the real world, situations characterized as Prisoner's Dilemmas often entail Coasean bargaining, or distributional conflicts. But our usual telling of the Prisoner's Dilemma story often obscures or ignores this issue.

What about the assumptions underlying the collective action model? Once again, "trade and" issues present a serious challenge. Let's consider the assumption that states are rational, unitary actors. This assumption is surely incomplete and misleading. Recall the lengthy and intricate political maneuverings behind the U.S. Clean Air Act provisions that Venezuela challenged in the very first "trade and environment" dispute filed at the WTO.[6] The history of these provisions reveals a variety of shifting and at times contradictory positions held by Congress, the State Department, the EPA, and the USTR regarding this law.[7] Traditional models that view the state as unitary actor seem ill-equipped to explain such behavior.

What of the assumption that states are the only key actors? Public choice scholars have properly emphasized the role of interest groups in the formation of trade policy, and I'd suggest that one cannot adequately understand "trade and environment" disputes—or other "trade and" disputes—if one ignores the critical roles played by industry, NGOs, and other nonstate actors. For example, is the Reformulated Gasoline case better understood as a dispute between the sovereign nations of Venezuela and the United States, or as a sophisticated multi-track political and economic dispute between Citgo and Sun Oil for the gasoline market in the northeastern U.S.? Similarly, how much does the WTO dispute over the European Union's banana import system implicate U.S. national interests, and how much does it involve the interests of Chiquita Banana?[8] Again, models that assume state interests and behavior are the key variables to be analyzed, as the collective action model does, will obscure the important roles played by private individuals and interests.

So, by suggesting that the critical issues are distributional, and that states are neither unitary nor the only important actors, the "trade and" issues challenge the collective action model. And while critique of the view of the state as unitary actor is not exactly late-breaking news, it bears noting that the international legal system—including WTO dispute resolution—still relies on archaic legal fictions in this regard.

The Embedded Liberalism Model

As discussed above, the "problem" here is how to preserve governments' ability to manage domestic economies, but avoid the restrictive trade policies of the 1930s. The "solution" is an open, multilateral system that permits domestic interventions. But the "trade and" issues challenge several elements of this model. I'll mention just two.

First, embedded liberalism promises nations wide latitude to intervene in domestic economies. But successful GATT challenges to environmental laws, and expanding disciplines in other "trade and" areas, tend to limit the regulatory tools that states can use. In other words, as GATT disciplines expand, governments may increasingly discover that they have inadvertently subverted their ability to manage the domestic consequences of economic liberalization.

This suggests a second challenge. This model is premised on a sharp distinction between domestic and international matters. But the emergence of the "trade and" issues reflects, in part, a blurring of this line. Today, the "international" increasingly includes any policy that impacts international trade flows. This explains the pressure for WTO disciplines in new areas. However, disciplines in "trade and" areas unavoidably challenge the assumptions underlying the embedded liberalism model.

In short, trade and environment disputes help illustrate how the embedded liberalism compromise has been inverted. Where economic liberalism used to be embedded within, and hence limited by, a larger commitment to state autonomy, it increasingly appears that state autonomy is embedded in, and hence limited by a larger, globalized economy.

For all these reasons, trade and environment issues, and the "trade and" agenda more broadly, call into question the adequacy and accuracy of each of the three leading models. They present serious conceptual challenges to traditional understandings of the trade regime.

WTO DISPUTE RESOLUTION

The challenges posed by "trade and" issues are not simply conceptual. They are also practical and political. So let's shift our attention from theory to practice. Many of the features that render "trade and" issues so difficult for the models also render them difficult for WTO dispute resolution. Many of us have criticized panels for resolving "trade and environment" disputes in ways that obscure or ignore the conflicting values at stake.[9] We have urged panels to more forthrightly articulate and balance the diverse interests at issue. But notwithstanding this scholarship, panels continue to slight the underlying values. What realities are the panels responding to—and the academics missing?

Perhaps we can enrich our understanding of these issues if we focus more closely on the institutional roles and politics of the WTO. When a domestic legislature confronts, for example, a trade-environment issue, there is relatively little cost in the candid announcement that it is resolving a value conflict through majority vote. But the same is not true of WTO dispute resolution panels. While we expect legislatures to confront and resolve conflicting values, WTO panels are not policy-making bodies. Instead, they are supposed to apply law to fact, to decide according to principle instead of politics. Indeed, WTO dispute resolution would be delegitimated if it were seen as a forum for the resolution of value conflicts. Panels would undermine their institutional position if they embraced tests for resolving "trade and environment" conflicts that would unavoidably appear political. Panels that created and applied sensitive, multifactored tests truer to the underlying values would be practicing a dangerous form of judicial activism.[10] But this poses an unavoidable obstacle to successful WTO resolution of "trade and environment" disputes. Why? Precisely because "trade and environment"—and other "trade and" issues—are so contested. While numerous issues are contested, the "trade and" issues today are contested in a way that appears to take them outside of the legal domain, and squarely into the political domain. Some of our best scholarship, in effect, asks panels to draw difficult lines in the midst of a larger political struggle; but it is precisely this contestedness that would make it difficult for panel to apply a test in a way that seems consistent. Inconsistency in these areas would, however, send an unmistakable signal that politics—and not law—is at play. But for the institutional reasons outlined above, panels should rarely send that signal.

"Trade and" issues pose another threat to the system. Precisely because they are so contested—and because panel reports in these areas are understood in politicized terms—the reports are frequently discounted and often do not actually resolve the dispute. Let me give a few examples. While the Tuna-Dolphin reports were never adopted,[11] there can be little doubt that the U.S. embargo was GATT-illegal. Nevertheless, the U.S. maintained the ban for several years, and did not lift the embargo until earlier this year. A similar pattern is seen in the Beef-Hormone dispute. While the panel and appellate body found the European Union ban lacked sufficient scientific justification,[12] the EU did not immediately lift its ban. Rather, the initial EU response was that it would conduct a risk assessment while maintaining the ban. But this course of action is surely contrary to the spirit, if not the letter, of the report. Finally, consider the U.S. response to the Shrimp-Turtle panel report.[13] The immediate U.S. response was to explicitly threaten noncompliance, a position urged by many environmental NGOs. Friends of the trade system cannot help but worry that this pattern of noncompliance is itself a serious threat to the WTO dispute resolution system.

In short, as former GATT Director General Peter Sutherland stated, "The WTO ultimately depends for its credibility on its capacity to objectively adjudicate, and on the acceptance of that adjudication by the parties who are litigants before it."[14] But a series of panel and Appellate Body reports over the last several years reveal that the WTO cannot objectively adjudicate trade and environment issues, and when it tries to do so the results are frequently not accepted by the litigants.

All this suggests a paradox. As a theoretical matter, it is critical to identify and weigh the various competing interests in "trade and" disputes. But to be useful, theory must be translated into practice. And one unavoidable dimension of current practice is the institutional constraints on panels. What an elegant theory of the "trade and" issues needs is a politically salient way to apply it.

Does one exist? Some have argued that the best panels can do is candidly and openly announce that they are struggling to resolve the value conflicts raised by "trade and" issues. But, as suggested above, that strategy may be self-defeating.

Instead, I suggest another possible way out of the problem, drawing on domestic law arguments that Alexander Bickel and other constitutional law scholars have made.[15] Bickel understood that courts and other adjudicatory tribunals must decide cases according to principle. He also understood that courts have limited political capital. He was deeply concerned about the legitimacy of unelected and unaccountable judges overturning laws passed by electorally accountable legislatures, particularly laws governing highly controversial issues. Finally, he recognized that relying on principle in the face of determined resistance can be counterproductive.

To grossly oversimplify quite an elegant argument, Bickel argued that, to preserve their legitimacy, courts must carefully and strategically deploy their limited political capital. They must prudently decide whether and when to address contested issues. At times, they should not decide—or defer decision of—certain contested issues.

Now, this argument may be rather disconcerting, but in fact it is a strategy that not only U.S. courts use, but also the ECJ, the ICJ, and various other domestic and international tribunals use in order to best deploy their scarce political capital. At a minimum, it is worth considering whether WTO panels should pursue a similar strategy. The arguments set out above suggest it is possible that more would be gained than lost if panels would, like U.S. courts, develop doctrines for avoiding the merits of disputes. While this proposal might sound troublingly unprincipled, the argument is that these techniques could be used by panels to acknowledge political realities without abandoning principle.

I believe that the trading community increasingly recognizes the WTO's shortcomings and the heightened risks of noncompliance in trade and areas, as well as the systemic costs associated with unsuccessful WTO attempts to resolve these issues. I'll mention just one example: shortly after release of the Shrimp-Turtle panel report, the WTO's Director General pleaded that the WTO not be asked to serve as "judge, jury, and police" on international environmental matters. He stated that "[a]sking the WTO to solve issues which are not central to its work, especially when these are issues which governments have failed to address satisfactorily in other contexts, is not just a recipe for failure. It could do untold harm to the trading system itself."[16]

There are a number of ironies in this call for moving "trade and" disputes outside WTO dispute resolution. One is that the Uruguay Round agreements are often celebrated for expanding trade disciplines into many new areas, and for formalizing and strengthening the dispute resolution system. But, as I have tried to show, these two accomplishments may be at war with each other.

Another is that, prior to the Uruguay Round, the GATT system included a number of procedural mechanisms that enabled panels to avoid decisions on the merits. At the time, this was seen as a serious problem to be remedied, and the system was tightened and legalized so as to make it more legitimate. So the second irony is that the GATT system included ample mechanisms for avoiding decisions on the merits when they were not needed, and took them away precisely at the time when they have become most desirable.

The final irony is the suggestion that to preserve the appearance of principled decision-making, WTO panels adopt politically expedient means of avoiding the merits of certain disputes. This argument deserves more attention than I can give it here, and poses certain obvious dangers: Can the "expediency" that this strategy would introduce to WTO dispute resolution be neatly cabined, or might it "infect" the entire process? What tools would panels use to decide whether and when to avoid the merits of a dispute?

While these are serious and difficult questions, they offer little guidance to panels caught in "no-win" situations. The newly formed WTO system should not be expected to ignore the political costs that accompany the unsatisfactory resolution of "trade and" disputes. More importantly, the suggestion that panels abstain from deciding certain issues is not a call for the exercise of unbounded discretion. Rather, it should be understood as a call for the exercise of prudence in the name of principle. More importantly, it represents an effort to begin a serious debate as to whether WTO panels might enhance their legitimacy and effectiveness by using tools similar to those used by U.S. courts and other adjudicatory bodies.

THE TRANSATLANTIC ECONOMIC PARTNERSHIP

These are all elements of a larger case against attempting to resolve trade and environment, and other "trade and" issues, at the WTO. But this negative case is of limited utility to policymakers. The obvious question is whether there are other institutions or fora that might be more appropriate?

I'd suggest that a more appropriate forum would consider these issues in a nonadjudicatory setting.[17] It would be a forum that, unlike the WTO, gives due consideration to both trade and non-trade values. It should be a forum that includes not just governments, but leading business and NGO voices. It should be a forum, in other words, that has many of the features of the Transatlantic Economic Partnership. So I believe that this initiative has tremendous potential to move the debate ahead in this area.

Of course, this potential has not yet been realized. It is not difficult to list the reasons why progress may not occur. But let me identify a few reasons why progress in this area now seems possible. First, as you know, the Commission's proposed Action Plan expressly identifies trade-environment as an action area. Significantly, the Action Plan explicitly calls for the WTO to give full weight to environmental considerations throughout the WTO agreements. It also, quite properly, seeks EU/U.S. agreement on how to approach and prioritize environment-specific issues in the run-up to the planned WTO High Level Meeting.

Moreover, unlike the WTO, the TEP initiatives will include participation by nongovernmental actors. Through the Transatlantic Business Dialogue (TABD), the business community has already made a significant contribution on many issues, and should have input into joint approaches to trade and environment issues. More importantly, the TEP contemplates a Transatlantic Environment Dialogue. While this Dialogue is in its infancy, it holds significant potential.

These are the structural reasons. There are also political reasons. On the government side, both the EU and the U.S. have a vested interest in a successful high-level WTO meeting on trade-environment next year. The domestic politics of the fast track in this country and the MAI both here and abroad have created significant political pressure for progress on the environmental front. Moreover, recent reports in the Shrimp-Turtle and Beef-Hormone disputes provide additional impetus to show progress in the WTO context in particular. Finally, the partial resolution of Helms-Burton at the last EU-U.S. summit has opened the political space necessary for progress on other fronts.

Other governmental dynamics are also promising. The U.S. State Department has taken a welcome and surprisingly enthusiastic interest in fostering the fledgling environment dialogue. On the European side, the "third way" apparently ascendent in Britain, France, Italy, and now Germany may open the political space necessary for trying creative approaches to trade-environment issues. In addition, the old distrust between the Atlanticists and those who see the EU as a shield against the U.S. appears to have subsided in recent years. In fact, contrary to stereotypes, it may be that the U.S. and France are actually closer on environment and labor issues than some of the other European governments.

There is also reason for optimism on the NGO side. The recent NGO meeting in Paris was very constructive. Having spoken at length with the NGO participants on the U.S. side, I can report that they want to build on the TABD model and proceed in a very pragmatic manner that will, I believe, maximize the possibility of success.

So, for all of these reasons, I am cautiously optimistic. But I should add that many NGOs remain skeptical about this process, and deeply troubled by what they see as a three-year head start by business within the Transatlantic Agenda. My sense is that NGOs will view the December summit and the WTO High Level Meeting as markers. If they feel they do not have adequate input into these events they may—rightly or wrongly—disengage from the process.

Let me mention one final, and closely related area, in which the TEP may be helpful. It is the area of investment and environment, which in the long run may be even more important than trade and environment. This is another area that presents a large and difficult series of issues. And, as the MAI negotiations reveal, these issues are politically explosive. These issues have started to percolate through the NAFTA system. As some of you know, Canada just paid $13 million to settle a claim that a law banning trade in a certain fuel additive was an expropriation.[18] Other arbitral claims have been filed against both Canada and Mexico over environmental actions. I think it unlikely that closed, adversarial proceedings between an investor and a state will produce the sort of political compromise necessary to move ahead in this area. But I wonder if a forum that is not adjudicatory, that includes substantial input from interested nonstate actors, and that considers issues outside of the context of particular, polarized disputes, might be better able to make progress on these issues. So my final point is to urge careful attention to this area, as well as to the important trade and environment issues that we will hear much more about over the course of this Conference.

Thank you very much for your attention, and for the opportunity to address such a distinguished gathering.

ENDNOTES

1. This argument is elaborated in John Gerard Ruggie, "Embedded Liberalism Revisited: Institutions and Progress in International Economic Relations," in *Progress in Postwar International Relations* (Emanuel Adler & Beverly Crawford, eds., 1991); John Gerard Ruggie, "International Regimes, Transactions, and Change: Embedded Liberalism in the Postwar Economic Order," *36 Int'l Org.* 379 (1982).

2. For influential discussions of this argument, see Robert L. Hale (1952), *Freedom through Law: Public Control of Private Governing Power*; Robert L. Hale (1943), "Bargaining, Duress and Economic Liberalism," *43 Colum. L. Rev. 603.*

3. "Agreement on Trade-Related Aspects of Intellectual Property Rights," Apr. 15, 1994, "Marrakesh Agreement Establishing the World Trade Organization, Annex 1C," reprinted in *33 I.L.M. 81* (1994)

4. A more detailed elaboration of this argument is developed in Brian Alexander Langille (1996), "General Reflections on the Relationship of Trade and Labor (Or: Fair Trade is Free Trade's Destiny)," in *2 Fair Trade and Harmonization*, Bhagwati, Jagdish and Robert E. Hudec (eds.), pp. 231, 246.

5. The Endangered Species Act and certain Clean Air Act provisions directing EPA to set national primary ambient air quality standards at a level that will protect the public health with an adequate margin for safety, without regard to the cost of attaining the standards, are examples of such legislation.

6. "United States—Standards for Reformulated and Conventional Gasoline," *WT/DS2/AB/R*, April 29, 1996, reprinted in *35 I.L.M.* 603 (1996); "United States—Standards for Reformulated and Conventional Gasoline," *WT/DS2/R*, January 29, 1996, reprinted in *35 I.L.M.* 274 (1996).

7. An extended discussion of this history is found in Jeffrey L. Dunoff (1998), "The Misguided Debate Over NGO Participation at the WTO," *1 J. Int'l Econ. L.* 433.

8. "European Communities—Regime for the Importation, Sale and Distribution of Bananas," (1997), *WT/DS27/R*, May 22.

9. See, e.g., Jeffrey L. Dunoff (1992), "Reconciling International Trade with Preservation of the Global Commons: Can We Prosper and Protect?," *49 Wash. & Lee L. Rev.* 1407.

10. Many argue that the Shrimp-Turtle Appellate Body Report, issued after this presentation, evidences a move toward a more sensitive, balancing test. See *United States—Import Prohibition of Certain Shrimp and Shrimp Products, WTO Doc. WT/DS58/AB/R*, October 12, 1998. For an argument that this movement is more apparent than real, see Jeffrey L. Dunoff, *Border Patrol at the World Trade Organization, 9,* Yearbook of International Environmental Law xxx (forthcoming).

11. *United States—Restrictions on Imports of Tuna*, GATT Doc. No. DS20/R (June 1994), reprinted in *33 I.L.M.* 842 (1994); *United States—Restrictions on Imports of Tuna*, GATT BISD (39th Supp) at 155 (1993), reprinted in 30 *I.L.M.* 1594 (1991).

12. "European Communities—EC Measures Concerning Meat and Meat Products (Hormones)," *WT/DS26/AB/R*, January 16, 1998; "European Communities—EC Measures Concerning Meat and Meat Products (Hormones)," *WT/DS26/R*, August 18, 1997.

13. "United States—Import Prohibition of Certain Shrimp and Shrimp Products," *WT/DS58/R,* May 15, 1998.

14. "Multilateralism Works, Former Director Says as GATT Reaches Fifty, Bridges," available at <http://www.ictsd.org/html/cover203.htm>. Visited on Sept. 23, 1998.

15. See, e.g., Alexander Bickel, "Foreword: The Passive Virtues," *75 Harv. L. Rev.* 40 (1961); Lawrence Lessig, "Fidelity and Constraint," *65 Ford. L. Rev.* 1365 (1997); Lawrence Lessig, "Understanding Changed Readings: Fidelity and Theory," *47 Stan. L. Rev.* 395 (1995).

16. "WTO Cannot be 'Judge, Jury, Police' of Environment Issues, Top Official Says," *BNA Int'l Env. Daily*, Mar. 18, 1998.

17. I've discussed these institutional issues elsewhere. See Jeffrey L. Dunoff (1994), "Institutional Misfits: The GATT, the ICJ and Trade-Environment Dispute," *15 Mich. J. Int'l L.* 1042; Jeffrey L. Dunoff (1994), "Resolving Trade-Environmental Conflicts: The Case for Trading Institutions," *27 Cornell Int'l L. J.* 607.

18. "Canadian Government Withdraws Ban on Trade, Import of Gasoline Additive MMT," *BNA Int'l Trade Daily*, July 21, 1998.

JURISPRUDENCE IN THE GATT AND THE ENVIRONMENT DEBATE

Kilian Delbrück
Federal Ministry of the Environment, Berlin, Germany

I have been working on trade/environmental policy issues in the OECD, GATT, and other related organizations since 1991. When the work in the GATT Committee on Trade and the Environment (CTE) came to a virtual standstill after the Singapore Conference at the end of 1996, I was asked to participate as a panelist in the Shrimp-Turtle case. The last year or so has therefore had some interesting experiences for me.

Jurisprudence is, of course, particularly important within the GATT and environment debate. GATT is not only a fundamental globalization and liberalization agreement, but it also has a highly developed rule-based system for dealing with disputes. It is a full-fledged court, making its decisions like any other court in the world—even if the members did not originally expect it to do so.

The WTO dispute settlement system is unique. There is no such system on the environmental side, and this may be a contributing factor to the conflict between trade and environmental policy. The reason why GATT jurisprudence is particularly important for the transatlantic agenda is that quite a number of the most contentious environment-related trade disputes have involved the EU and the U.S., more often than not on different sides of an issue. The most important environmental disputes of the past couple of years concerned the famous Tuna-

Dolphin case decided in 1991 and in 1994 and the Shrimp-Turtle decision of 1998.

The central legal provisions for environment and trade decisions are the exception clauses in GATT rules: Article XX and its sub-sections (b) and (g), as well as the "chapeau" of Article XX. Article XX(b) relates to the protection of life and health—human and animal—pre-conditioning that the measures have to be necessary. Article XX(g) relates to the protection of exhaustible natural resources, and pre-conditions that the measure has to be related to the protection of these resources. The chapeau's main criterion is that the measures do not arbitrarily or unjustifiably discriminate between countries where the same conditions prevail.

Other environmental provisions of the WTO agreements include the preamble (which talks about trade liberalization and sustainable development), the agreement on technical barriers to trade, and the agreement on sanitary and phytosanitary measures (SPS agreement). We will now consider the specific disputes.

The 1991 Tuna-Dolphin case resulted from an import ban by the U.S. against tuna products from tuna fishing with nets which did not conform to the U.S. requirements on the safety of dolphins. The main finding was that Article XX(b) and XX(g) do not cover measures to protect human, animal, or plant life or health outside the jurisdiction of the party taking the measure. This was the fundamental, very broad-based ruling, questioning not only the measure in place, which was rejected, but also a number of other environmental policy measures, both unilateral and multilateral.

The decision was heavily criticized for this broad scope. In 1994 the same case came again to the GATT because of a secondary U.S. embargo affecting nations that imported products from countries targeted by the primary embargo. The Netherlands was among the complainants against this secondary ban. This second decision was more cautious, stating, in principle, that the location of the protected resource—territorial or extra-territorial—is not decisive. It thus deviated from the road that the Tuna I panel had taken, but it maintained that Article XX(b) and XX(g) do not cover measures aimed at forcing other countries to change their policies.

This would leave open the question of the GATT compatibility of other measures such as certain multilateral agreements aimed at members of the WTO who did not participate in the multilateral environmental agreements.

Let us now consider the case of reformulated gasoline. This was the first WTO case on trade and the environment and it was a case ultimately decided by the appellate body. The appellate body included among its main points the finding that the words of the GATT text are to be given their ordinary meaning. This may sound self-evident, but it amounted to a rejection of the panel report in this case, where the panel had deviated considerably from the ordinary meaning of the GATT text.

The appellate body further stated that air is an exhaustible natural resource within the meaning of GATT Article XX(g). This in itself may not appear of interest, but the consequence was that, for such trade measures as the U.S. ban on tuna, the necessity test of Article XX(b) was no longer valid, as XX(g) calls only for a measure related to the protection of an exhaustible natural resources. The question of necessity therefore lost a part of its importance in the trade and environment debate.

The fundamental purpose of the Article XX chapeau is to prevent abuse or illegitimate use of the exceptions in Article XX, and it was ultimately the basis for the rejection of the U.S. measure. The appellate body found that the U.S. measure was an abuse of the exceptions of Article XX and an arbitrary or unreasonable discrimination between countries.

In the Beef-Hormone case, the EU was the defendant and the U.S. the complainant. This also went through two stages—first a panel report, then an appellate body decision. The finding clarifies the obligations of the Sanitary and Phyto-Sanitary (SPS) agreements, and in particular the need for a risk assessment. The trade measure of the EU was an import restriction for beef containing certain growth hormones. The dispute revolved around whether or not this import restriction was acceptable. The appellate body found that while the precautionary principle has been incorporated into the SPS agreement, it does not override the specific provisions. This is one of the reasons why the precautionary principle is now a central issue in the political debate about trade and the environment.
The details of this case were very complex, and it contained a number of statements that the EU appealed. The fundamental issue behind all these specific questions was the balance between the sovereignty of members of the WTO and restrictions in national policy making. For example, how far is it possible for one country to restrict imports to protect their own population when there is no certainty on the relevant risks?

Again, the ordinary meaning was quite important in this case. The main message of the appellate body report, changing to some degree the panel report, was much more cautious than the latter in restricting national sovereignty. The panel report would have resulted more or less in a world internal market because many products had to be allowed freely into the territory of every member. The report, I believe, went in some respects further toward opening up markets than is now required in the relationship between the EU and its members, or the U.S. and its states. Specific points that have been raised and upheld by the appellate body concern the burden of proof and the question of how far risk management has to go before such measures can be introduced. There is also the question of whether only the potential of threat or the probability of risk can justify enactment of an import restriction.

The Shrimp-Turtle case must be simplified here, and I speak now only for myself, not for the rest of the panel. The panel's conclusions are written in a 400-page report, which I will here attempt to summarize. The trade measure at stake was an import ban by the U.S. on shrimp and shrimp products from countries not certified by the U.S. Government as pursuing specific turtle protection policies comparable to the U.S. policy. In this regard it was similar to the Tuna-Dolphin cases.

This import ban was applied originally by the U.S. administration only to countries of the Caribbean Western Atlantic, with a three-year grace period. During this time, an international agreement was concluded covering this region. Then, four months before the end of this phase-in time, a U.S. court ruled that the ban had to be applied to all countries worldwide. There were some specific conditions but in principle it had to be applied generally outside the Caribbean Western Atlantic region. In fact, there were four U.S. court decisions during the proceedings. Within the remaining four months, the U.S. made no effort to reach a multilateral solution with those countries not in the Caribbean Western Atlantic region. While on the one hand, this was not surprising given the limited time available, the relevant U.S. law called, nevertheless, for such efforts. The findings of the panel were, in my view, an exercise in prudence. The report is very much linked to the specifics of this case, and it did not try to solve the whole question of unilateralism vs. multilateralism or the whole MEA trade and environment debate in one panel.

A key sentence in the findings is that the chapeau of Article XX does not cover a measure conditioning access to a country's markets for a particular product upon the adoption of certain policies by the exporting member. This is because such a measure could lead to multiple conflicting policy requirements for the exporting member. For this reason—bearing in mind we are simplifying the issue here—the U.S. measure was ultimately rejected. The reasoning behind this finding has been interpreted as implying that in general, trade concerns are higher than environmental ones. While neither I nor the report itself would accept such an interpretation, the reasoning could perhaps have been made clearer. The appellate body may say something specific on this point.

The next point in the findings was that the risk of conflicting policy requirements is reduced when requirements are decided in multilateral settings. This is an opener in the MEA debate, although of course it was not an MEA issue that was at stake in this case. As it is formulated in the report, this language is not restricted to cases where two parties of an MEA are in conflict, but could also cover conflicts between parties and non-parties of an MEA.

The panel explicitly left open whether recourse to unilateral measures is always ruled out, particularly after serious attempts have been made to negotiate. This was not decided in this particular case as the U.S. admitted there had been no attempts to negotiate, and consequently the issue was not disputed. As in the case of the second Tuna I panel decision, the panel confirmed that the jurisdictional scope of Article XX is not decisive. Although there had been arguments on extra-territorial or extra-jurisdictional issues during the proceedings, we did not deal explicitly with this. The reason, very simply, was that GATT Article XX does not mention this aspect.

In the end there is no finding on the Process and Production Methods (PPMs) in general. The PPM issue arises from the distinction between measures relating to the product characteristics and measures relating to the production method of a specific product. Up to now, traditional GATT law has preferred measures dealing only with product characteristics, while measures dealing with the exporting country's methods of production are normally viewed in a critical light. In fact, there is little jurisprudence but many political statements in this direction.

A closer look at the panel report thus reveals that it deals with conditioning market access on certain policies, but it does not say "on certain products." The report points out that one of the important features of the specific measure at stake was that the U.S. demanded a general change in policies from the exporting country, not just with regard to non-turtle safe products imported into the U.S. Having completed the presentation of some cases of GATT jurisprudence, I have two further short comments that go beyond the status quo. The status quo as it is described now by the jurisprudence is not satisfactory. The panel and appellate body reports do not rule out a reversal in the future. The German government and the EU are very much in favor of new negotiations in the WTO on trade and environment after the Third Ministerial meeting at the end of 1999. There are two main messages relevant here. First, it is, in my view, inconceivable to have any future major liberalization agreement without dealing with environmental issues. Second, developing countries will in future play a much bigger role in any negotiations. It will neither be possible or acceptable to ignore their interests.

In conclusion, let me touch on what could be some key trade and environment issues during the new round of trade negotiations. MEAs have already been mentioned. In addition, attention should be given to eco-labelling, market access, and environmental principles that would include the precautionary principle. Another major issue for me is cooperation between WTO and the UN Environment Program (UNEP). In this context, the discussion should not be restricted to UNEP, but could also be used to discuss some of the broader institutional issues in the trade and environment debate.

Transparency for civil society is also an issue that should be discussed, and investment may become part of the new negotiations after possible failure of the MAI. Of course, developing countries will insist on discussing technology transfer and the so-called "positive measures," that is, incentive measures rather than sanctions, to further their environmental policies. Another question that will undoubtedly come up is if and how an environmental assessment can be included in the new round.

Finally, there is the whole matter of the relationships between national sovereignty, environmental policy harmonization, and the elimination of barriers to trade. This goes beyond the simple issue of whether the WTO should allow these measures, embracing also the extent to which harmonization makes sense and should be promoted.

VOLUNTARY ENVIRONMENTAL MANAGEMENT SYSTEMS AND REGULATORY RELIEF

Eberhard Bohne
Professor, Speyer National School of Administrative Sciences
Speyer, Germany

ISSUES

I would like to address several issues: First, what are the main differences between the European Union "Eco-Management and Audit Scheme" (EMAS) and the international standard ISO 14001 in terms of concept and implementation in EU member states? Second, which conditions justify regulatory relief for certified or registered companies from environmental command and control requirements? And, finally, is there a need for regional environmental management standards such as EMAS in addition to the worldwide standard ISO 14001?

MAIN DIFFERENCES BETWEEN ISO 14001 AND EMAS

The basic elements of ISO 14001 and EMAS are very similar. Both standards require companies to establish an environmental management and audit system. Common system elements are:

1. environmental policies with a commitment to continuous improvement of environmental protection,
2. environmental objectives and programs to achieve them,
3. management structures and procedures for developing, implementing and reviewing environmental policies, and
4. audit procedures for evaluating the environmental management system.

Assuming that you are familiar with the elements of environmental management and audit systems, I will not go into a detailed description of EMAS. I will rather give a brief overview of three conceptual differences between ISO 14001 and EMAS which account for much of the ongoing controversies on both sides of the Atlantic. These differences relate to the legal nature, performance or systems orientation, and external controls and the role of the public of the two standards.

Legal Nature

The ISO 14000 series standards are private standards that have been developed by industries from all over the world. Standardization work takes place within the institutional framework of the International Standardization Organization (ISO), whose members are private national standardization bodies. This means that ISO 14001 is a product of the business world and primarily serving corporate interests.

In contrast, EMAS is an EC regulation that is legally binding on all EU member states, other actors involved, and on all companies once they have decided to voluntarily participate in the scheme. EMAS is the European equivalent to a U.S. federal law. Thus, EMAS is a product of the political process and designed to serve private as well as public interests.

The different institutional and political origins of ISO 14001 and EMAS have to be kept in mind when comparing and assessing the two standards and designing strategies of regulatory relief.

Performance or Systems Orientation

ISO 14001 (No. 4.2) calls for a company environmental policy which "includes a commitment to continual improvement and prevention of pollution." However, there are no substantive criteria which determine the level of commitment. The informative Annex A (No. 3.3) to the standard gives only the non-binding advice that a company "may consider the use of best available technology where economically viable, cost effective and judged appropriate."

Hence, any dirty industry with outdated technical equipment and old permits can meet the ISO requirement as long as it commits itself to reducing its present level of pollution in the future, and ensures legal compliance with old permit conditions.

In contrast, EMAS (Article 3 lit. a) calls for a commitment aimed at the continuous improvement of environmental performance which reduces environmental pollution to levels that can be achieved by the "economically viable application of best available technology." This criterion is known under the acronym of "EVABAT."

From an economic and environmental perspective, the lack of substantive performance criteria is the greatest weakness of ISO 14001 (Roht-Arriaza 1996: 108), for it invites unfair economic competition and ineffective environmental protection.

External Controls and the Role of the Public

The following EMAS elements are absent in the ISO 14000 series standards:

1. environmental statement prepared by participating companies and designed for the public (Article 5 EMAS),
2. independent environmental verifiers who check the environmental management system, the results of internal audits, and validate the environmental statement (Article 4[5] EMAS),
3. registration of sites which have received validated environmental statements (Article 8 EMAS),
4. permission for companies to use an official "statement of participation" with the EC logo for their registered sites (Article 10 EMAS),
5. repetition of the control process, at least, every three years (Article 4 [2] EMAS).

These elements serve control and incentive functions.

Independent environmental verifiers exercise external professional controls that are supplemented by public controls through environmental statements and site registers. These periodic controls are intended to enhance the credibility of EMAS with the public. Simultaneously, public credibility of EMAS and the permission to use the EC logo provide incentives for companies to participate in the scheme and to build and maintain a positive public image.

Figure 1 shows the official "statement of participation" that may be used by registered sites.

Let me now turn to the implementation of ISO 14001 and EMAS.

Implementation

Table 1 gives a worldwide overview as of April 1999 of countries with companies certified under ISO 14001, and companies registered under EMAS.

Figure 1. Statement of Participation

EC Eco-Management and Audit Scheme	This site has an environmental management system and its environmental performance is reported on to the public in accordance with the Community eco-management and audit scheme (registration no...)
EC Eco-Management and Audit Scheme	All the sites in the Community where we carry out our industrial activities have an environmental management system and their environmental performance is reported on to the public in accordance with the Community eco-management and audit scheme (plus optional statement regarding practices in third counties).
EC Eco-Management and Audit Scheme	All the sites in [name(s) of the Community Member State(s)] where we carry out our industrial activities have an environmental management system and their environmental performance is reported on to the public in accordance with the Community eco-management and audit scheme.
EC Eco-Management and Audit Scheme	The following sites where we carry out our industrial activities have an environmental performance which is reported on to the public in accordance with Community eco-management and audit schemes: — site name, registration number — — ...

The numbers clearly indicate that there is no worldwide run toward certification. Japan is the leader with almost 2000 certified companies followed by Germany with 1300 certified companies. The U.S. holds 6th place with 450 certified companies. The numbers have probably increased since April 1999. But I doubt that the pattern of implementation—as shown in Table 1—will have changed much.

When comparing ISO certification to EMAS registration in Europe, two things come as a surprise: first, the ISO 14001 is the preferred standard in all

European countries—except in Germany. And second, Germany is the European EMAS champion. Even if you weigh the number of EMAS registrations with population size or gross national product, Germany is still the leader—though closely followed by Austria.

This pattern is even more surprising when you look at the almost negligible number of EMAS registrations in the UK and the Netherlands. These two countries had been the strongest supporters of EMAS during the legislative process at the EU level, while Germany opposed EMAS until the final meeting of the EU Minister Council in 1993. The German opposition did not come from the Environment Ministry but from the Ministry of Economics and the German Federation of Industries. They disliked the elements of external controls and public participation in EMAS and considered them an intrusion into "corporate privacy." Only when Germany was completely isolated in the Ministry Council, did German industries give their consent to the EMAS regulation. They requested, however, the inclusion of BAT in the standard in order to prevent unfair competition. The UK, Spain, and other countries grudgingly accepted the German request in return for the German approval of the EMAS regulation. The outcome of the negotiations was a typical European compromise: the slightly convoluted policy concept of EVABAT.

I have no fully satisfactory explanation as to why German industries are now embracing EMAS whereas British and Dutch industries have a clear preference for ISO 14001. My personal guess, however, is that German industries see greater chances to achieve regulatory relief from environmental command and control regulations through EMAS registration than through ISO 14001 certification.

The call for deregulation in the environmental sector is much stronger in Germany than in other European countries. After German industries decided to abandon their opposition to EMAS, they have emphasized over and over again that they expected regulatory relief in return for their endorsement of EMAS.

In general, EMAS enjoys more public credibility in Germany than ISO 14001. Therefore, deregulation appears politically more feasible in conjunction with EMAS than with ISO 14001. This assessment may, in part, explain why German industries prefer, at present, EMAS over ISO 14001.

Table 2 supports this interpretation.

A comparison of two recent surveys of European and German companies indicates that German companies rank legal compliance—a prerequisite for deregulation—among the three most important objectives and benefits of EMAS participation. In contrast, this aspect plays no significant role in a European wide context.

Let me now turn to the issue of regulatory relief.

Table 1. ISO Worldwide and EMAs EU-wide

County	*ISO 14001*	*EMAS*	*Country*	*ISO 1401*	*EMAS*
Japan	1.960		United Arab Emirates	4	
Germany	1.300	2.020	Croatia	3	
United Kingdom	800	70	Colombia	3	
Sweden	520	153	Barbados	3	
Korea	463		Morocco	3	
USA	450		Costa Rica	3	
Taiwan	423		Mauritius	2	
Netherlands	360	22	Pakistan	2	
Denmark	350	99	Guatemala	1	
Switzerland	336		Jordan	1	
Australia	300		Lebanon	1	
France	238	32	Malta	1	
Austria	200	175	Oman	1	
Spain	175	30	Peru	1	
Finland	160	18	Rumania	1	
Belgium	130	9	Russia	1	
Italy	120	14	Saudi Arabia	1	
Thailand	121		Uruguay	1	
Canada	100		Venezuela	1	
Brasil	88				
Ireland	82	6			
Malaysia	80				
Singapore	78				
China/Hong Kong	81/40				
India	60				
Norway	72	52			
Argentina	54				
Indonesia	48				
Turkey	45				
Hungary	52				
Mexico	40				
South Africa	30				
New Zealand	28				
Philippines	23				
Czech Republic	20				
Egypt	15				
Israel	13				
Slovak Republic	13				
Poland	11				
Portugal	8	2			
Greece	6	1			
Luxemburg	6	1			
Slovenia	6				
Iran	5				
Chile	5				

Source: Reinhard Peglau, Umweltbundesamt (Federal Environmental Agency), D–14191 Berlin; e-mail: reinhard.peglau@uba.de; last update: 24 April 1999

CONDITIONS FOR REGULATORY RELIEF FROM ENVIRONMENTAL COMMAND AND CONTROL REQUIREMENTS

Types of Regulatory Relief

The German Federal Environment Ministry has recently proposed a draft regulation on regulatory relief for EMAS registered sites. The draft regulation covers command and control requirements of air and water pollution control and waste management with emphasis on the operation of industrial installations.

According to the proposal, registered sites shall be relieved from certain regulatory requirements concerning

- notification of authorities in various cases,
- documentation of monitoring results and other data,
- company reports to public authorities in several areas,
- self-monitoring, and
- the assignment of environmental responsibilities within an organization.

It is assumed that these regulatory obligations are automatically met by the EMAS environmental management system.

All 16 German Länder have implemented some of these proposals. Several Länder have also directed their inspectors to exempt registered sites from routine inspections.

Technically speaking, these types of regulatory relief measures do not deregulate environmental law in a literal sense. At least under German law, statutory provisions remain unchanged. These relief measures only direct inspectors and enforcement authorities to regard information, documentation, reports, monitoring results, and other organizational activities resulting from an environmental management and audit system as meeting respective regulatory requirements. Furthermore, it is assumed, while there is no evidence to the contrary, that registered sites are operated in compliance with environmental law.

More far-reaching proposals such as exemption of registered sites from environment permit requirements have presently no political support in Germany.

Functional Equivalence

The crucial questions of all regulatory relief measures center on whether and to what extent the results of environmental management and audit systems are functional equivalents to the results of command and control measures.

How does one determine functional equivalence?

Table 2. Three Most Important Objectives/Motives and Benefits of EMAS Participation in EU Member States[1] and Germany[2]

Objectives/Motives				*Benefits*			
EU Member States (N=140)		Germany (N=271)		EU Member States (N=140)		Germany (N=271)	
1. Reduce waste	56%	1. Continual improvement of environmental performance	76%	1. Cost savings	31%	1. Improved organization and documentation	76%
2. Reduce energy consumption	52%	2. Increased legal compliance	67%	2. Better image	29%	2. Better image	67%
3. Reduce water pollution	29%	3. Identify shortcomings	65%	3. Improved employee morale	26%	3. Increased legal compliance	67%

[1]Telephone survey by Centre for Environmental Technology, London, February 1998
[2]Written survey by Federal Environmental Protection Agency, Berlin, July 1998

There is probably a consensus that environmental management and audit systems and command and control systems are functionally equivalent if both systems serve the same objectives and have the same control-effectiveness. Since legal compliance is part of a company environmental policy one could argue that both systems serve the same objectives.

However, it is difficult to compare and determine the control-effectiveness of environmental management and audit systems and command and control systems.

The two systems are designed to influence company behavior, though the means of control are different. Command and control systems influence behavior through coercion while participation in environmental management and audit systems is voluntary and based on incentives such as cost reductions or a positive public image.

Figure 2 tries to conceptualize the requirements for "functional equivalence" of command and control systems and EMAS. The left side of the figure shows the command and control system. The right side presents EMAS in conjunction with regulatory relief measures. The dependent variable is the degree of legal compliance in company behavior (inner white box).

The boxes on the left and right margins represent sets of independent variables.

Command and control systems treat companies as a "black box." They prescribe certain behavioral requirements and objectives but leave to companies

Figure 2. Functional Equivalence between Existing Command and Control (C & C) System and Deregulated Command and Control System with EMAS

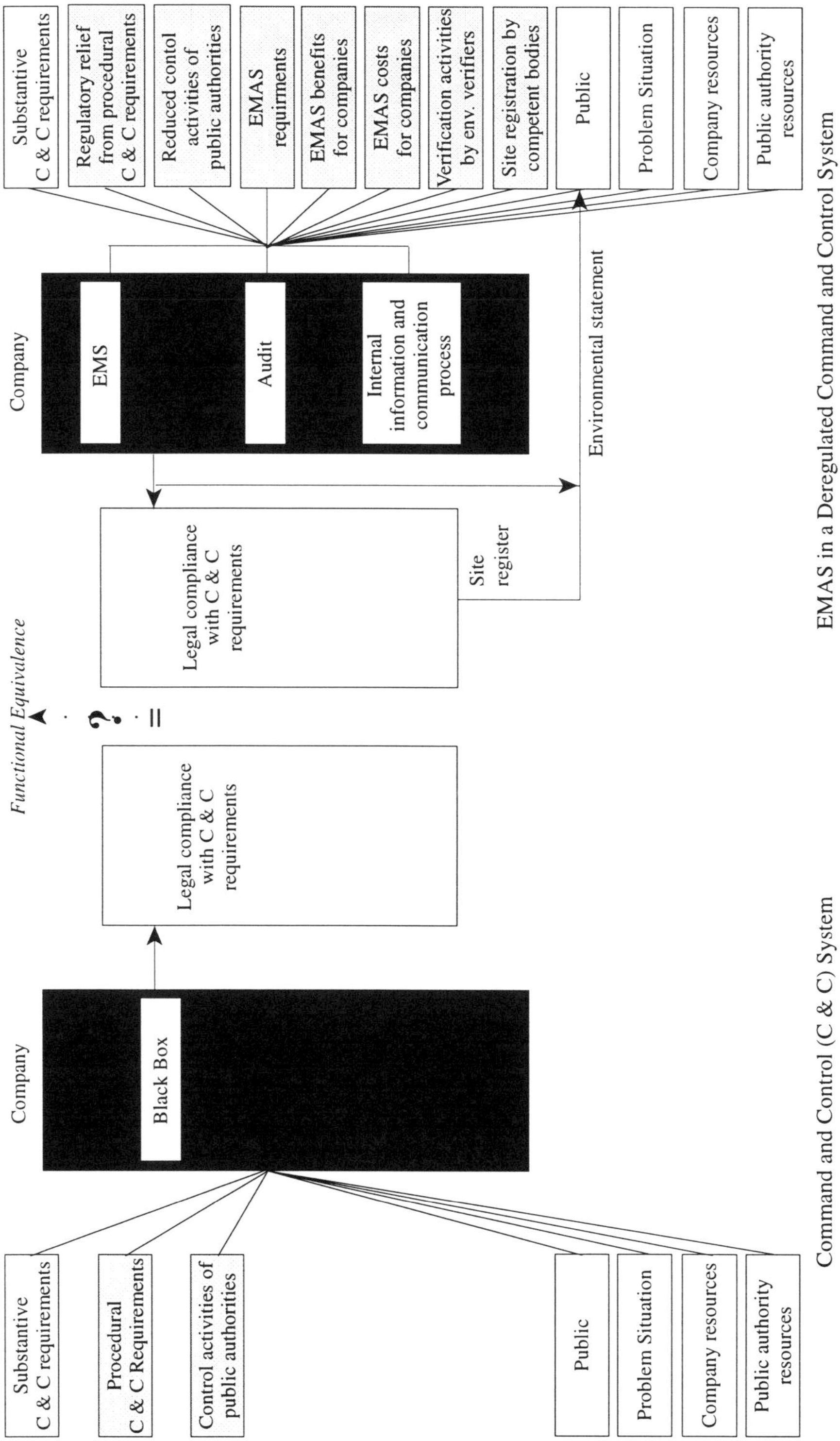

how to achieve them. They do not affect the internal organization of companies. In contrast, ISO 14001 and EMAS "open" the "black box" and set rules for the management and internal organization of companies. In addition to that, EMAS introduces external verifiers, site registers, and public environmental statements in order to guarantee the functioning of environmental management and audit systems.

The question is now: Will EMAS compensate for the reduced control effectiveness of a deregulated command and control system, and, thus, ensure legal compliance of companies?

Functional equivalence between the command and control system and EMAS can be assumed if both systems produce the same output in terms of legally required information, documentation, reports, self-monitoring, and the like. The most difficult question to answer is whether EMAS will also ensure compliance with substantive environmental requirements such as legal emission standards or environmental quality standards.

The control effectiveness of EMAS in this regard can probably be determined only in a negative way: If a given environmental management and audit system *does not* provide for specific organizational safeguards to guarantee compliance with substantive legal requirements such as emission limits in permits, it is plausible to conclude that this system does not justify regulatory relief from command and control measures such as exemption from inspections or from permits for new or modified installations. A detailed empirical analysis of functional equivalence between German environmental command and control regulations in the industrial sector has been recently completed by Bohne and Wagner (1999) and will be published in 2000.

NEED FOR REGIONAL MANAGEMENT STANDARDS

Let me now turn to the third issue: Is there a need for regional environmental management standards such as EMAS in addition to the worldwide standard ISO 14001?

The U.S. and other promoters of the ISO 14000 series standards are likely to answer this question in the negative. A regional standard appears to be superfluous if there is a worldwide international standard. Governments that are not satisfied with present levels of environmental performance, so goes the argument, should legislate appropriate command and control regulations and enforce them in order to achieve the desired level of environmental protection. However, if regulatory relief from command and control requirements is considered desirable for certified companies, then the picture looks different. In a democracy, governments have the constitutional responsibility to ensure that the law is obeyed. They do not meet this responsibility if they simply hope that citizens will voluntarily comply with the law. Governments must establish mechanisms of controls and sanctions to ensure legal compliance. This mechanism need not be exclusively based on coercion. On the contrary, it should be supplemented by incentive systems. Incentive systems must include control mechanisms which guarantee that the rules of the incentive systems are observed. Hence, it follows that regulatory relief must be compensated by effective non-regulatory control mechanisms.

EMAS includes such control mechanisms. External controls are provided by independent environmental verifiers, site registers, and public environmental statements.

These elements are lacking in the ISO 14001 standard. Consequently, regulatory relief is not justified if this standard is not supplemented by external control mechanisms.

In council resolution No. 97–05 (June 12, 1997) on "Future Cooperation regarding Environmental Management Systems and Compliance" under the "North American Agreement on Environmental Cooperation" it was concluded by the U.S., Canadian and Mexican Governments that:

> Adoption of an environmental management system pursuant to ISO 14001 does not constitute or guarantee compliance with legal requirements and will not in any way prevent the governments from taking enforcement action where appropriate.

Therefore, my personal guess is that in the U.S., too, regulatory relief from command and control measures will only be realized if federal or state governments or the U.S. standardization organization supplement the ISO 14001 standard with additional control mechanisms.

Call them what you may, there will be regional standards or no regulatory relief.

REFERENCES

Bohne, Eberhard and Wagner, Hellmut (August 1999). *Öko-Audit und Deregulierung im innerstaatlichen Recht auf Gesetzes- und Vollzugsebene nach der Verordnung (EWG)* 1836/93, research report No. 297 18 086 for the Federal Environmental Protection Agency. Speyer: Forschungsinstitut für öffentliche Verwaltung.

Roht-Arriaza, Naomi (1996). "Private Voluntary Standard-Setting, The International Organization for Standardization, and International Environmental Lawmaking." In: Handl, Günther (ed.), *Yearbook of International Environmental Law*, Vol. 6, 1995, p. 107–63, Oxford: Clarendon Press.

VOLUNTARY ENVIRONMENTAL MANAGEMENT SYSTEMS IN THE FRENCH CONTEXT

Marc Aviam
Ministry of the Environment
Paris, France

Everybody agrees on the necessity to make environmental policies move in order to face the new challenges, which are, of course:

- economic and ecological globalization,
- sustainable development, and
- increasing requirements for firms.

The foundation of our environmental policies is a traditional regulation or command and control approach, based on norms and permits. We need regulation. It is essential when safety and human health are on a similar course or when there are rather similar problems.

Economic instruments in the field of the environment emerged in the '60s, and they complement regulation. But we know regulation and economic instruments have their limits.

In order to adapt to the new context, is necessary to complete those commitments, those mechanisms, and those partnerships with economic actors in defining and especially in implementing environmental policies. Today we need a multiplication of institutional arrangements based on the voluntary involvement of companies in order to reach our environmental goals.

I think it is important to stress the diversity of those arrangements taking place in the most developed countries. They are called voluntary programs, voluntary agreements, and sometimes codes of conduct. The most recent are EMAS (European Management and Auditing Systems) and, of course, ISO 14000 normalization.

Those mechanisms are different. Their implementation depends on our national histories and cultures, the role of the state, their status (normative or not), and their diverse functions. We can discuss a point, but in my view, they constitute the branches of the same family that we can call environmental commitments on a voluntary basis. I will try to classify those commitments in the second part of my introduction. But I would like first to present the French experience in this matter, before finally, and with the help of the two enlightenments, pointing out three key issues.

Voluntary commitments emerged in France in 1971 with the creation of the Ministry of the Environment. I will distinguish three periods expressing different contexts, issues, and tools.

The first period extends to the end of the 1970s. About 20 commitments were signed between the Ministry of the Environment and companies whose goals were to help the latter respond to the requirements of the regulation. This negotiated approach evolved through branch contracts signed with nine professional organizations representing small, high-polluting, companies having economic difficulties. The contracts included financial aid from the state representing 10 percent of the anti-pollution investment.

Characteristically during this time, their challenge was local and concerned small groups. Moreover, the Ministry was young and had to legitimize its action and prove that it could settle its policy with constraint. And, too, this policy concerned the pollution coming from the process of fixed installations.

The second phase started in 1986, when this approach was extended to the producers of products containing detergents, followed by the CFC's users.
It corresponded to a new generation of diffused environmental problems:

Successive agreements with detergent producers were characterized by an uncertainty about the role of phosphates in the eutrophication process. Their intent was the reduction in the quantity of detergents and an increase in public information. CFC's commitments referred to a global problem. The administration intended to favor companies' mobilization in order to organize national demand. Users involved 26 professional organizations.

You can notice that, during those two phases, initiatives came from administration and at the end of this period, global problems and economic challenges were also emerging.

The third period doesn't correlate to France specifically. It began at the end of the 1980s and was due to the rise of these challenges. It was characterized in France and in other countries by an eruption of voluntary approaches generally led by the firms themselves. In this period, the international context was more and more prominent and the economic pressures in the environmental field were stronger. Firms were more conscious of the strategic role of the environment; they modified their organization and increased their communication efforts

At the same time, French companies seemed to be late and had a bad ecological image. The bottom of the list, published by consultants, didn't correspond to the reality of the largest and multinational firms because they were well-respected and often deemed beyond regulation. They utilized internal eco-audits and signed the International Chamber of Commerce Charter concerning the environment. But that is the reason why our Environmental National Plan, in 1991, started rebuilding and recommended a partnership policy with the companies through eco-auditing and what we call enterprise environmental plans. Those plans are voluntary, strategic, pragmatic, and flexible. The administration suggested a methodology for their elaboration, but didn't control or label the plans.

All firms, sectors, and functions were potentially concerned. The policy began with 60 large companies and is today developed in the direction of medium and small enterprises by our agency, ADEME, using a regional approach. The method complemented regulation and took place in the set of environmental management systems. It was a good step toward EMAS or ISO 14000 normalization.

Today, European companies can adopt those two main environmental management systems, eventually simultaneously with a double recognition. French companies, once again, are not so enthusiastic. Only 25 of them were ISO certified in 1997, representing 3 percent of European certified firms versus 60 percent for the UK sites. Their adhesion to EMAS is very weak, with only 0.5 percent of the European sites versus 80 for the German companies. Probably this is because firms' initiatives are numerous outside normalized systems.

Figure 1 examines the classifications of those commitments. The combinations of three aspects highlight eight categories of agreement. These aspects are: their individual or collective character, how much public authority is involved, and their status, determining the existence of sanctions in case of non-compliance.

Those, in turn, can be organized into two opposing institutional arrangements: the traditional public intervention and the laissez-faire policy, corresponding to the market logic.

First, the position and number of voluntary agreements give them a central role. They are collective and negotiated with public authorities. They correspond to the French "branch contracts" and to the detergents and CFC's agreements.

There are two variants. One variant is called the "Dutch covenants." Covenants are coupled with regulation and are also articulated with tradeable permits. Another category concerns the Public Voluntary Programs, like the 33/

Figure 1. Environmental Commitments on Voluntary Base: Between Public Intervention and "Laissez-Faire" Policy

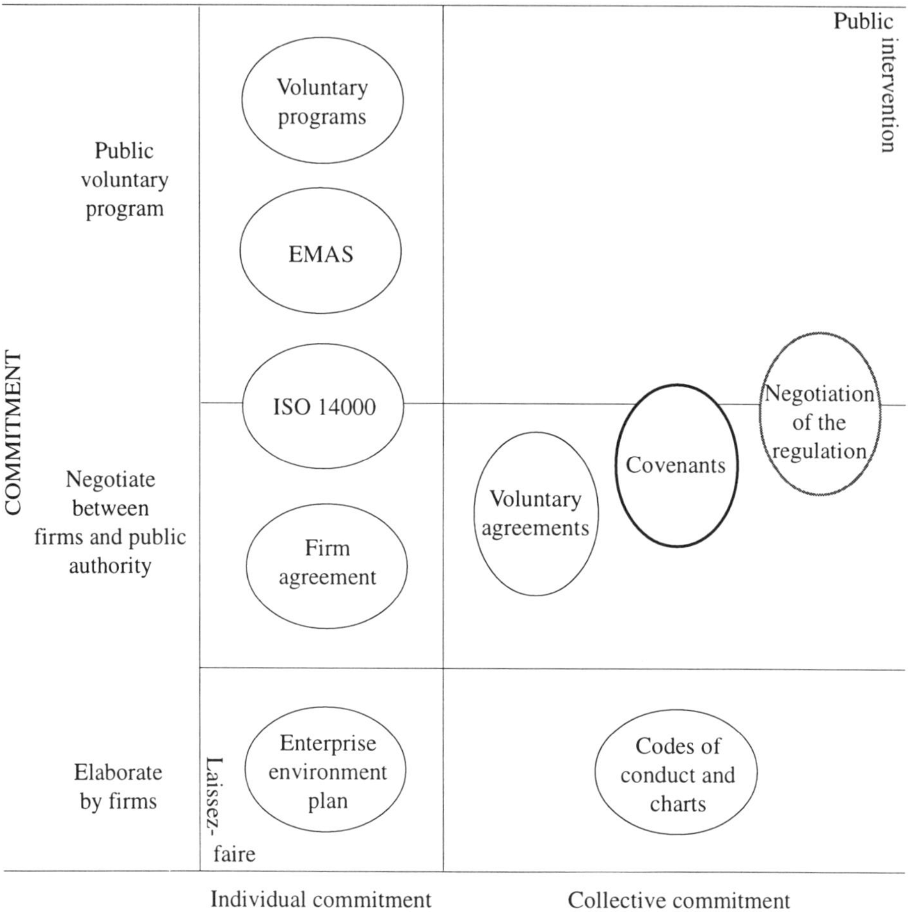

Source: "Voluntary Commitments in Environment: Advantages and Disadvantages," *Cerna*, June 1997, for the Ministry of the Environment, Research and Economic Affairs Service, France.

50 and green lights program in the U.S. where companies are invited to adhere to a de-pollution program defined by the EPA.

Belonging to the same category, EMAS, is a European environmental regulation encouraging companies to adopt a normalized program of management.

ISO 14000 is a hybrid system, positioned between Public Voluntary Program and negotiated systems, because it is a non-public regulation, elaborated with companies themselves.

Some commitments are very closed to regulation when the collective rules are submitted to administrative sanctions; among those is the German Dual System (GDS), devoted to the packaging waste recycling and its equivalent Eco-Emballage in France.

The analysis of those mechanisms should show that they are used in any pollutant sector for any type of pollution. They are not used in a specific strategy that could be adapted to a particular problem. So, which are the companies entering those systems and why do they do it? This will be my first key issue. The second will concern the question of the efficiency of these environmental commitments and management systems. Finally, I will consider the regulation-commitments dialectic and the state responsibility today in the globalization context.

One can identify three main sources of possible gains explaining the firm commitment in environment actions:

- the existence of a regulatory menace;
- the opportunity for non-regret investments, which means that firm investment is profitable, at last; and
- the benefit due to the ecological image gain with consumers, neighbor populations, and employees.

Today, the largest companies mainly have those motivations and are able to use those main systems, particularly the ISO normalization. The situation seems to me different with the smallest firms. In France, for example, they don't have the time, the money, or the competence to do it. They respect, more or less, the regulation (generally less), but they don't follow its evolution. This is probably the real challenge, because there are thousands of medium or small firms.

My questions center on why companies make or do not make the choice to enter the ISO or EMAS systems. What are their gains? Are those mechanisms necessary to make environmental progress? Do the permits anticipate regulation of the smallest companies? How can we help them to join those normalized systems?

Efficiency is my second issue. Are those different commitments cosmetic mechanisms? The answer depends on the nature of the commitment and is certainty negative concerning EMAS and ISO. The question of efficiency can be explored for the commitments that are negotiated with public authorities.

I invite you to distinguish between environmental effectiveness and economic efficiency. Concerning environmental effectiveness, how can we prevent regulatory capture that means that the company involvement in defining the commitment can conform to very modest goals. The second question is, can we prevent the risk of free riders in the absence of control and sanction?

Concerning economic efficiency, the problem is related to the allocative efficacy when the repartition of efforts between companies doesn't take into account their abatement pollution cost differences. In that case, the global cost is not minimized, and that is generally the case.

Then, should we consider a reduction of public intervention without a parallel development of environmental management systems? This can have important consequences both on environmental effectiveness and on economic efficiency. My third issue concerns the regulation-commitment dialectic. Complexity and uncertainty are increasing in the environmental field. More and more frequently, governments have to act and make choices in this context and in taking into account companies, consumers, and citizens new attitudes. The choice of instruments becomes crucial.

The French experience shows that voluntary commitments complement regulation and economic instruments, but can also be a step in the implementation of regulation.

On the other hand, regulation can offer a framework where companies can enter on a voluntary basis, and that's the case for EMAS and ISO normalization. Some other commitments are negotiated in view of transcription into regulation. This suggests that regulation and voluntary commitments are not opposed to each other, but exist in a complementary way. But beyond complementarity, practice at work demonstrates that public authorities are developing hybrid instruments and policies mixing regulation, economic instruments and/or voluntary commitments.

In summary, it seems to me that complementarity and the combination of instruments are probably the best and most pragmatic way to face the new environmental problems.

ISO 14001: REAL WORLD IMPLEMENTATION AND STATUS

Randy Dougherty
Vice President, NSF International
Ann Arbor, Michigan

WHAT IS THE ISO 14001 ENVIRONMENTAL MANAGEMENT SYSTEM STANDARD?

ISO 14001 is an international voluntary consensus standard developed by the International Organization for Standardization (ISO) for developing and implementing an organization's environmental management system (EMS). It requires that an organization establish an environmental policy with a commitment to regulatory compliance, develop procedures to identify environmental aspects and legal requirements of its operations, and implement programs to manage the associated impacts, focusing on continual improvement and prevention of pollution. ISO 14001 is the only standard out of the ISO 14000 series by which an organization may objectively audit its EMS for self-declaration of conformance or for third party certification.[1]

History

ISO was established in 1946, with a mission to promote international trade by harmonizing international standards. It is comprised of national standards bodies from over 100 countries, and it has developed numerous international voluntary consensus standards, including ISO 14001. In 1991 ISO created the Strategic Advisory Group on the Environment (SAGE) which determined the need for international environmental management standards and recommended that ISO develop them. Consequently, ISO created Technical Committee 207 (TC 207) in 1993 of which the U.S. Technical Advisory Group (U.S. TAG) is a part, along with other national delegations from ISO member countries. TC 207 was charged with the development of the ISO 14000 series of standards based upon consensus among stakeholders including industry, government, not-for-profit organizations, standards organizations, and environmental groups. Ultimately, the ISO 14001 EMS standard was published in September of 1996 after a development process of approximately five years.

Purpose and Benefit

Much of the impetus for drafting ISO 14001 came from four main factors: (1) the development of ISO 9000 standards for quality management systems, (2) increased international interest in sustainable development, (3) private sector programs (i.e., Responsible Care) and public concern for the environment, and (4) national EMS standards (i.e., BS 7750, NSF 110) and the European Eco-Management and Audit Scheme (EMAS) which was adopted by the European Union in 1993 (Diamond 1996). Two main purposes of the standard are to obtain international consistency in private sector approaches to environmental management and to guide environmental performance through a flexible, voluntary system.

There are several benefits expected from the implementation ISO 14001, the first of which is the promotion of innovation at the manufacturing plant level to improve environmental performance through efficient strategies. Organizations implementing the standard also expect to realize a broadened customer base (especially in Europe and the Far East), competitive advantage, reduced costs and increased revenues due to increased efficiency of operations, and improved regulatory compliance. Certification to the standard may also result in improved public perception due to improved environmental performance.

Both government agencies and business associations report that environmental improvements have followed ISO 14001 implementation in large and small enterprises (BATE August 1998). The U.S. Environmental Protection Agency (EPA) and NSF International (NSF) have also carried out numerous ISO 14001 EMS pilot projects in which participants have realized benefits including: improved communication and environmental awareness, improved procedures and documentation, enhanced awareness of risk-related budgetary needs, time savings, identification of local regulatory requirements, and increased capacity to improve environmental performance (Davis 1998; Davis and Branson

1998). Thus, execution of the standard may reveal results that are beneficial for both the environment and the organizations that are implementing it.

LESSONS LEARNED: REALITIES AND PROJECT RESULTS

One reality with regards to the usefulness of the standard is that small and medium-sized enterprises (SMEs) may collectively have a key affect on the usefulness of ISO 14001 implementation in that they represent the majority of overall pollutant emissions in the United States. However, they do not typically have the time or resources to develop an ISO 14001 EMS. Registrations in the U.S. are increasing as more companies embrace the standard. However, the majority of these companies are large, multinational entities. SMEs may lack the information, resources, or managerial awareness of environmental impacts, such that they do not understand or cannot use ISO 14001. Consequently, controversy exists over whether a separate EMS standard should be developed for SMEs. ISO explored this idea over the past two years and recently decided not to develop a separate standard, but to simply provide assistance to SMEs in implementing ISO 14001 (BATE August 1998).

In addition to these realities, participants in and sponsors of EMS demonstration projects over the past two years have learned several "real-world" lessons about implementing ISO 14001 in a wide range of organization types and sizes. Based on the results of projects funded by the EPA in partnership with NSF International, the main lessons regard motivations for EMS development, common challenges, and implementation advice. Common motivations for developing an EMS are to counter negative public perceptions of an organization, to distinguish a company from those which do not have an EMS in place, to use EMS as a defensive tool with regards to documentation and information retrieval, to follow the new "wave" of the future in environmental protection, and to obtain ISO 14001 registration. Motivation to move from EMS development into ISO 14001 certification stems from benefits mentioned previously, including regulatory and legal conformance and flexibility, fulfillment of contract requirements, expansion of customer base, market advantages, and potential reduction in insurance premiums (Davis 1998; Davis and Branson 1998).

Many of the challenges encountered in ISO 14001 implementation stem from a lack of organizational support. Early warning signs of inadequate organizational support include passive management support, a lack of personnel necessary to lead EMS development, and resistance to spending the time and effort required for implementation. The need for cultural change may be a barrier as well if implementation would require an organization to adopt unfamiliar structure, formality, and controls. Project managers may combat these organizational problems by incorporating EMS training into existing employee training programs and by continually "selling" the effort to management and employees by highlighting and demonstrating benefits. Another important strategy is to spend time planning, rather than focusing immediately on integrating an EMS into existing management programs. A final challenge of ISO 14001 implementation, especially in SMEs, is difficulty in interpreting and understanding the standard itself. This problem is mainly due to the abstract nature of some of its requirements, project leaders' lack of experience in environmental management, and the perception that implementation is not necessary since much of its requirements are already being met in broad terms (Davis 1998; Davis and Branson 1998).

Organizations pursuing ISO 14001 may take several pieces of implementation advice, based upon the experience of NSF/EPA EMS demonstration project participants. The first is that top management support is needed as well as the support of supervisory and line management. Second, many organizations already have relevant EMS policy and practices in place. Thus, project managers should identify these elements of management in initial EMS project stages. Managers should also strive to use cross-functional teams in EMS implementation as they are critical to obtain the necessary expertise, consensus, and acceptance corporate-wide. Development and use of a network of organizations pursuing ISO 14001 is also a helpful option. Two final components of ISO 14001 success are the demonstration of early success and the sustenance of overt, consistent actions to support EMS procedures and policies (Davis 1998).

STATUS OF ISO 14001 REGISTRATION

National

Approximately 220 sites in the United States are registered to ISO 14001, in over 35 states. Currently, the industries of electronics, utilities, chemicals, and instruments (for measuring, analyzing and controlling) represent the largest portion of ISO 14001 registrations in the nation. Other industry sectors that have obtained certification include the defense, plastics, auto, health care, and pharmaceutical industries. As of October of 1997, the U.S. was lagging well behind other countries in the level of ISO 14001 registrations, especially when evaluated in terms of registered sites per million population (ENDS 1997). However, both public and private-sector organizations have shown increasing consideration for the standard, and experts have speculated that for each registered site in the U.S., roughly 25 companies are implementing an EMS based on the ISO 14001 standard (globeNet 1997). Given the increase in the number of U.S.

registered sites since this estimate (~55 total in 1997 to ~220 in 1998), the nation is likely to be moving into a higher-ranking position, as was expected by many leaders in the field. The year of 1998 was expected to present significant increases in ISO 14001 registration in North America, and current results confirm this trend (NSF research 1998; globeNet 1998; IESU May 1998).

International

In contrast to U.S. industry focus on the internal benefits of ISO 14001 registration, European companies view certification as a means by which to ensure proactive compliance with mandates for environmental performance (globeNet 1997). Registration activity reflects this approach as European countries have been the leaders in international ISO 14001 certifications. However, the amount of Asian registrations also continue to increase rapidly as companies respond to a strong fear that ISO 14001 may be used as a barrier to Asian export trade.

As of October 1997 the United Kingdom, Japan, Germany, and The Netherlands lead the world with 440, 425, 320, and 230 ISO 14001 registered sites, respectively (ENDS 1997). In terms of registered sites per million population, the top countries in decreasing order were The Netherlands, Switzerland, Sweden, Denmark, and Austria. However, these rankings have likely changed due to rapid increases in registrations in both the U.S. and the Far East. As of June 1998, Asian certifications to ISO 14001 (numbering 1,517) accounted for one-third of the global total, which was estimated to be 4,400 (BATE, July 1998). The leaders in this region with their respective number of ISO 14001 certificates are Japan at 1,018, Korea at 247, Taiwan at 195, India at 60, and Malaysia also at 60 (IESU August 1998). Last, despite significant training needs, a base for EMS development is emerging in Central and Eastern Europe, with a total of 39 ISO 14001 certifications as of June 1, 1998 (BATE August 1998).[2]

GOVERNMENT RECOGNITION AND USAGE OF ISO 14001

On March 12, 1998 the U.S. Environmental Protection Agency's Office of Reinvention published its position statement on EMS and ISO 14001, stating that it supports the development of ISO 14001 EMSs and it will partner with states in pilot projects to collect data on implementation. It will not, however, base "any regulatory incentives solely on the use of EMSs, or certification to ISO 14001." An important result is that this statement gave ISO 14001 the status of a true public policy issue (IESU April 1998). Many other federal agencies are also investigating the usefulness of ISO 14001 within the context of their regulatory and procurement programs (Hemenway and Gildersleeve 1995).

Among state agencies, the level of implementing ISO 14001 EMSs varies widely, although they have made significant progress in understanding the standard as it relates to and complements their goals for protecting public health (MacArthur and Bellen 1998). Along with the federal government, most state agencies provide no formal regulatory relief for ISO 14001 registered organizations, but they participate in continued efforts to improve understanding and use of ISO 14001 EMSs. The Multi-State Working Group (MSWG) on Environmental Management Systems is one group of state regulators that is investigating strategies for inter-state collaboration in EMS implementation while also making suggestions for revising ISO 14001 in the near future. Some local agencies are also taking initiative in implementing ISO 14001 by participating in EPA-sponsored EMS demonstration projects (Davis 1998; globeNet 1998).

In international governments, ISO 14001 has met varying acceptance, with little formal establishment of regulatory benefits for certification. For example, the Chinese National Environmental Protection Agency encourages implementation of the standard in state-owned industries and The Netherlands' Central Ministry of the Environment provides "outline licenses" to companies that, among other requirements, demonstrate an effective EMS based on ISO 14001 or the EMAS (IESU April, June 1998). Despite this lack of government coercion to adopt ISO 14001, international companies do take the most initiative in becoming certified to maintain their ability to market themselves worldwide, reduce liability, and to lessen negative impacts on the environment.

Across all levels of government, debate exists over the proper perspective to take regarding the relationship between ISO 14001 and command and control (CAC) measures for environmental protection. Some fear that as governments try to implement more innovative strategies for regulation, ISO 14001 may "replace" traditional strategies. However, ISO 14001 cannot (and was never intended to) replace CAC regulations for environmental protection. Rather, it is a tool to supplement or complement CAC measures. ISO 14001 sets no specific limits on emission levels (such as CAC), but it puts in place a framework within which an organization may meet such limits. Ultimately, an ISO 14001 EMS should build the capacity of an organization to meet compliance measures consistently in an efficient manner. This result could free up time and resources for the organization and for the regulating agency, as both entities could maintain a good grasp on the organization's overall approach to managing environmental performance. Based upon this understanding, regulatory bodies may be able to ultimately realize a more efficient method of enforcing regulatory compliance.

ENDNOTES

1. The 14000 series includes standards for EMS (14001, 14004), auditing (14010, 14011, 14012), labeling (14020 14021, 14024), environmental performance (14031), and life cycle analysis (14040).

2. Countries included in this estimate are Croatia, Czech Republic, Hungary, Lithuania, Poland, Slovakia, and Slovenia.

REFERENCES

Business and the Environment (BATE) (1998). "Asian Certifications to ISO 14001 Account for One-Third of Global Total," *Business and the Environmen,* Volume IX, No. 7, p. 8, July, Cutter Information Corporation.

Business and the Environment (BATE) (1998). "ISO 14001 at Two," *Business and the Environment's ISO 14000 Update*, Volume IV, No. 8, p. 2, August, Cutter Information Corporation.

Business and the Environment (BATE) (1998). "No Special Guidance for SMEs on ISO 14001," *Business and the Environment's ISO 14000 Update*, Cutter Information Corporation, Volume IV, No. 8, p. 1, August.

Davis, S.P. (1998). *Implementing an EMS in Community Based Organizations*. Ann Arbor, MI: NSF International.

—— and Branson, C.A. (1998). *EMS: A Guide for Metal Finishers*. Ann Arbor, MI: NSF International.

Diamond, Craig P. (December 1996). *Environmental Management System Demonstration Project—Final Report.* Ann Arbor, MI: NSF International, Ann Arbor, MI.

Environmental Data Services, Ltd. (ENDS) (October 1997). "Global Uptake of ISO 14001 Shows Uneven Picture," *The ENDS Report.* United Kingdom.

globeNet (1998). "Municipalities Feature: Implementing ISO 14001 Environmental Management Systems at the Municipal Level," Global Environment and Technology Foundation, reported at <http://www.iso.14000.net>.

globeNet (1997). "UK Publication Reports Strong ISO 14001 Growth Despite U.S. Registration Activity," Global Environment and Technology Foundation, reported at <http://www.iso.14000.net>.

globeNet (1998). "US States with ISO 14001 Certified Organizations," Global Environment and Technology Foundation, reported at <http://www.iso.14000.net>.

Hemenway, C.G. and Gildersleeve, J.P. (1995). *What is ISO 14000? Questions and Answers.* Fairfax, VA: CEEM Information Services.

International Environmental Systems Update (IESU) (1998). "Dutch Government Issues Environmental Licenses," Fairfax, VA: CEEM Information Services, Vol. 5, No. 6 (June).

—— (1998). "ISO 14000 Interest Gains Momentum in China," Fairfax, VA: CEEM Information Systems, Vol. 5, No. 4 (April).

—— (1998). *Special Supplement,* "EPA Publishes Position Statement on ISO 14000," Fairfax, VA: CEEM Information Systems, Vol. 5, No. 4 (April).

—— (1998). "The Asian Contagion," Fairfax, VA: CEEM Information Systems, (August) Vol. 5, No. 8.

—— (1998). "U.S. Sites Known to Be ISO 14001 Certified," Fairfax, VA: CEEM Information Services. Vol. 5, No. 5 (May).

MacArthur, John and Bellen, Gordon (1998). "ISO 14001 in State Regulatory Offices: A Survey of Activities," *Environmental Quality Management.* New York: John Wiley and Sons, Inc.

THE EFFECTIVENESS OF INSTRUMENTS FOR ENVIRONMENTAL POLICIES IN THE INDUSTRY: REGULATING PACKAGING WASTE[1]

Arthur Ringeling
Professor
Monique Hozee
Research Associate
Erasmus University,
Rotterdam, The Netherlands

EUROPEAN ENVIRONMENTAL POLICY*

The EU plays a role of growing significance in the environmental policy making processes of its member states. Since 1973 the EU has had its own environmental policy and by now EU environmental regulation includes more than 200 pieces of legislation. In many member states the amount of environmental community law outweighs that of purely domestic origin (cf., Majone 1996). The Environmental Action Programs set out the broad outlines of EU environmental policy. As the environmental problems increased in range and complexity, the scope of the Action Programs broadened over the years. The fifth and most recent Action Program was adopted in 1992 and focuses on sustainable development. In order to successfully apply this concept of sustainable development it is important to pay attention to the precise means by which the environmental policy is implemented in the member states. As a supranational organization the EU has the ability to adopt legislation that binds its members. When the policy takes the form of a *directive*, member states are required to translate it into their own national policy. In case of a *regulation*, which is directly applicable, it might be necessary to take complementary measures to enable the proper functioning of the regulation. In other words, the directive or regulation needs to be embedded in the national policy of the field in question to make it an integrated part. Therefore, EU decisions have a direct influence on the member states, which in return encourages involvement in the development of those policies.

Even though the EU has become a key source of environmental legislation for its member states, it can only influence the implementation of its policy indirectly because the direct and final responsibility for carrying out EU environmental policy lies in the hands of the member states. The EU is dependent on the willingness and the ability of national administrative actors for the realisation of EU policy objectives (cf., Hanf 1996). Since the implementation is left to the member states themselves, it is dependent on historically determined national administrative practices and traditions of those countries (cf., Olson 1997). Besides being dependent on governmental bodies, the EU is dependent on the cooperation of a number of other actors as well, such as civilians, companies, and interest groups. In order to successfully implement environmental policies and achieve sustainable development, actors are expected to adapt their behaviour.

It is important to note that within the process of implementing EU legislation two phases can be distinguished. The first phase consists of the legal steps taken in response to a directive, the *formal implementation* or *transposition*. The second phase is the *practical implementation*, i.e., what is done in practice to put policy into effect. The record of the member states in carrying out environmental policy has left much to be desired—they seriously fail to implement EU legislation in a timely and correct fashion and integration of environmental policy in other policies is slow. As a consequence the impact of EU environmental policy is poor. EU statistics are mainly concerned with the formal implementation; whether or not a member state executed these rules and enforced them is hardly taken into consideration due to lack of manpower and competencies. Therefore, it is difficult to get a picture of how and with what effect practical implementation takes place. Nevertheless, it can be concluded that the EU is faced with an implementation deficit. This implementation gap may in the long run undermine the legitimacy and credibility of the EU.

In this study we will focus on the practical implementation phase of the packaging directive (94/62/EC). The central assumption is that the characteristics of the prevailing environmental policy instruments and the ways they are applied, restrict the policy's effectiveness, because they do not sufficiently take into account the institutional setting in which actors take decisions that affect sustainable development. In other words, the effectiveness of environmental policy depends on the fit between the characteristics of the environmental instruments on the one hand, and the "setting" in which actors take decisions with environmental consequences on the other.

Accordingly, the goal of the research project is to examine how the relation between the characteristics of the policy instruments and the specific institutional setting of the implementation of policy in the EU member states influences the realisation of environmental aims as phrased in the Fifth Action Program—thus gaining knowledge and insight in the relation between instruments, institutional setting and effectiveness.

RESEARCH DESIGN

Our research[2] consists of a cross-national comparative case study. In the comparative design two clusters of countries can be distinguished: Northern European countries that are characterized by a developing environmental policy and complex procedures, and Southern European Countries that are characterized by a quicker ratification of EU directives and a less well-developed "domestic" environmental policy. The Netherlands, Germany, and Belgium are selected as representatives of the North European countries. Greece and Spain are selected as representatives of Southern European countries. France is expected to take more or less a position in between.[3] As far as the policy sector is concerned, the packaging industry was selected. At the end of the 1980s packaging, both for industrial and household purposes, was identified as an important national environmental policy problem. Several European countries initiated approaches with respect to the packaging problem. These differing national measures became an obstacle to the objective of a single market. The push for harmonization of these different systems to the development of the EU directive on packaging (94/62/EC). As a consequence, all member states needed to create some government regulation regarding packaging waste, forcing some countries to change their approach, and others to start developing a system, while leaving room for various systems to develop. In the member states involved in this research, the packaging problem is integrated in the national and sectoral setting although through different institutional arrangements, making it a very interesting case for testing our central assumption.

CONCEPTUAL FRAMEWORK

Central in our research is the idea of "fit"—basically, the more fit, the more effective the policy. Fit is a concept that is well-known in policy sciences, which essentially comes down to correspondence in relationships. That correspondence can take different forms. For instance, it can be a compromise between different actors, or policy choices that look much the same, or even a measure taken that is adequate when circumstances are taken into account. In the concept of fit, ideas about rationalism of policy processes can be recognized. The concept can be found in organizational theory-based ideas about contingency. It can also be found in network thinking and institutional theory in the policy sciences.

The concept of fit is measured in these cases by looking at the characteristics of the policy and the instruments of the private sector as well as the different levels of government. In Figure 1, Hemerijck et al. (1998) distinguish four kinds of questions about fit which can be considered as an operationalization of the more general idea of fit that we have in mind.

The different questions that are asked in one way or another play a role in our research and in the theories we tried to develop. This is most clear for the question on effectiveness, but also the question on feasibility had been there constantly as the question to what extent courses of action were permitted. The more we pay attention to the networks developing and implementing policies, the more that question becomes important. The legal question of whether it is permitted what the member states decide in the light of European legislation is always present, as well as the normative question. We took a normative stand as a starting point. That normative stand was the policy of the European Union on packaging waste.

A question that can be asked is: What has to fit? The general answer to that question is choices. Without choices of policymakers or other actors no attempt exists to reach a feasible policy. Now two other questions can be asked: Choices

Figure 1. Four Types of Questions

	Structural-Formal	*Cultural-Normative*
Logic of appropriateness	Feasibility *(Does it suit?)* 1	Acceptability *(Is it normative correct?)* 2
Logic of consequences	Effectiveness *(Does it work?)* 3	Legality *(Is it permitted?)* 4

Source: Hemerjick et al. 1998.

of what and choices by whom? The "what" question can be answered by referring to policies and instruments. By policies we understand a combination of normative positions and goals to be reached and the policy theories behind these goals. To put it differently, a policy consists of problem analysis, problem definition, solutions of the problem, and strategies to do so. By an instrument, the type of means to reach these goals is meant. Governments, both national and EU may formulate instruments. They are elements of policies, referring to specific means (legal, financial, procedural, etc.) that are applied in the implementation of a specific policy. The "who" question refers to the EU, national governments, and the national/international business community or private sector.

The variables and actors mentioned can be related in a number of different ways. We make a choice of the relationships that seem most relevant for our research. That leads to the following seven fit relationships:

1. The fit between policy of the European Union and the policy of the member states with regard to a certain policy problem.
2. The fit between the policy of the member states and the policy of the national business community.
3. The fit between the EU policy and the policy of the business community.
4. The fit between the policy of the member states and the instruments chosen in a certain country.
5. The fit between the policy of the European Union and the instruments the member states have chosen.
6. The fit between the policy of the national business community and the instruments the member states had chosen.
7. The fit between the instruments of the member states and the instruments of the business community.

The first type of fit seems to be self-evident. When a member state takes another direction than European regulatory policy intends, implementation in that country will lag behind. The relationships that exist or develop in a certain country can lead to more consensus between the public and private sector. We presuppose in the second type of fit that such a phenomenon leads to better results. The third type of fit refers to the phenomenon that industry, among which U.S. based multi-nationals, is lobbying intensively in Brussels. In a number of circumstances industry shares sectoral interests on the field we studied. Moreover, the business community uses the European level simultaneously with the national level of the member countries, the first more to the extent that they seem to loose their case on the national level. The choice for an instrument is not a question of policy optimization alone. It also is a question of tradition, of routine, and of political pressure, to mention a few reasons. That is our consideration for formulating the fourth type of fit. The fifth type of fit is formulated because there can be consensus on the policy level between the European Union and the member states, but a tension stems from the instrument choice of the member state. The sixth type of fit is in particular important in a case where instruments of the member state and the policy preferences of the business community coincide or differ. The seventh type of fit refers to the consensus in instrument choice between the public and the private sector.

Certainly, in theory, more potential fit relationships are possible. For instance, we can pay attention to the fit between the policy of the European Union and the instruments of the EU. However, it is doubtful to what extent this relationship is worth considering since this relationship goes beyond the object of our project. Our research concentrates on the relationship between the European Union and the member states and the different implementation practices in the member states. It is not aimed in researching and analyzing the policy of the European Union itself. Second, we have to be more specific with regard to which the extent of the policy of the European Union also contains instruments. In the case of directives the European Union leaves the implementation of its policy to the member states. So, most of the instruments are chosen at the national level. Therefore, our primary interest will be the national implementation of the directive on packaging and therefore on the instruments chosen and applied by the member states. Third, a potential fit can be imagined between the policy of the business community and the instruments this community applies. However, with that we also come outside the scope of our project, because we are no longer in the public domain.

In order to simplify our analysis we take policies and instruments together when we analyze the ideas of the business community. We realize that reality is more complicated than this. For instance, we considered business as one entity. With regard to the policy problem we studied, the business community is split. The makers and the users, the producers, the fillers, the distributors, the consumers of packaging do not have the same interests and preferences. Also, there are relationships between business organizations in different countries. Furthermore, they manifest themselves not only on the national but on the international and European level as well. However, these phenomena will eventually manifest themselves in the country studies and in our comparative analysis. A second complication is that we considered the member states to act as one entity, while we have both centralized and federalized member states included in our project. Therefore, this supposition is not without drawbacks either. The implications of federalization on environmental measures will also become evident in the country studies and in the comparative analysis. A third complication is that there are relationships between the different kinds of fits mentioned. With regard to this, our research strategy has been that this will surface later on when we have done the case studies, and we will try then to compare them. In our comparative analysis, this is one of the subjects to focus on.

Another idea behind our project is that national governments follow certain governance models. These governance models are not the same in the countries studied and the effects are not the same either. All kinds of different governance models can be distinguished. We have focused on the following four:

1. command and control;
2. governance on main policy lines;
3. selective governance; and
4. facilitating governance.

There is no direct correspondence to the governance models a specific government is following and the instruments applied. Nevertheless, a connection can be distinguished between these governance models and policy and instrument choices made. Governance models tell us something about the arena, the relationships between different entities, which policy choices are feasible and which are not, and which instrument options play a role. They can help us to better understand why certain possibilities were taken into consideration in the policy processes studied and why other possibilities were not. Choices made in the context of these different governance models produce different effects.

In the course of our project, it became more and more a study of dynamic effects—effects of the policy of the European Union, to be more precise. To an important extent this is the result of the difficulties we encountered in operationalizing the concept of effectiveness in its various aspects. Also, our project is becoming a study of dynamics: the process of formulation and implementation of the policy the European Union is highly non-linear, complex, and, to some extent, chaotic, with focus on the national as well as on the EU level.

COMPARISON OF PACKAGING WASTE POLICIES

In this section a descriptive comparative analysis across the cases is given, while trying to understand the effects (of policies) in countries in relation to (a) instruments and their use and (b) the institutional setting. We will start by comparing the cases with regard to the national settings. Next, the entities/actors involved in the process will be compared, paying particular attention to their interests and their perceptions and definitions of the policy problem. Further, we will focus on the dynamics—i.e., the process of policy formulation. We will compare the differences between countries in the process, the patterns of interaction, cross-country links, and the interaction between the national policy arenas and the EU policy arena. We will also compare the result of this process in terms of formal policy and the use of instruments. Finally, a comparison of effects will be made on the following dimensions: environmental quality, goal attainment, costs, and other effects.

National Settings

Legislation on waste precedes environmental policy and legislation by (many) decades in all cases (second half of the 19th century post-war era). A more or less identical starting point for each case is that waste disposal is considered a public responsibility. Competencies are allocated to national, regional, and municipal authorities. The latter ensure rapid and safe disposal, because of the hazard for public health. Households and industry pay directly for these public services—for households mostly a flat rate, for industry a tariff structure (volume, weight, type, time-dependent).

Initially, all waste went to landfills, mostly uncontrolled, which at some point in time will lead to problems. The resulting nuisance and soil and water contamination cause a not-in-my-backyard (NIMBY) syndrome for landfills. In densely populated areas municipalities shifted, if only partially, to incineration (more costly, but more readily available). Aggravated by the dioxin scare, incineration also evokes a NIMBY reaction.

Over time waste disposal ceased to be just an issue of environmental hygiene, to be dealt with in a professional, responsible way; it moved toward the center of environmental policy and became an issue of resource management, source-oriented policies, economic incentives, policy planning. At this point the national settings of the cases start diverging. In most countries this development led to new efforts in policy planning, in particular in France, Germany, and The Netherlands (early 'eighties), while Belgium and Spain published comprehensive waste plans around 1990. In The Netherlands and Germany, and to some extent in France, packaging waste was identified as a policy issue along with other categories of waste (hazardous, organic, sludge, etc.). Packaging waste, with a high volume-to-weight ratio, became more and more visible. In Spain and Greece, packaging waste, for several decades, was a smaller fraction of a smaller (per capita) waste flow in comparison to other OECD countries. However, this difference has decreased over the last ten years. Main differences in national settings are that waste is a non-issue in Spain, while Greece is facing increasing difficulties in finding new locations for waste processing at all (although they are not ready to consider packaging waste a separate, but related policy issue).

Key elements in national (packaging) waste policy formulation in Germany, The Netherlands, and, to a certain extent, Belgium are:

- Environmental hygiene; the effects of incineration and landfill on the quality of air, soil and groundwater are a major concern. This (in particular through public health risks), along with the nuisance of increasingly large-scale waste processing (odor, noise, landscape effects) causes NIMBY effects.
- The prevention ladder; it is not just the back end of the materials cycle (i.e., waste processing) which causes concern, there are also concerns at

the front end: resource depletion. Solutions for waste processing should therefore be found considering entire materials cycles. The prevention ladder is adopted as a guiding principle: prevention at the top followed by re-use, recycling, incineration with energy recovery, incineration, and landfill at the bottom.

- Producer responsibility; the responsibility for waste processing traditionally lies with the government, often partly delegated to local authorities. In the development of waste policy and legislation in the 'eighties Germany and The Netherlands reformulated this notion: the government retains certain responsibilities and competencies, but industry ("producers" of waste) is assigned the prime responsibility for its waste. For hazardous waste this brings the notion of *entsorgungspflicht* and *zorgplicht*. For packaging waste (in fact, for all products) this leads to the concept of "extended producer responsibility," where the producer remains responsible for the product (including packaging) even after distribution and consumer use. These concepts, although strongly advocated by environmentalists, are not yet fully adopted in the packaging policies of those countries.

Actor Groups[4]

In Germany, The Netherlands, and Belgium (Flanders) *environmentalist groups* have been instrumental in the problem definition of waste. This dates back to the early 'seventies when they started denouncing consumerism and its constant flux of "throw-away" articles and packaging, completely in the spirit of that time. Ever since, these organizations played an agenda-setting role: soil contamination on uncontrolled landfills, public health risks near incinerators, identifying the dioxin hazard, causing NIMBY syndromes in nearly every siting of waste disposal facilities, exposing—often illegal—international transports of waste (hazardous, DSD, and other). All along they considered packaging waste a substantial problem within the context of waste-related problems. The problem definition of environmentalist groups in those countries evolved—in the light of sustainable development—from a waste issue to an issue of managing energy and materials flows.

The environmental organizations were among the first to formulate a key principle of waste policies, the prevention ladder (proposed in the 'seventies and still a hot subject today). They are strong advocates of the principle of extended producer responsibility as well. They see a strong regulatory role for government if industry does not adopt this responsibility, or does so without satisfactory results. Most importantly, they are rather strict in adhering to the prevention ladder, taking a principle for a commandment, distinguishing rather sharply among prevention, re-use (in various grades), recycling (in various grades), incineration (with energy recovery before without), and landfill.

Environmentalist groups are reluctant to participate in interactive policy processes, especially if the other actors expect their commitment to the result. In The Netherlands they did participate in the formulation of waste policy, but not in the negotiations on the packaging covenant, or in its implementation. A similar process could be seen in Germany. Environmentalist groups are strong in the public and political debate and exert their influence wherever they can.

Environmentalist organizations play a less explicit role in other countries. The Spanish case, for example, describes the role of NGOs in environmental policymaking in general terms. Packaging appears to be no specific issue for them. In Greece packaging waste is not perceived as a particular environmental issue by environmentalist groups and in the public opinion. They resist very strongly any type of large-scale waste processing facility (landfill and, even more, incinerators).

In all cases the key actors are government and industry (associations or relevant industries). Governments in countries with a history in waste policy (Germany, Belgium, The Netherlands, and France) take an interest in extending this policy to packaging, beginning in the1980s. The governments in Germany and The Netherlands are comparatively proactive. There is a more or less comprehensive, integrative approach to environmental policy and legislation, in which packaging waste has its place. Government attitude reflects the strong pressure of environmentalist organizations, which is amplified by public opinion. Because of this, the economy-environment balance (reducing packaging waste vs. free trade/low costs) tips clearly toward the environment. Governments of two other countries (Spain, Greece) perceive the implementation of the EU packaging directive in itself as an interest. In Greece, contrary to Spain, the siting of any disposal facility (landfill or incineration) becomes increasingly problematic.

In most countries regional authorities (prefectures, Länder, provinces, etc.) have important competencies in policy and legislation on waste, shared with municipalities. Municipalities and regional authorities do not play a role in formulating packaging policies, or in the design and implementation of national schemes, except through their national associations (for Germany and The Netherlands). Packaging is not a big issue for them since they have no competency in addressing industry on the issue. Yet, various cases (France, Germany, and Belgium) show that these actors do have high stakes and a strong influence on the actual implementation of national packaging schemes. In Spain and Greece, for example, they are involved in pilot projects and demonstration schemes. In newly federalizing countries like Belgium and Spain, they are involved fully in the policy process.

The attitude of industry is fairly homogenous across Europe. It varies from largely defensive to proactive. Industry does not recognize packaging waste as an issue in the first place since it only constitutes a small fraction of total solid waste. To the extent that packaging waste is a problem, industry rejects the prevention ladder so strongly supported by environmental organizations. It does so by arguing that there are ample cases where this ladder simply does not hold—for example, when recycling can be proven to have less environmental impact than re-use. Industry also points out that, if prevention and re-use have a lower impact than recycling or incineration, the cost increase may be very high. Industry generally rejects the (extended) producer responsibility ("we are at the mercy of the consumer"), preferring the notion of shared responsibility.

Industry wants no government interference in packaging systems. Fillers and wholesale/retail argue that this will negatively affect price and quality of its propositions to consumers. It is considered not just an issue of cost (which it certainly is), but even more an issue of autonomy in customers and of principle (state interference is in no proportion to the environmental issue at stake). This becomes even more of an issue as fast-moving consumer goods are going through a process of scale increase, both for production and distribution. This means a geographical scale increase to the level of Europe. The single European market is a necessary condition for this process, which is at stake when individual member states of the EU develop policies on packaging waste which constitute de facto trade barriers. Clearly, industry is keen to have a level playing field. Producers of packaging materials argue against policies and legislation that discriminates against specific packaging materials, rather than sets environmental standards. Industry forms associations to represent itself in the policy formulation process (and often later on in implementation process), both at a national level and at the European level (ERRA).

On a more comparative note: the differences in problem perception, normative points of departure and positions on policy options, are larger between different categories of industry (materials, packaging, fillers, and wholesale/retail), than between countries.

Consumers, buying packaged products and discarding their packaging as waste, are key actors in the process of materials flows from packaging to waste. Yet, in the policy process they are not present themselves. Rather, all others claim to represent them. According to industry, the consumer is not well understood by environmentalists and policymakers in his demand for convenience, quality, and price. According to environmentalists, the consumer is certainly willing to pay for re-usable packaging and recycling, as is proven across markets in Germany and Denmark, while the consumer is also willing to participate in separate collection schemes. In fact, the German and the Greek case show some unexpected results on consumer acceptance of separate collection of packaging waste. In Germany, consumer participation was much higher than initially expected. In the Greek case, the pilot projects of HERRA show that the consumer is highly sympathetic toward the idea of recycling, and eager to participate in separate collection of much more than just packaging waste. In

The Netherlands, consumers proved to be quite responsive in collection recycling schemes throughout the 1980s and 1990s (especially for paper/cardboard and glass).

The Process of Policy Formulation on Packaging Waste

The process of policy formulation on packaging waste in Europe can hardly be described in a single sequence of the policy cycle. In fact, several cycles can be distinguished over a period of more than 25 years.

The First Cycle: National Initiatives on Beverage Containers

In the 1970s, packaging waste was not a policy issue in most European countries. The Dutch case mentions how environmentalist groups, concerned with litter, started a campaign against one-way packaging. In the ensuing policy debate among government, industry, and environmentalists SVM (the Association for Packaging and Environment) was founded, which later on represented industry in the Dutch packaging covenants. The debate did not lead to specific policies or legislation on packaging, but to the more generic Waste Substances Act that was submitted to parliament in 1975 and adopted in 1977. Although at the time no coherent network of environmental NGO in Europe (such as FOE or EEB) existed, environmentalist groups in Denmark and Germany made efforts to put packaging waste on the political agenda's of their countries simultaneously. In fact, a negotiated agreement was concluded between the German government and industry on stabilizing the existing refill system (an agreement which had no effect, as it turned out later on).

The Second Cycle: European Involvement, Still on Beverage Containers

From the early 'eighties on there is a policy debate in several European countries, which extends to the EU level. In France the debate is mostly domestic, resulting in *contrats de branche* which eventually do not prove to be effective. In Denmark, The Netherlands, and Germany, the debate focuses on beverage containers. Initially, industry in The Netherlands is able to "fend off" actual government policy formulation and legislation (prohibiting one-way packaging for beverages) by signing a "code of conduct" (1985). Under this code, industry would not advertise for one-way packaging, and it would expand its comprehensive program of bottle banks (started in 1981).

A brief aside: Denmark adopted a mandatory return and refilling scheme for beverages in the early 'eighties that effectively ruled out all one-way packaging. This was challenged in the European Court of Justice, which published its famous Danish beer bottle arrest in 1986. The EU adopted its Directive 85/339/EEC on beverage containers. Germany introduced at that time a mandatory deposit scheme for beverage bottles that had to be revoked after protests from the European Commission.

Simultaneously, Germany—after the adoption of the German Waste Management Act—implemented the above Directive 85/339/EEC in the Ordinance for returning one-way plastic beverage containers. This ordinance constituted an obligatory refill system for plastic bottles (also known as the "Lex Coca-Cola"). This was later included in the packaging ordinance. The Federal Ministry of Environment drafted an ordinance for labeling beverage containers. The cycle ends here: the policy approach of "packaging avoidance" instead of "packaging waste avoidance" meets too much resistance. The packaging debate in Germany moves from avoidance to the full range of avoidance/re-use/recycling, and from bottles to all consumer goods plus transportation packaging.

The Third Cycle: National Initiatives on Packaging Waste

In Germany, the policy debate, and negotiations between government and industry on the reduction of packaging waste, continued in the late 'eighties. The influence of environmentalist organizations was very high and constant over time. As a result, the problem definition and the normative points of departure adopted by the German government were largely those of the environmentalist groups.

The German government publishes targets for re-use and recycling for several materials (glass, tin-plate, paper, plastic) in 1989 and 1990. These targets are not accepted by industry. Early in 1990, a dual waste system (later DSD) was proposed as a means to achieve policy targets after all, while leaving prime responsibility with industry. After the government adopted this proposal, the policy arena changed: The discussion was no longer on quantitative policy targets, and policy selection but on how to implement a DSD. The necessary legislation was provided in the Packaging Ordinance (adopted in May 1991). Producer responsibility is the pivotal element of this legislation. It addresses both transport packaging and consumer packaging (sales and secondary). It stipulates that all transportation packaging must be taken back by producers and re-used or materially recycled. It stipulates the same for consumer packaging, with an exception for companies that participate in a private disposal system (the "Dual System"). Thus, industry is forced to participate in such a system, since the cost of taking back packing by individual companies is clearly prohibitively expensive. Industry itself further developed and proposed the system. The key features are:

- DSD sets up the separate collection system and implements it, in communication with municipalities,
- DSD contracts out all of the processing activities to private companies,
- It does so with an overall effectiveness that meets the targets for recycling of various materials specified in the ordinance,

- Industry pays DSD for collection and processing, and prints a green dot on every package. The fees depend on material type, weight and volume of a package.

Key instruments in the German policy are the rigid quota for refillables, and the obligatory take back of packaging (leading to DSD). This result of the policy process in Germany has strong effects across the German borders, (a) on the policy process in Belgium and The Netherlands and (b) on the industrial community

In The Netherlands and Belgium, negotiations between government and industry took place in the same period (late 1980s), under an observable shadow of the German process of policy formulation. The governments were not ready to take the drastic step of the German Packaging Ordinance, while industry wanted to avoid a dual system at all costs. These negotiations led to negotiated agreements on the reduction of packaging waste. In Belgium the regional governments initially acted independently. It seems that industry achieved consistency through "upward co-ordination" in this case; PRO (for elaborating a prevention and recycling policy) and FOST (for operating a waste separation plant) were established in 1991/92. FOST failed to select a site for the separation plant (another case of NIMBY), while the Belgian government proposed the introduction of eco-taxes (in part on packaging) in 1993. It was the only country proceeding along this line. At this point in time the process ground to a halt in distrust and conflict between Belgian government and industry.

In The Netherlands the negotiations took place between government and SVM, the Dutch industry "Association for Packaging and Environment." The starting point for the new negotiations was the Dutch National Environmental Policy Plan (NEPP 1989), along with a 1988 Memorandum on Waste Policy. Both documents laid out the targets and principles for packaging waste (similar to those in Germany). The negotiations were in part successful because the Dutch government was preparing its version of DSD. This was considered a threat by industry. As a result of this, and because it expected more flexibility (both in time and options) in a negotiated agreement, SVM opted for a "Packaging Covenant." This covenant is enforceable by law, and contains goals for quantitative and qualitative prevention and for product/material re-use. Key words are self-activation, lifecycles, and chain responsibility. The agreement was signed June 1991. It calls for individual "packaging chains" to draft and carry out implementation plans. Industry will switch from one-way to re-usable packaging, if lifecycle analyses show that this is environmentally superior, and if there are no overriding objections on "market economic grounds." The Covenant stipulates no scheme for separate collection and treatment or for financial contributions by industry as in most other cases in this study.

The developments in The Netherlands, Belgium, and especially Germany cause deep concern within industry. In particular, multinational companies not only consider the packaging ordinance (with quota for refillables, and DSD as a consequence) as impractical and costly, but they also consider it a serious infringement on the single European market. The same applies to companies in the EU, who export their products to Germany—e.g., the orange producers in Spain. Industry takes the issue to other policy arenas, in France and Brussels.

In 1990, the French government, in particular the minister for environment, Brice Lalonde, started preparing a packaging ordinance both in response to the development of DSD in Germany, and in anticipation of the EU packaging directive. It is not clear how multinational companies in Germany actually moved the debate to France after DSD was adopted. Was it a direct line, or did it go through ERRA or the US Chamber of Commerce? The government asked industry, in the persons of Riboud and Beffa who manage two major French enterprises in the food industry, to study the issue and propose solutions. Their reports are the basis of the later French ordinance. Main points in the ordinance are the obligation to recycle/recover packaging to *the extent feasible*, and the distinction between *waste and ultimate waste*. The ordinance contains no specific goals, quantitative or qualitative. Other than in Germany and The Netherlands, incineration of waste is labeled "recovery" and "valorization" if the energy content in the packaging material is recovered. However, Belgium (in FOST Plus) seems to make that distinction as well, while from the German case it appears that a current re-enactment of the German ordinance allows for "thermal recovery" of up to 50 percent of recoverable materials.

French industry, in order to implement the ordinance, establishes "Eco-emballage," which takes care of the recovery of consumer packaging. French industry pays Eco-emballage (depending on type and quantity of packaging sold) which contracts out to municipalities and private waste treatment companies the collection and treatment activities. Eco-emballage compensates additional costs of recycling and valorization to municipalities. They supply recyclable materials recycling companies (*filieres*), who also have a contract with Eco-emballage, under which they are compensated for the difference between recycling costs and the market value of recycled materials.

The Fourth Cycle: Harmonization in the European Union

As a result of the policy processes in, especially, Germany and France (and to a lesser extent in Belgium and The Netherlands) the European Commission started preparing a Directive on Packaging Waste in 1990. The same value conflicts between environment and free trade that appeared in the German and Dutch policy arenas characterize this process, first of all. This time however, the "weights" of the actors involved were different. The Commission and the European Parliament, certainly at the first reading of the Directive in 1993, leaned toward the problem definition, the policy principles and the ambitious quantitative targets of Germany, The Netherlands, and Denmark. It aimed at free trade by harmonization and at high environmental performance. Most other countries (except for Belgium, and Luxembourg) were opposed to the principles proposed (waste management hierarchy) and to the ambitious targets proposed (for prevention, recovery, and recycling). The latter would require substantial changes in the waste management infrastructure of some countries, and lead to high costs. Also, they opposed the (potential) infringements on free trade caused by the radical policies of some member states (e.g., Germany). The packaging directive became the most lobbied piece of EU environmental legislation so far. As a result of (1) the concerted efforts by industry, (2) the relatively small effort by environmentalist organizations, and (3) the majority vote exercised by the (non-front runner) member states, the directive contained only few remaining aspects that are contrary to the industry position. The debate on the basis for the directive, art. 100a vs. art. 130s, will not be discussed here, but the fact that eventually it was based on art. 100a underlines its prime goal: harmonization and free trade. On the environmental side, the directive was watered down, providing ranges of targets for recycling and recovery which are easily met by all member states.

Even so, the effects of Directive (94/62/EC) are not to be neglected:

1. It had a catalytic effect on the policy process in Belgium. What is more, it did allow for the introduction of economic incentives and, thus, for the eco-taxes adopted in Belgium.
2. Germany and The Netherlands interpreted the directive as consistent with their domestic policies, and their implementation.
3. It started off a process in Greece and Spain which otherwise would not have started at that time, with the risk of serious free trade disputes in later years.

Per the first point, Belgian government and industry closely monitored the work of the commission, and participated in it. Also they studied closely the (drafts of) the French ordinance. It is characteristic for this policy process that in Belgium strategic, SWOT-type, analyses were carried out, and scenarios were developed for the domestic process. Similar analyses were later carried out in Greece and Spain.

As a result, the Belgian process continued. FOST Plus was established (1994) for the co-ordination of individual collection and recycling initiatives, to avoid (for industry) eco-taxes on drink containers, and to "fulfill the requirements of the Belgian interregional co-operation agreement." Like DSD, FOST Plus collected payments from industry (which industry considered a viable alternative for eco-taxes), related to weight and type of packaging material used. Although it had to organize a separate (dual) collection system initially, it did not organize a separate collection system, but it had contracts with both municipalities and private waste treatment companies for collecting, sorting, transporting, and recycling of packaging waste. Another important difference with DSD is that

FOST Plus started locally, in 1994, serving only a small part of Belgium. In 2000 it is expected to serve 90 percent of Belgium. By 1999 an 80 percent valorization target is to be reached, along with a 50 percent recycling target.

Regarding the second point, after the adoption of Directive 94/62/EC by the EU the process of implementation by member states started. Germany, Belgium, and The Netherlands considered their national policies and instruments used adequate implementations of the Directive—although the European Commission holds that, even to date, Belgium and Germany have not implemented all articles of the Directive. Since an EU directive requires implementation through legislation, in The Netherlands the signing of a covenant was not sufficient anymore and all possible measures were open to discussion again. The following negotations ended in a ministerial guideline and a new packaging covenant.

And as per the final point, Greece and Spain, which both participated in the EU negotiations on the Directive, started the implementation process. In Greece there was no established policy or legislation yet toward the implementation of the Directive. However, the policy process started in 1994, when the Greek government appointed a committee on legislation for management of municipal waste. One of the objectives of this committee was to achieve compliance with EU legislation (including the Directive). In this committee all relevant actor groups were represented (except, again, municipalities/regional authorities). Also, the Greek government started a comprehensive survey of packaging waste, which was to evolve into a monitoring system. The Ministry of Environment funded local initiatives on separate collection and recycling of packaging materials. There were a number of local initiatives, aimed at separate collecting and recycling of materials (paper, glass, plastic, steel, and aluminum). Most notable are the pilot programs by HERRA (the Hellenic Recycling and Recovery Association) in two municipalities (86.000 inhabitants), and to a lesser extent ACMAR, which organizes separate collection of paper in the Athens agglomeration.

Spain has a large number of local initiatives toward the separate collection and treatment of waste as well. Spain seems to follow the approach adopted in France, since Spanish industry launched a proposal for the management of packaging waste in 1992, later formulated in a voluntary agreement signed by national and regional governments, municipalities and provinces, as well as industry. This agreement proposes ASODECO, a new organization that takes up the same responsibilities as Eco-emballage in France. More recently, a law on packaging and packaging waste was adopted (Law 11/1997), which is a framework law. It outlines the system for management of packaging waste: principles for authorities in promoting prevention, re-use, recycling and valorization, quantitative targets and time horizons (in line with those of the Directive), role of central government and ACs, etc. Further regulations within this framework law will deal with the practical implementation. Under this law, there is an obligation for companies to set up a deposit, collection, and return system for packaging waste. They can be absolved from this obligation if they participate in an integrated system of management of packaging waste, organized through ECOEMBES (which basically emerged out of ASODECO). ECOEMBES will be the equivalent of Eco-emballage (France) and FOST Plus (Belgium). Like Eco-emballage, ECOEMBES is expected to set up subsidiaries for particular waste flows (e.g., Ecovidrio for glass and ECICLOPLAST for plastic). The Spanish case reports that industry, governments, and these new organizations have quite a way to go before the system is operational. Spain, as well as Greece, has yet to set targets for packaging waste within the range of the EU directive.

Effects and Assessment

Effects on Environmental Quality

Little empirical data exist on the effects of packaging policies (national or EU) on the actual environmental quality in the six countries studied here. In an attempt to find some effect we will descend the prevention ladder, the leading principle of both the EU and most national packaging policies.

One tangible result is the effects of the policies in terms of *prevention* or *avoidance*. The German and the Dutch cases indicate that the overall volume of packaging has decreased by about 10 percent (in 1995 compared to the 1990/91 level). The German case reports that the major prevention effect was achieved in 1992 and 1993, after which it leveled off. The question is whether there is a continuous prevention effect. Prevention of packaging has a positive environmental effect throughout the lifecycle of packaging material: extraction and production of raw materials, production of packaging materials and systems, energy used in storage/handling/transportation, and disposal/landfill/incineration of waste. This is a significant, positive result, especially when considering the real increase of consumption over the same period.

The environmental advantage of *re-use* over single use (with recycling at the material level) is not beyond dispute. Lifecycle analyses carried out in the German process of policy formulation indicate that re-use (with relatively short transportation distances for products and packaging) has a lower environmental impact than material recycling. The lifecycle analyses carried out under the Dutch packaging covenant are at best inconclusive. They do show those hybrid systems (e.g., for detergents) and well-selected mono-material single uses packaging (e.g., PE-sachet for milk) are superior. In other cases the differences between re-usable and single use are small and sensitive to assumptions made (e.g., on product spillage, transport distances, process efficiencies). They also show that both re-usable and single use have large, unexplored potentials for environmental improvement. It can be concluded that the impact of shifting from materials recycling to re-usable packaging is still under question and that the potentials for improvement of both re-usable and single use packaging stand to remain unused if either system is enforced by regulation.

Controversy certainly exists over the environmental quality improvement obtained by incineration (with energy recovery), also described as thermal recycling, over *material recycling*. The German case reports that an increasing volume of packaging waste with caloric value (i.e., plastic, paper, cardboard) is incinerated as feed stock in blast ovens. This causes emission levels (of various pollutants) that are considerably higher than in (regular waste, state-of-the-art) incinerators. A further result is that regular waste incinerators receive a load with a lower caloric value. In order to meet their emission standards they need additional fuel. There are also counter-arguments from the (waste) industries; the caloric content of waste for incineration is reduced only marginally when plastic packaging waste is removed because it is such a small fraction. The environmental quality improvement obtained by a shift from landfill to *incineration* is hard to quantify. It is qualified as an improvement by many and as deterioration by others. It remains a contentious issue.

An overall assessment of the effects of packaging policy on the environment is difficult to give, at best one can say that things did not change much for the best, but certainly not for the worst.

Goal Attainment

First we need to answer the question which set of goals we must use for reference when discussing goal attainment. When we use the goals of the Directive, we see that Germany and The Netherlands are near or over the maximum targets specified in the Directive. Belgium and France will easily reach the range specified in the Directive, once Eco-emballage and FOST Plus are fully operational (in geographical scope and processing facilities). For Greece and Spain it is too early to draw conclusions, since they are in the stage of implementation and experimentation.

We can also discuss goal attainment in terms of the targets set within the national systems. In Germany the separate collection in DSD was an immediate success, due to the high level of participation by consumers. Initially, DSD had great difficulties in handling the supply of packaging waste: (il)legal exports to developing countries and other countries in Europe; "free rider" problems and too-low license fees caused near bankruptcy of DSD in 1993. After 1993 events took a turn for the better. A re-enactment of the Packaging Ordinance is reported to be necessary for dealing adequately with free riders. For transport packaging, which falls within the scope of the Packaging Ordinance, little actual data are available. So far, there have been no administrative steps taken, nor monitoring or sanctions.

While the German ordinance caused a tidal wave in the national packaging chain, in the other cases national policies caused ripples: Belgium, according to its policy, is a "slow starter"; FOST Plus was expected to reach 35 percent of geographical coverage in 1996. In fact, the speed is increasing: the Belgian case reports that FOST Plus covered two-thirds of Belgium by 1996, where it reaches or exceeds the goals of the Directive. This is not the case for the national goals; it can be doubted if FOST Plus will be able to reach the targets of the eco-tax law.

In France, Eco-emballage has a slow start as well. An evaluation of the first phases of the system shows that the 75 percent valorization and 20 percent materials recycling goals will not be reached (actual data are not available, although ADEME seems to have them). The fees are low, and Eco-emballage provides little incentive to municipalities to invest in the required technology (incinerators, separation centers, etc.). Even more, since municipalities are reluctant to make such investments while financially depending on a private organization. Finally, if municipalities invest in technology for recycling and valorization they generally opt for valorization. This matches their current expertise and hardware, while less expensive than the other options.

The Dutch packaging covenant reaches its goals. The 10 percent overall reduction target for 2000 may be reached since the total volume of packaging stabilized in 1992, while gradually decreasing since then. This is largely the result of preventative efforts by industry (less packaging material, smaller number of materials, less weight/volume; sometimes a tradeoff between prevention and recycling). In the same period consumption kept increasing. A 50 percent material recycling interim target was reached in 1995. At that time, the 100 percent valorization target was not yet reached. However, since 1996 the landfill of packaging waste is legally prohibited. All incineration has to be done with energy recovery.

Finally, although Spain and Greece have not yet implemented the EU directive, the local initiatives, experiments, and pilot programs are promising (to be elaborated some more). It is unlikely that targets of the Directive will be reached within the specified time period.

Costs

It is difficult to make a proper cost comparison over the six cases, since they offer little information on the subject. The Belgian and French cases contain a table with the license fees for industry. The Belgian case presents fees in BEF per kg of material. The consumer seems to pay 5–350 ECU per ton (from glass to plastics). The French case presents fees in FF per hard-cover package (from the 0.01 FF for a .2 to 3 liter bottle, at 400 grams for a glass 0.70 liter bottle and 100 grams for 1.5 liter PET bottle I construe 4–18 ECU per ton, from glass to plastic).

The Dutch case contains no cost data. The prevention efforts of industry are said to have had no effect on cost prices (they were often reduced—e.g., the hybrid packaging of more compact detergents or the lightweight refillable bottles). In other cases, certain segments of consumer markets appeared to be willing to pay for a more expensive, lightweight PC refillable bottle. Materials' recycling is mainly done for single-use glass, where Dutch industry started separate collection (in bottle banks) in the early 1980s. The net costs of this system are zero (or marginally positive). The apparent cost difference with France and Belgium (4–5 ECU per ton) can be explained from both the longer experience and the higher population density in The Netherlands. The cost of valorization (incineration with energy recovery) varies from 90–140 ECU per ton (depending on a large number of parameters). Including the cost of collection and handling (separate or not), these costs are 200–350 ECU (again, these are rough estimates). It is conceivable that these costs are covered from the Belgian license fees, especially since in Belgium more concerted efforts are made to make the required capacity available. The French fees are too low to make the desired recycling facilities economically viable.

The total cost of the dual system in Germany can be estimated at 2 billion ECU (DSD turnover in 1995), for the recovery of 5 million tons of packaging waste (about 400 ECU per ton). However, the German case reports that this average cost per ton is deceptive, because before DSD there were already self-financed (revenues of secondary materials) recycling schemes for about 2 million tons of glass, tin-plate, and paper packaging. This means that DSD cost about 660 ECU per ton packaging *additionally* recovered.

For Spain and Greece, the current experimental character and small scale of packaging recycling activities make it difficult to draw conclusions on the costs of entire national systems for packaging waste. Looking at the costs, then, it can be concluded that, although specific data is missing, a great variance exists between the countries.

Other Effects

So far, the effects of implementation of packaging policies were discussed in terms of changes in the collection and processing of packaging waste, and the costs for industry and households. Still, there are other effects, which deserve attention:

- Market distortions—in Germany, the Bundes Kartell Amt has a particular interest in the packaging ordinance since it gives a monopoly to DSD, and it may discriminate against foreign imports (in fact there is the issue over refillable quota, in which the mineral water industry seems to use the quota for market protection purposes).
- Municipalities and public utilities in waste management were generally not involved in developing the national systems. In particular France and

Germany defend their interests (competence, already existing collection, and processing systems).

- The German case reports that the impact of the packaging policies on innovations in packaging systems is low. The Dutch case reports a substantial impact on packaging innovations.

CONCLUSIONS

First of all, we conclude that there are all kinds of fit, lack of fit, and development towards fit in the policy field studied. We will elaborate a bit on that. The policy problem studied showed a development of a greater fit between the policy of the European Union and the member states. As a consequence, the policies of the member states compared to each other became more the same as well. It can be concluded that the measure the European Union took, led to more policy harmonization among the member states. Looking at the systems implemented as a result of the packaging directive it seems as if they are gravitating towards two general systems (DSD-like or Eco-emballage-like). This is the more remarkable considering the fact that no preference for a specific system was given in the directive.

Another consideration is how the national policies are made. Some countries, e.g., France, used patterns of consensus building more than other countries, e.g., Germany. Other countries, e.g., The Netherlands, made use of only regulation first, and seeing that it did help quite a bit, consequently changed their patterns of policy-making toward consensus-building.

However, there is a special intervening factor here. The business community has the opportunity to interfere and to deal two times. If it is not satisfied with the results on the national level, it can try again on the European level. Important lobby groups are active in the decisionmaking process in Brussels. And not without success, in the packaging field an europeanization of the German solution was effectively blocked.

We have to remark, however, that in the cases studied there exists a partial fit with regard to the policy and instruments preferred by industry, because the business community mostly is a divided house. Producers of packaging material or of hazardous waste do not have the same interests as fillers, distributors, or transporters.

The fit countries tried to reach between their policies and the instruments used is also interesting. But fitting national policies toward European standards is not the same as a choice of the same instruments. Even more, several countries opted for unique instruments like the eco-tax in Belgium and the covenants in The Netherlands. They demonstrate a high fit with national policy-making, but whether it fitted in the European policy is heavily discussed.

What member states and industry in general tried was to obtain the most fit between the European policy and their own policy or between policies and instruments used. When they succeeded in that, what were the consequences for the EU policy? Did it lead to better results? And from which point of view were they better? It is not easy to give a good judgement on these questions. A high degree of fit is not good or attractive in all circumstances. It depends on the standards we use.

The research also makes clear that a strong fit between the preferences of different actors do not always lead to a more effective policy. There are circumstances where a strong fit between the preferences of member states and industry exists but environment is paying the price. Eco-emballage in France seems to be the prime example of that. What can be said is that a strong fit leads to better implementation of a certain policy, an implementation with less resistance, blockades, and what is more. This interesting administrative phenomenon is not to be confused with the effects on environment and the development of environmental quality. In essence that is the confusion between outputs and outcomes.

Policies

EU policy did harmonize the national policies on packaging to some extent. So we conclude it had effect. Countries that did not have very much environmental policy of their own copied what they saw from other countries. They did not copy haphazardly, but rather transplanted what fit in their own country. The EU policy put some countries in motion that were not active with regard to the problems in question. This, too, can be considered an effect.

Despite one policy of the European Union, different national policies exist with regard to the issue we have studied. The national setting does have influence on the policy development in the member states. We conclude that those differences between the instruments the different member states use can be explained to an important extent by the attempts to reach agreement with the private sector in a specific country. This national setting is more important in countries where there is more policy development with regard to the problems in question.

Instruments

Instrument choice follows interesting patterns. It is not so that the Northern countries opt for horizontal or modern instruments and the Southern for classic, traditional regulation. A lot of different factors are important here. First of all, there is the obligation for the member states to adopt EU regulation in their national legislation. So, there is a juridical base for the national policies anyway. Furthermore, we can not conclude that one type of instrument is superior to another. Instruments are mostly selected within a certain national context. That limits the choice/options. But it can also be said that there is experience with the application of certain instruments in a specific country.

The negotiation processes in the member states between public and private parties can lead to the choice of different instruments when the member states are compared. Despite these differences, the instruments of the countries concerned can have important results. We may even speculate that a harmonization of the instruments in the member states would not have lead to the level of performance we can see now.

Horizontal instruments are not superior to vertical ones. They just fulfill other functions than these other instruments. They have more to do with the policy-making process and stimulate consensus-building. There is no reason to underscore these functions. On the contrary, in a number of countries studied we see how important it is that consensus between different actors is facilitated. And with representatives of the private sector that are benevolent toward the solution of environmental problems such a consensus benefits all.

Not every voluntary agreement is acceptable for the public sector. It depends among others from the results it will have and also from the extent to with the agreement is binding according to the law.

Monitoring

The European Union seems to have serious monitoring problems. The authorities in Brussels do check whether the member states take over regulations and rules in their own legislation, but there the monitoring seems to stop due to lack of manpower and competencies. To control the practical implementaion the Commission is dependent on the reports of member states and complaints of citizens. The former source is not very informative and the latter mainly deals with isolated cases. So there is little information on the Brussels level about differences in implementation practice in the member states. Without information on how well EU policy is practiced by member states' administrations and to what effect it is of course impossible to learn from past experience and improve policymaking.

General Conclusion

In general, we can conclude that the so-called implementation deficit is less a deficit than is easily assumed. Perhaps the term is coined too easily. To be sure, there is a certain distance between high expectations and what is realized in day-to-day practice. The policy of the European Union we studied is no exception. But the phenomenon of different policies and different instruments of the member states easily trip us up. We might consider the fact that a more common market can be reached, despite different implementation practices.

With regard to the packaging policy we concluded that policies of the member states were harmonized more than before the European Union took action. Although we observed differences with regard to the instruments, we also concluded that the national setting and the consensus-seeking in national policy-making processes to an important extent, influenced instrument choice.

So, in short, the measures of the European Union were effective, but their effects did not always go into the desired direction, nor did they do so very quickly. Packaging was not a directive once and for all and the European Union is still in need of a lot of activities.

ENDNOTES

1. This paper is based on Hafkamp, W.A., M. Hozee, A.B. Ringeling (eds.) (1999), *The Effectiveness of instruments for Environmental Policies in the Field of Industry: Regulating Packaging and Transport of Hazardous Waste*. Final Report, Volume I and II.

2. The research was funded under the framework of the EC Environmental Research Program *Economic and Social Aspects of the Environment* of DG XII.

3. The national case studies were carried out by researchers of Erasmus University Rotterdam (The Netherlands), Free University of Berlin (Germany), Ecologic (Germany), National Technical University of Athens (Greece), University of Gent (Belgium), and Autonomous University of Barcelona (Spain).

4. The characteristics of the actor groups concerned in the various countries are summarized in the table in Appendix 1.

REFERENCES

Hanf, K. (1996). "Implementing International Environmental Policies. In: Blowers, A. and P. Glasbergen, *Environmental Policy in an International Context: Prospects for Environmental Change*. London: Arnold.

Hemerijck, A. et al. (1998)."Vier beleidsvragen. Naar een grotere coherentie in de beleidswetenschap (Four Policy Question: Towards more Coherence in the Policy Science)." Unpublished manuscript. Rotterdam: Erasmus University.

Majone, G. (1996). *Regulating Europe.* London/New York: Routledge.

Olson, J.P. (1997). "European Challenges to the Nation State." In: Steunenberg, B. and F. van Vught (eds.), *Political Institutions and Public Policy. Perspectives on European Decision Making.* Dordrecht: Kluwer Academic Publishers.

Appendix 1. Actor Groups and their Characteristics

Actor Groups	*Belgium*	*Germany*	*France*	*Greece*	*Netherlands*	*Spain*
Environmentalists' Attitude	Proactive	Highly Proactive	Active	Active	Highly Proactive	Active
Problem Definition	PW important fraction of HH waste, to be reduced	–	–	No landfill No incineration	–	–
Principles	Prevention ladder producer resposibility	Prevention ladder producer reponsibility	–	Public health	Prevention ladder producer reponsibility	–
Government's Attitude						
—National	Proactive	Proactive	Reactive	Reactive	Proactive	Reactive
—Regional[1]	Proactive	–	–	–	–	Proactive
Problem Definition	PW important fraction of HH waste to be reduced	see B	continued utilization of waste management infrastructure in France	siting of landfills free trade	see B	
Principles	Prevention ladder, not so strict	Prevention ladder strict producer responsibility	free trade presentation with valorization		Prevention ladder to be tested for individual packaging system	
Industry Attitude General Waste Industry	Defensive Active	Defensive Active	Defensive Active	Defensive Active	Defensive Active	Defensive
	1. There is no problem with packaging waste 2. Interfere with free trade					
Principles	Free trade proportionality					
Consumers, Household Attitude	–	Highly responsive		Responsive	Responsive	
Problem Definition		Largely absent; "yes, waste is a problem"				
Principles		"Recycling is a good idea, but price, comfort, and quality are important, too"				

[1]Associations of municipalities and regional/provincial/prefactural authorities play a role in the policy process
[2]In all countries; in countries going through a process of federalization, individual regions play an important role as well

VOLUNTARY APPROACHES TO ENVIRONMENTAL PROTECTION

Thomas P. Lyon
Associate Professor
John Maxwell
Assistant Professor
Kelley School of Business, Indiana University, Bloomington

This talk summarizes the results of a series of papers that John Maxwell and I (along with colleagues at other universities) have been working on for some time. Our goals are to understand why companies voluntarily engage in environmental protection, and to understand the implications of these actions for social welfare and for government policy.[1]

I want to begin by distinguishing three types of voluntary programs. (I should note that this typology is entirely consistent with the one Marc Aviam presented earlier.) First of all, we can identify *unilateral programs* that companies themselves initiate. Second, we can identify *public voluntary schemes,* i.e., programs initiated by governments in which corporations are invited to participate but the government is really the prime mover. Third, we can identify what are often called *negotiated agreements* in which both parties are bringing something to the table and there is a process of negotiations between them.

To start with the first of these, *unilateral corporate actions*, I would like to give you some examples. Earlier you heard a lot about ISO 14000, something that is really a private sector initiative. There are also lots of other more limited examples. ARCO, for example, brought out a set of reformulated gasolines that were designed to be cleaner than ordinary gasoline. The market for these fuels focused on the Los Angeles Basin, with its extraordinary pollution problems, and they were brought out in the early 1990s to great public acclaim. That is one example of a unilateral action. Many of you are familiar with another such action: McDonalds Corporation's move away from the styrofoam clamshell container to a cardboard paper-based container for Big Macs and other sandwiches. Finally, the chemical industry has engaged in a collective form of unilateral action with its Responsible Care Program, which is also a corporate-sponsored type of activity.

Turning to *public voluntary schemes*, the one that you heard a lot about earlier is EMAS, which is a government-initiated program in Europe. In the U.S., probably the best known example is the 33/50 Program that was instituted by the Environmental Protection Agency to encourage 33 percent and then 50 percent reductions in toxic emissions over a period that goes from, I believe, 1988–1995. That is a particularly important and interesting program because it is one of the few programs where there is extensive data that can be used to study the program's effectiveness. There have been a number of studies using these toxics data, and if I have time I'll discuss those studies briefly.

Finally, in the area of *negotiated agreements*, the Dutch are very strong proponents of this approach and they have used it extensively with their national environmental policy program. The German CO2 reduction program is also what I would characterize as a negotiated agreement. In the U.S., the EPA has a negotiated agreement program under the name of Project Excel. I would like to turn now to the different motivations for companies to be involved in these different types of voluntary programs. First of all there is what you might call the "happy-happy" approach: "I'll improve my productive efficiency, lower my costs, make more money and, by golly, the environment will be better off at the same time, so we're all happy." 3M is probably the best-known proponent of this approach, at least in the United States. They claim to have saved many millions of dollars by preventing pollution.

A second type of motivation is that of shifting market demand and supply. On the demand side, a company might hope to attract "green" consumers, by which I mean people who typically have high incomes and are willing to pay a premium for an environmentally friendly product. The Body Shop is a corporation that has played very successfully to this market. On the supply side, firms may be trying to attract a supply of funds from green investors, often through socially responsible investment funds that are willing to allocate money toward responsible corporations. I am not really going to emphasize either of those although there is some evidence to support the idea that both of them matter.

What we've been more intrigued by is the interplay of corporate and regulatory activities. I believe that a lot of corporate activities in these areas are designed to influence how government regulations play out. There are several ways that companies may influence government policy. We had several talks earlier that touched on this topic—in particular, Dr. Bohne talking about regulatory relief in return for the adoption of certain kinds of programs, such as the ISO 14000 or the EMAS programs. So one thing that might be a payoff for a company is a reduction in regulatory monitoring: "If I commit to environmental improvement up-front, maybe the regulators won't pester me so often." A second motive may be to preempt the emergence of stricter regulations that might be forthcoming otherwise. A third possibility is that if a firm can't prevent regulations from emerging perhaps it can at least weaken them. Finally, sometimes companies can actually benefit from stricter regulations if those regulations will squeeze out other firms with higher costs.

I want to talk about each of those in turn. First of all, let's take the notion of deflecting regulatory monitoring; I think the EMAS and the ISO 14000 examples fit well in this context. If a company can make a public commitment—which regulators have reason to believe is credible—that they are going to be cleaner in their production processes, then a rational regulator should respond to that by saying "I am going to divert my resources for monitoring away from you and toward other firms that have not made similar commitments." Of course, for this to work those commitments must be credible and the firm's promises to reduce emissions must be believable. If that condition can be met, however, then this might be a perfectly sensible reason for companies to engage in voluntary pollution abatement. In fact, there is some empirical evidence that regulators do indeed adjust their monitoring practices in response to the voluntary abatement activities of corporations.[2]

Of particular interest is the question of whether, for a given corporate motivation, voluntary actions lead to socially beneficial or socially detrimental results. In the case of deflecting regulatory monitoring, we would expect the results to be socially beneficial. This assumes that regulators are rational in shifting their monitoring resources away, and assumes regulators are actually acting in the public good (we could have a whole conference about that question) but if these assumptions hold true then this kind of activity ought to be welfare enhancing.[3]

The second motivation that I mentioned was preempting government regulations that might otherwise be coming down the pike. This assumes an interest group perspective on the politics of regulation and assumes that there is pressure from certain interest groups to adopt more stringent regulations. Companies can look down the road and foresee such interest-group activity, and they may be able to take actions that will forestall interest group intervention. If they can do that they may be able to avoid strict regulations. For example, the Responsible Care program in the chemical industry has often mentioned preemption as a goal.

Now, one implication of the preemption motive is that one ought to see more voluntary activity when the pressure for regulation is higher. In the United

States there is some evidence in support of this proposition. If you look across the 50 states, focusing on states that have more environmental group members, those tend to be the states where you see more voluntary reductions in toxic chemical emissions. This analysis makes use of the EPA's TRI, Toxic Release Inventory, to measure the reductions. So there is some evidence that firms are responding to the threat of regulation.[4]

It is also important to ask whether preemption hurts the public. My answer is "no" if the public still has the option to press for regulations if the voluntary actions aren't good enough. However, preemption may be harmful if the government commits itself to keep citizens out of the political process should industry take some specific action. The reason is that politicians might cut a bad deal and citizens might be made worse off. But if citizens retain the right to come in and press for new regulations if they want them then, I would argue, preemption is not going to be harmful. The basic reasoning here is pretty simple: if a company does something voluntarily to improve the environment, then if citizens later decide they want to press for even tighter regulations they are going to be better off in the aggregate. They got some free cleanup through the company's voluntary action. Now they can go in and spend their lobbying resources to mandate some additional cleanup and, on net, they are going to get a cleaner environment at lower lobbying cost than they would have gotten if the firm didn't do anything voluntarily. That means that if interest groups allow themselves to be preempted, if they decide not to participate in the political process, they must be calculating that they're better off than they would have been if they had gotten in there and fought for tighter regulations.

Let's turn now to the third category I mentioned before: companies may be able to weaken future standards they can't fully preempt. The first two categories involved situations where we think welfare is improved. Now we are starting to get into the categories that are damaging. For example, regulators often set a standard that is somewhere below the truly best practice that is available in the business world. Oftentimes the EPA will set a standard that is supposed to be "best available control technology" (BACT) but if you follow the details, the EPA doesn't necessarily require the very best thing that is on the market. It will actually back off from that by, for example, using an average across a variety of companies that are considered to have "good" emissions technology. In this case, leading-edge companies can influence the standard regulators set by adopting something that is not pace-setting. If an industry adopts a less impressive best practice it can induce regulators to set a weaker standard and there is no reason to expect that to make citizens better off. So this is the first example of voluntary action that we are rather worried about. I don't know how often this happens, but consider situations where a piece of legislation comes down the pike and says that in ten years regulators must set a new rule. For example, this happened with the 1990 Clean Air Act amendments. They set a variety of air pollution requirements for toxic chemicals that had to be implemented within ten years. That gives companies a long time to position themselves in a way that could influence the regulations.[5]

Finally, I want to mention the possibility that companies may take voluntary environmental improvements in order to encourage regulators to set tougher standards. In most cases companies have no reason to do this since it's going to increase their costs. But there may be special times in which companies find this type of activity profitable. For example, large companies may be able to meet stiffer standards more easily than small companies. A large company may then have reason to lobby the regulator for more stringent regulation, in the hope that the new regulation will force some smaller firms to exit the industry. By taking a voluntary action, e.g., adopting a new technology voluntarily, the firm may be able to signal to the regulator that the cost of the new technology is modest. The regulator may then draw the inference that society would be better off if all firms were required to install the new technology, since it cleans up the environment at a modest cost. If small firms can't afford the new technology, however, then the regulator may inadvertently induce exit, making the industry less competitive, raising prices and allowing the large firm to profit at the expense of consumers.

The possibility of anti-competitive regulation may be a particularly important issue for less developed countries. Consider a situation in which a developed-world company enters the market with the technology it's been using in the United States, and then attempts to convince the regulator that all local companies should be required to adopt the new technology too. These firms might not be able to afford the new equipment and they may be forced out of the market in that case. There is no reason to presume that citizens in that country are then better off if they have to pay higher prices in a more concentrated industry. Even if they are getting better environmental performance, the price hike may more than offset the environmental gains. This is another case where we are concerned that social welfare may be reduced as a result of voluntary corporate actions to improve the environment.

I have offered you a whirlwind tour through four possible motivations for corporate environmentalism. What can governments do to try to encourage beneficial corporate actions while discouraging detrimental ones? I think there are several things they can try. One is supporting the provision of public information that allows interest groups to be more effective in pressing for new regulations. This has been a very important effect from the EPA's Toxic Release Inventory (TRI). Information on the toxic chemicals released in any community in the United States is now easily available to the public through the Internet. The Environmental Defense Fund has set up a very user-friendly site at <www.scorecard.org> that uses the TRI data to provide information on toxic chemical releases from thousands of individual plants around the country. The site also provides information on the toxicity of the various chemicals released, the location of the plant, and even includes the phone numbers of managers at individual plants along with the addresses and phone numbers of the members of Congress responsible for that particular part of the country. Environmental groups and concerned individual citizens can use this information to bring political pressure to bear on local, state and federal authorities to press for cleanup. They can also pressure companies directly with the information. In my view, information provision is one of the most effective regulatory strategies available and governments can play a very important role in creating and disseminating information about the environment and the actions of individual corporations.

A second thing governments can do is to be very clear about regulatory threats. Some of the negotiated agreements and the public voluntary schemes I referred to earlier make very good use of regulatory threats. They state quite explicitly: "We're going to regulate you if you don't meet certain requirements voluntarily." By making the threat clear and precise, the government allows companies to make plans based on a fair amount of clarity about the future rather than under great uncertainty as to what the government is likely to do. Corporations are much more comfortable making investments under conditions of certainty rather than uncertainty. Thus, making a clear regulatory threat may be a very useful way for governments to encourage "voluntary" corporate actions. Indeed, I am increasingly convinced that most "voluntary" corporate action to improve the environment comes about due to explicit or implicit threats from government.

The third action governments can take is to ensure that voluntary programs are monitored carefully. It is amazing to me the number of public voluntary programs that go essentially unmonitored, especially in Europe where there is more of a tradition of informal cooperation between government and industry. Industry may offer to take beneficial actions but I think it is very important for governments to be sure that monitoring happens so that the government can be certain that industry has really fulfilled its promises. It is not really going to do society much good if industry can promise future actions, thereby preempt mandatory regulations, and yet not have anyone monitor to make sure that the promised actions actually do occur. The temptation for companies to fail to deliver under such circumstances is simply too great. Thus, supporting monitoring is also a very important role for governments.

Finally, governments should be a bit skeptical about what constitutes "best practice" regarding environmental protection within an industry. Industry may have strategic reasons to claim that best practice falls rather short of the technological frontier, so as to encourage regulators to set weaker standards.

The title of this session referred to multinational enterprises. Are there any specific things we can say about those? Well, first of all there does seem to be some empirical evidence that firms that operate in multiple countries tend to be better environmental performers. So I think we ought to look at multinationals as a potentially positive player on the environmental scene rather than necessarily a negative. At the same time, though, we need to recognize that a small country may have a hard time influencing large multinational companies. A larger country is going to be a much bigger influence simply because they have a bigger market to offer. As a result, multilateral agreements may sometimes be needed to bring about adequate voluntary activity.

Let me conclude by noting that negotiated agreements hold some promise for dealing with multinational enterprises. Picture a nation such as The Netherlands that is next door to a highly polluting company in Germany but can't influence that company directly through its own regulations because it doesn't have sovereignty. Nevertheless, with a negotiated agreement it can cut a deal with that company. It can, in effect, write a contract offering certain benefits if the company is willing to reduce its pollution, which is spilling across international borders. Thus, the negotiated agreement may be a very nice tool for dealing with multinationals.

Overall, the arena of voluntary corporate action offers the potential for significant environmental benefits if governments understand their own important role in supporting the process.

ENDNOTES

1. For a much more thorough treatment of this topic, see Thomas P. Lyon and John W. Maxwell (1999), "Voluntary Approaches to Environmental Regulation," in Franzini, Maurizio and Antonio Nicita (eds.), *Environmental Economics: Past, Present and Future,* Ashgate Publishing.

2. See Christopher Decker (1999), "Voluntary Environmental Investment and Regulatory Responsiveness: An Empirical Analysis," mimeo, Indiana University.

3. For a rigorous analysis of the issue, see Christopher Decker and John W. Maxwell (1999), "Voluntary Environmental Investment and Regulatory Flexibility," mimeo, Indiana University, September. Note that Decker and Maxwell show that investments designed to fend off regulatory monitoring may in certain cases reduce social welfare.

4. For further details, see John W. Maxwell, Thomas P. Lyon, and Steven C. Hackett (October 2000), "Self-Regulation and Social Welfare: The Political Economy of Corporate Environmentalism," *Journal of Law and Economics.*

5. For a rigorous analysis of this possibility, see Stefan Lutz, Thomas P. Lyon, and John W. Maxwell, "Strategic Quality Choice when Regulations are Forthcoming," *Journal of Industrial Economics*, forthcoming.

COMPANIES PERCEPTION OF ENVIRONMENTAL ISSUES

Stefania Borghini
Fondazione Eni Enrico Mattei
Milan, Italy

What incentives must be in place to convince multinational corporations (MNCs) to dedicate more private resources to serve public environmental interests?

The usual approach to understand and compare the efficiency and effectiveness of different environmental policy instruments is to put them directly in relation with the obtained levels of environmental performances; more rarely it has been studied how and whether these instruments influence the firms' perception of environmental issues' significance.

These issues have been studied by a recent European project (Barometer 1997) that tried to understand companies' perceptions of the most important environmental issues, environmental management driving factors, and barriers. It was assumed that only a deep understanding of the companies' priorities could lead to the identification of the appropriate environmental policy instruments. This presentation illustrates the firms' ranking of the environmental aspects, driving factors and barriers, compares the general results with the perception of only large multinational firms, and finally analyses policy implications.

The first result is that companies consider relevant those environmental issues that are mostly regulated and this result does not change across industry. That is, the perception of environmental issues' significance is clearly related to the pressure coming from regulators, rather than to the companies' activities.

Moreover, among these issues firms focus their attention on those that are more costly. In particular the results of the survey indicate waste, energy consumption, air emissions, and wastewater the most important effects (Figure 1).

Another important result is that this perception does not change between small and large companies; both concentrate their strategies mainly on solid waste and energy consumption.

As a consequence the first recommendation could be that regulators should put more attention on companies' activities and companies' sizes when developing public policy. It could be even acceptable when a small company that produces textile products does not consider risks of accidents and soil contamination among the most important impacts, but it is not acceptable when a big multinational petroleum or chemical company has the same perception.

Voluntary agreements with large multinational companies or with industrial association that take into account the peculiarities and the environmental consequences of different industry activities could be a solution. National legislation, even necessary to guarantee a minimum level of environmental protection, may lead to a similar perception of environmental issues by industries that have different risks and environmental effects or by small local firms and large multinational companies. Voluntary agreements, on the contrary, being a more flexible tool may be used for achieving specific firm/industry objectives. The second result is that national and supranational European companies still perceive legislation as the most relevant driving force and, consequently, those companies' strategies are mainly aimed at achieving compliance. Environment is not considered a competitive factor and is not considered of interest to the financial community (Figure 2).

Figure 1. Environmental Consequences of Manufacturing Processes

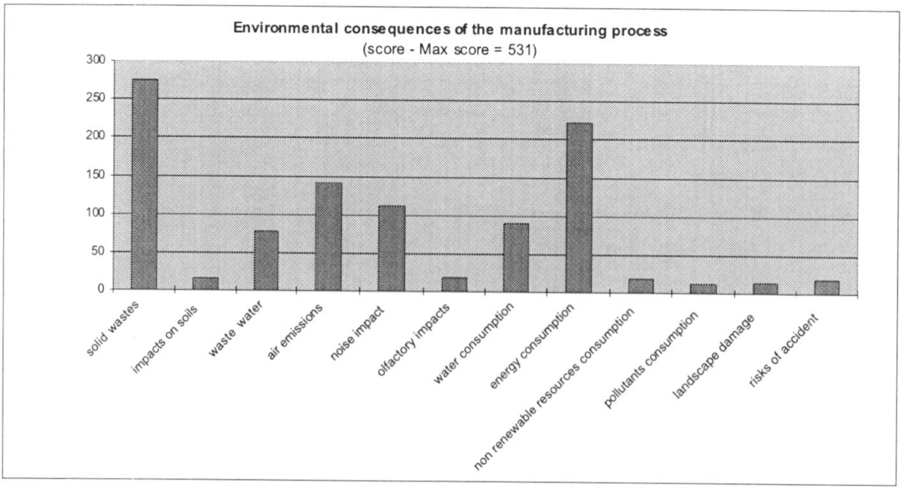

Source: Barometer 1997

In MNCs, apart from regulators, the actor that is perceived as one of the main driving factors is the top management commitment, as obvious, in big multinational organization environmental strategy is strongly linked with the top management orientation.

From a policy perspective, the role of the pubic authority should be to implement policy that may raise the interest of actors other than the manufacturing companies such as banks and insurance. For example, one way could be the enactment of legislation that requires environmental disclosure, as already happened in Canada with federal legislation that requires disclosure of environmental liabilities in annual financial statements. Another way could be to find new channel for public participation in environmental legislation enforcement and monitoring.

Concerning MNCs, the relevance that management commitment has for their environmental strategy should be taken into account. Regulators and policymakers should start looking inside the "black box." There are reason for noncompliance that are strictly linked with failures of companies organization and not with willful behaviors. For example, disseminating methodologies that make the language of environmental management as close as possible to the financial one, companies' internal monitorings may be more effective. Indeed, to achieve better environmental performances—especially in MNCs—the top management should be aware of the companies' environmental performances and should easily evaluate the effort that employees put in environmental actives.

Figure 2. Environmental Driving Forces

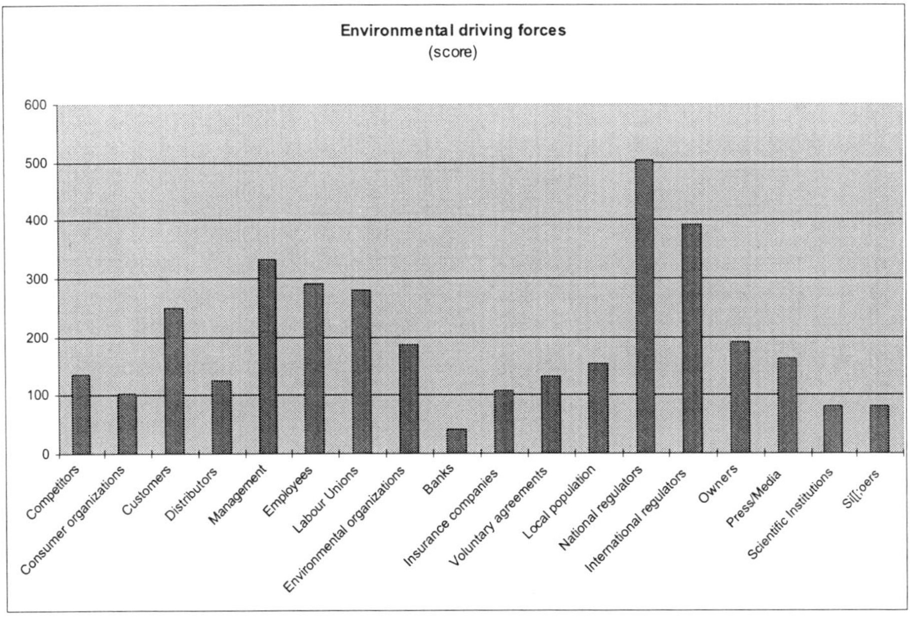

The EPA is working in this direction, for example through the development and dissemination of methodologies of environmental management accounting.

The last question that I will analyze in this presentation is related to the obstacles that companies meet when they have to implement an environmental strategy. The first result is that this perception is strongly country-based. For example, in Italy, the absence of regulatory advantage and the presence of unclear regulation are seen as the main barriers. In the North of Europe, however, companies consider the fact that when they implement an environmental strategy they do not gain any comparative advantage and moreover have to carry big costs to be obstacles.

In MNCs the obstacles that are considered more relevant than the others are the ones related to organizational problems. This result is not so surprising; these companies do not have problems in finding the right technological solutions. They have enough resources; moreover, they are always subject to stronger external pressure so that they are perfectly aware of the reasons to implement environmental measures since. For them the real obstacle is the organizational problem. From a public policy perspective the diffusion of standardized Environmental Management Systems as EMAS or ISO14001 could help in solving these problems.

POLLUTION HAVENS AND INDUSTRIAL FLIGHT: WEIGHING THE EVIDENCE

Matthew Auer
Associate Professor, School of Public and Environmental Affairs
Indiana University, Bloomington

There is increasing interest among environmentalists, academicians, and also the business community about the so-called "industrial flight" phenomenon. The concern boils down to whether strict regulations in the advanced industrialized countries compel industries to move their operations to countries with less-exacting environmental rules and regulations. By and large, the latter countries are poor. It is suggested that these poor countries are becoming "pollution havens" for dirty industries. Here, I attempt to draw a distinction between industrial flight and pollution havens. Briefly, one can exist without the other.

First: a warning. Those seeking to confirm or alternately refute the industrial flight and pollution haven hypotheses are challenged by the poor quality of relevant data sets. Consider, for example, data on firms' capital expenditures for pollution control and pollution abatement. To illustrate, a particular factory may be operating an old boiler that relies on a coal feedstock. Factory officials replace that boiler with an energy-efficient fluidized bed boiler. The new boiler generates less dust and sulfur dioxide. But the new device also enhances the overall efficiency and productivity of the factory. Some firms will identify the boiler as a purely environmental investment and all benefits derived from it as consequences of spending on environmental improvements. These firms, then, tend to exaggerate market-oriented advantages of their so-called environmental investments.

Uncertainty about industry's spending on environmental infrastructure is complemented by equally unclear accounting practices governing environmental operating costs. To illustrate, a key task of a particular employee at a particular factory may be to clean, maintain, and optimize the performance of a newly installed fluidized bed boiler. But perhaps that employee also performs non-environmental duties, like bookkeeping or answering the phones. How does one tease out that fraction of the employee's job that deals with environmental management? Some firms may be inclined to report that employee's total annual compensation as an environmental expense. For some firms, this type of accounting is not intentionally deceitful. Rather, it is a customized way to report a liability that has no standard location in the firm's balance sheet. Needless to say, data on different firms' environment-related operating costs are unreliable and often, incomparable.

The problem of data comparability worsens when the analysis encompasses firms that are based in nations outside of member countries of the Organization for Economic Cooperation and Development. Indeed, comparing environmental accounting data among firms in OECD countries is a hazardous undertaking in and of itself.

In summary, there are fundamental problems of data quality and comparability in this area of inquiry, complicating not only an effort to measure the problem, but even to verify that the problem exists.

Keeping these warnings in mind, we may now consider the evidentiary basis for the pollution haven hypothesis and draw some preliminary conclusions. There are a number of studies on how environmental regulations affect foreign direct investment (FDI) flows from wealthy to less-wealthy countries and vice versa. There is especially avid interest in the investment behavior of multinational corporations (MNCs). FDI is a good proxy for the investment behavior of MNCs because most FDI constitutes MNCs' investments. Some environmentalists propose that MNCs are expanding their investments in poor countries primarily because of environmental regulatory pressures in the MNCs' parent countries. The evidence substantiating this conjecture is thin, at best.

It is instructive to focus on the behavior of pollution-prone industries in particular, because these firms have relatively high pollution abatement costs and hence, would appear to have the most incentive to move to countries with lax environmental standards. Studies by multilateral financial institutions like the World Bank and NGOs such as Resources for the Future indicate that developing countries are gaining a comparative advantage in the manufacture of pollution-prone goods, including industrial chemicals, pulp and paper, non-ferrous metals, and refined petroleum. During the mid-1970s to mid-1980s, world trade of so-called dirty goods originating from North America fell from over 20 percent to less than 15 percent. On the surface, this data would appear to bolster environmentalists (as well as some apologists for industry) who assert that pollution-prone industries are exiting the United States and Canada to exploit less strict environmental regulatory regimes overseas. Environmentalists might also point to data showing that during the 1970s and 1980s, the share of dirty goods in world trade originating from Southeast Asia increased from less than 5 percent to almost 10 percent. Some are quick to conclude that Southeast Asian countries are gaining a comparative advantage in the production of dirty goods because of the industrial flight phenomenon. These observers are probably only half-correct. The share of world trade in pollution-prone goods originating from that region *is* increasing. But the laxness of host country's environmental rules and procedures probably only plays a small part in this trend.

Alternative explanations for the trend are more compelling. First, the growing presence of dirty industries in developing countries may be due to increasing demand for these goods in these countries. As developing countries' economies grow, and as incomes rise, demand increases for goods like petroleum, coal, chemicals, metals, and pulp and paper.

A related point: the expanding presence of dirty industries in developing countries may be a reflection of the "normal" course of industrialization. As countries become industrialized, the first industries on the scene are extractive industries and primary industries and these sectors tend to be pollution-prone. This early stage of industrial economic development began in England in the early nineteenth century and the U.S. passed through this stage a few decades later, with primary and heavy industries dominating the American scene into the early twentieth century. Most developing countries entered this stage of fossil fuel-intensive, pollution-prone manufacturing in the 1960s and 1970s. As much as we might aspire for these countries to gain access to knowledge and technologies that permit them to leap-frog over this pollution-prone period in their economic development, the truth is, global economic growth is fueled mostly by relatively dirty sources of energy and even some of the most environmentally conscientious firms remain major byproducers of wasted materials, wasted energy, and pollution. Despite their efforts to reduce pollution loads per unit production, many firms remain major polluters as aggregate production levels rise. For industries in developing countries, environmental efforts at the per unit level may be neutralized as production expands at the firm, industry, and sector levels.

Third, comparative advantage partly explains the growth of dirty industry sectors in developing countries and it also influences migration of dirty industries to developing countries. For example, Finland and Sweden with their abundant taiga forests are logical centers for pulp and paper production. Venezuela, Saudi Arabia, Indonesia, and, more recently, many African countries attract petroleum industries to their shores (and off their shores) because of the presence of large oil and natural gas reservoirs in these countries.

Fourth, there are a host of macroeconomic factors that might compel industries to relocate from wealthy to developing countries. Among the most important are the quality and cost of labor. I would guess that nine out of ten citizens in Bloomington, Indiana would rank labor costs above environmental costs as key reasons for recent defections of major industrial employers from Bloomington. Official explanations by the companies themselves tend to support this supposition. Other factors that weigh into industries' decisions to relocate to developing countries include industrialists' expectations and knowledge of: property taxes, income taxes, and other taxes in the candidate host country; availability of tax holidays; access to special economic zones; availability of low-interest credit; exchange rates; stability of the economy; government stability; the security of property rights; rules governing repatriation of profits; proximity to markets; and the quality of transportation and communication infrastructure. To this list, one might add the relative strictness or laxness of environmental rules and regulations in the candidate host country. But in most cases, other factors in this list will be as or more important in coaxing industries to relocate abroad, or alternatively, to remain in the parent country.

Finally, many multinational companies that erect new subsidiaries in developing countries claim that the new firms institute the same, strict environmental management procedures that are in place at the parent firm. Some researchers find evidence that these companies practice what they preach. But in my own experience as an environmental auditor overseas, I have found that companies' rhetoric does not always match companies' performance. It is conceivable that efforts to standardize good environmental practices, for example, through the ISO 14000 scheme, will help MNC subsidiaries as well as indigenous firms achieve consistently good environmental management procedures and results, regardless of the firm's location. However, a key challenge remains for industries to not only reduce per unit pollution burdens but also aggregate pollution burdens as industrial production expands.

Those who doubt the pollution haven and industrial flight phenomena will hasten to note that wealthy countries still account for the largest share of world trade in dirty goods. There are around 25 countries in the world that account for about 85 percent of all trade in dirty goods. Ten of those countries are non-OECD members but they account for less than 15 percent of total world trade in dirty goods. So, this game remains dominated by the wealthiest countries.

Nevertheless, there *is* evidence that developing countries are gaining in the commerce of dirty industry goods that originate from developing countries and that the latter's "advantage" in these industries will grow over time. But we must be careful in ascribing causes for this trend. Developing countries may, indeed, become pollution havens for dirty industries. But available evidence suggests that the alleged industrial flight phenomenon does not account for this trend.

POLLUTION HAVENS: A KOREAN CASE STUDY

Roy Shin
Professor, School of Public and Environmental Affairs, Indiana University, Bloomington

When we discuss development, environment, and multinational corporations (MNCs), a major concern has been that differences among countries in environmental standards and costs may cause relocation of economic activity, especially "dirty" industries, from countries with rigid standards and strict enforcement to those regulations and enforcement are lax. Perhaps the most significant change in the environmental politics of the 1990s is that environmental protection has moved from the margins into the mainstream. As such, environmental protection has become a salient issue in the global community. This paper is based on an earlier work published in the *International Journal of Public Administration*. The study explored the question of industrial flight by examining DuPont's decision to locate its titanium dioxide producing plant in Korea in the late 1980s. The industrial flight and pollution haven hypotheses are relevant here to the investigation of the role of environmental factors in determining new plant location in foreign direct investment. Furthermore, DuPont's entry into Korea illustrates the complexity of industrial location decisions involving the dynamics of international trade, the production and the investment. The international issues are of two types in this respect.

First, it should be noted that environmental controls affect the level and pattern of international trade and investment patterns. Second, there is the question of what should be the appropriate role for the home governments in industrial countries in regulating the export of such hazardous products as pesticides and in controlling the workplace environmental policies of MNCs in their overseas operations.

Both the industrial flight and pollution haven hypotheses seek to explain how and why environmental regulations would alter the prevailing allocation of comparative advantage in industrial production. Just briefly, the first hypothesis, the industrial flight hypothesis, states that more stringent and rigorous regulations would push an increasing number of industries out of industrialized countries—the "Push Factor." The second one, the pollution haven hypothesis, posits that differences among countries in environmental standards and environmental control costs may cause transboundary movements of foreign firms in pollution intensive industries. This is what is known as the "Pull Factor."

Thus, the combination of the "Push" and "Pull" factors was expected to exert a powerful influence on the international pattern of trade and industrial location and also to complement the industrial development strategies of what you called Third World nations. The principle findings of this study as well as other prominent studies done on this subject on several industrializing countries as Ireland, Mexico, Spain, and Romania, suggest that strict environmental regulations in the environmentally less sensitive countries are unlikely to result in widespread loss of investment in industrial production.

Let's consider the Korea and DuPont titanium dioxide case. Titanium dioxide (the symbol for which is TIO_2) has been considered a superior white pigment used in coating plastics and paper markets. The problem with the production of titanium dioxide is the disposal of waste from the production process. Although they use very highly sophisticated processes—they moved from what they call the sulfate process to the chloride process—there is, even so, a residual that warrants proper disposal of waste from the production process. This residual consists of solid as well as liquid waste and especially toxic emissions such as the hydrochloride and the hydrocarbon. These residuals or emissions are tremendously large and also problematic because even in the United States disposal of this waste relied on mainly ocean dumping and landfill after neutralization.

Congress in the mid-'eighties banned ocean dumping and they tightened the landfill. That, of course, created a disposal problem (not only for DuPont) but also, as DuPont tried to find a new production site, location immediately became suspect even in Korea. The issue that emerges from the interplay of trade and environmental policies has to do with the extent to which an unfair trade restriction is or could be disguised as an environmental measure.

Although it is generally recognized that natural environmental endowments of a country are a luring factor to a MNC, these factors do not favor Korea. The scarcity of land and subsequent exorbitant land prices would rule out the landfill method. From DuPont's perspective, Korea presents a favorable business climate because there are markets, domestic market consumption, and infrastructure as well as the government-offered financial incentives for general manufacturing in Korea. Furthermore, I think DuPont's market projection indicated that all TIO_2 manufactured in Korea's plant could be consumed in Korea within several years after start-up.

So that the interesting thing is that the initial rejection by the Korean EPA of DuPont's application was made pursuant to the act based on the grounds that the proposed application was deficient both in scientific data as well as in the planned course of action concerning the removal of toxic waste. The application was rejected because it triggered the political process in the United States. The DuPont issue had been stalemated for four years since the Korean EPA rejected the initial application. There was a considerable political pressure exerted upon the Korean government. Then the U.S. Vice President Dan Quayle made a special visit to Korea.

From the U.S. perspective, Americans thought the trade protection measure was disguised in the name of the environment. After long stalemated processing reviews, DuPont filed a supplemental information document with the Korean authority. In it the company would operate the plant in Korea under the same conditions as in the U.S. with respect to compliance with environmental requirements. Finally, in 1990, DuPont got the Korean government's approval. Therefore, it is quite plausible to suggest factors other than environmental concerns might be more applicable to DuPont's decision to enter the Korean market. The question is then, what are the factors that might have contributed to DuPont's project after four years of all this political negotiations? From the economic development point of view, the project was obviously attractive to Korea's economic ministries—especially since it involved large sum of foreign direct investment. It would also contribute to improving the balance of international payments through import substitution and, of course, export increases.

From the industrial policy perspective, the transfer of high-technology management know-how as well as advanced industrial technology was a welcome addition. The most troublesome matter for the Korean EPA was from the legal perspective, because the legal equity between domestic and foreign presented questions of unfair treatment. There was a small Korean manufacturer engaged in titanium dioxide production. Logically, if DuPont could not be approved for environmental reasons, the Korean firm should be shut down as well. If not, this might be a case of violation of the Section 301 of the U.S. Trade Act. Therefore, it may have very well become another source of trade friction between the two countries.

There are two lessons that we could draw from this Korean case. One, although DuPont's initial plan to treat solid waste from the production unit through ocean dumping made its project of the plant unit suspect, this is an example of industrial flight in the first instance. The project as approved in 1990 by the

Korean government cannot be considered as such in light of DuPont's compliance with all of the measures that it would have been taking in the United States, using the same technology. Therefore, there was no environmental control cost advantage to be had by DuPont by its moving a plant to Korea.

The second lesson that we could draw from this is that although the Korean EPA was involved in the initial stage of investment negotiations for DuPont—along with relevant ministries (especially the Ministry of Finance—who had to approve the inflow of foreign direct investment), the Korean EPA had no final authority to veto the investment project. As the Korean government is now trying to decentralize most of authority to local government, the question of final authority on the matter occupies all the more significance today.

It is worthwhile to note that U.S. foreign investment in pollution-intensive industries grew no more rapidly than for all manufacturing. The share of U.S. foreign direct investment in pollution intensive industries that went to developing countries or the less environmentally sensitive countries compared with other industrial countries did not increase significantly. More importantly, host countries that received most overseas investment in pollution-prone chemicals, papers, metals, and petroleum-refining sectors were other industrialized countries, not developing ones. There is no credible evidence that environmental regulations have caused a widespread relocation of U.S. industries to so-called pollution havens.

The case of German industry, a study done by Knodgen, for example, examined industrial siting for a German foreign investment. His findings are again consistent with my findings and those of other research, which indicated that there is no evidence that German firms have reallocated production to pollution havens in other countries. An interesting finding was that 90 percent of German firms surveyed claim to use the same environmental protection techniques in developing countries as in Germany.

Finally, what are the policy implications? To the extent possible, the environmental standards in any country should be established within a local cost/benefit framework. That is to reflect more accurately local environmental economic factors. Perhaps the suggestion could be made that an environmental impact assessment or ecological accountability at various stages should be required of any MNC for a major foreign direct investment when they make an application. An environmental impact assessment should include anticipated effects, baseline environmental data, environmental protection, pollution abatement technology and procedures for a pollution emergency, for example, and then targets for environmental protection.

The purpose for making these policy suggestions is twofold. One reason is to transmit useful information to environmental regulators. The second, to form the basis for explicit environmental provisions in the investment agreement when the host government and the MNC are engaged in any type of discussion. In this respect, environmental provisions of investment agreements should be made public. Public disclosure provides a check on a cozy investment and host government deal and it may also avoid any political embarrassment to both the host and the MNC over issues that might emerge later.

A GERMAN PERSPECTIVE ON GLOBALIZATION AND POLLUTION HAVENS

Wolfgang Hass
Ministry of Economics
Berlin, Germany

Germany is at the forefront of strict environmental rules. For many years Germany has had a large negative balance of investments; foreign investors seem to avoid Germany more and more, while German investors seem to prefer outside locations. An issue of concern here is whether this is a result of strict environmental rules?

The answer is not so easy. The quality of a location depends on many factors. These include: economic and social conditions, education, technological surroundings, infrastructure, and environmental rules.

The German environmental policy is based on three equally important pillars: economic growth, social security, and ecological balance.

Germany has been engaged for some time in a discussion about the nation's quality as a location for doing business in global competition. In this debate, environmental rules are playing an important role. Of course there still exists a high level of harmonization in the European Union, but member countries may exceed this level in many areas.

One of the issues debated concerns emission limits for large combustion plants or, more generally, the introduction of special taxes on energy products as an incentive for energy savings and emission reductions (CO_2). In April 1999, the German government introduced ecological tax reform on a national level, following other EU countries (all with different solutions.) A tax on energy consumption was the mechanism. The expected revenue from this tax is about 8.5DM, which will be returned in equal parts to companies and employees to lower pension insurance contributions.

A stated purpose of the tax is to provide an incentive to improve the efficiency of the production of goods and services, and therefore to contribute to sustainable development. The reduction of social costs will also have a positive impact on employment in Germany. The government recognizes the need to carefully examine the impact of the tax on the international competitiveness of German companies in energy sensitive industries.

German industry has been complaining for many years that German standards and the level of taxation are still too high, compared with their international competition. They fear a greater shift, for instance, of energy-intensive production to locations in Eastern Europe, with negative impacts for the economy and employment in Germany. They argue that the environment would not benefit from such a development; it will have the opposite effect unless it is introduced on an at least EU-wide level.

But to complete the picture, there are many people—parties like the Greens and some scientists—of the opinion that being at the forefront with environmental standards and rules would have no negative impact on national industry. They could offer more environmentally friendly and efficient products and become therefore *more* competitive, also benefiting employment.

In my view, if we are to reduce the risks of industrial dislocation, the only solution is international cooperation and harmonization of environmental rules and targets. There still exists an international basis under the roof of the United Nations for doing so, namely:

- Agenda 21 ("Rio Process"), with the three international conventions on protection of global climate (Framework Convention on Climate Change), biological diversity, and combating desertification;
- The Montreal Protocol; and
- The Basel Convention on hazardous waste.

From my experience in the field of climate change, I think that there should and could be better coordination within the industrialized countries in preparing international negotiations; the Organization for Economic Cooperation and Development (OECD) could perhaps improve its work in this field.

Appendix I. Direct Investments 1995 (Mio. $)

EU Investment in Third Countries	
United Kingdom	42,360
Germany	34,890
France	18,734
Other EU countries	53,079
EU total	149,063
Investment of Third Countries in the EU	
Of which:	
France	23,735
United Kingdom	22,030
Schweden	14,273
Netherlands	10,766
Belgium/Lux.	10,299
Germany	8,940
Other EU countries	20,973
EU total	111,016

Source: International Monetary Fund, International Financial Statistics

OVERCOMING U.S./EU OBSTACLES TO TRADE/ENVIRONMENTAL COOPERATION

Montserrat Cuchillo
Professor, University Pompeu Fabra
Barcelona, Spain

There are many obstacles and problems building up a cooperative trade and environmental policy. One of the difficulties is the fact that trade policy and environmental policies have different, often contradictory objectives, as they on many occasion tend to put forward different and even contradictory values. It is therefore quite difficult to find a way whereby the two policies can work together.

Trade policy has the clear objective of freedom of trade and this has been translated into the elimination of trade restrictions. This is the basic idea surrounding all the globalization problems. It is very easy to trace the person or persons or group of persons or companies who are being benefited or endangered by a trade policy or a trade issue. It is easy to put forward in an adjudicatory manner which are the objectives, which are the values, which are the standards whereby a conflict between two parties in a trade relation are to be solved, and how these problems can be solved.

When we consider property rights, individual activity, or economic growth, we find common values based on traditional individual rights that can easily be seen as deserving of protection or deserving of a public intervention. On the other hand, with the environment, the identification of objectives and of values is much more difficult. Environmental issues entail a great diversity and the values they put forward include those from the relatively new but clearly accepted individual rights, such as the right to health, to the very broad, hazard and uncertain right of future generations to health, beauty, or perhaps survival. They range from very local problems such as water pollution or soil pollution, to broad global problems involving global considerations with transboundary problems. In these cases, the complexity of resolving conflicts between trade and the environment is readily evident in that trade, the rights and values affected, and the approximate number of persons involved can be clearly identified, while environmental interest and values and the person or persons suffering environmental harm is much more difficult, sometimes impossible, to identify.

So it is not simple to find a common ground in the global world for protection of the environment that goes beyond such very general propositions as sustainable development. (Even the meaning of sustainable development is still unclear.) Therefore, when dealing with environmental issues, we often have to accept the fact that the trade issue always takes precedence. Many of the conflicts we face are a reflection of different political situations regarding trade, the resulting and different approaches to trade, and their influence on approaches to environmental regulation.

Freedom of trade is very much connected to globalization. The free trade philosophy is compatible with the ideas of deregulation, economies of scale, and the idea of limiting the power of states and of building a global community. But environmental issues do not so easily mesh with these principles because environmental issues tend to focus first on local problems. They put forward the possibility of specific instruments, of a specific development in every state in order to face specific problems and priorities, connected to peculiar conditions of natural resources and to diversity of cultural and civic values and traditions, promoting non-unitary action and strengthening local communities.

Because of this situation, I suggest one of the problems with U.S. and European relations is the instability or unfinished construction of the common organization that we are trying to build in Europe. As is already known, this common organization is based on the idea of a common market as its central feature. The enhancement of freedom of trade is a clear foundation for unitary action in Europe and for the existence of a unitary organization. But we also find many challenges to this idea of building a unified community, because the weight of the individual states forming this community, and their refusal to lose substantive weight, has to be balanced by measures tending to allow this unified community to rest on the idea of being state- and local-centered.

So maybe this major push forward in environmental policies that is taking place in Europe may be connected with this importance of local issues in the environmental area. Environmental policies and environmental issues can be both an asset and an obstacle in the building of a unitary organization. They can be an asset in the sense that, given their connection to local conditions and their participatory character they are basically left, apart from the general policies fixed by the European Community, to state and local governments, through the subsidiarity principle, providing a sense of involvement, intervention and decision in the European institutions. On the other hand, they can be an obstacle in the sense that, given the non-unitary approach to specific local conditions, environmental measures and regulations adopted by state and local government already constitute serious obstacles, in a growing number of economic sectors, to freedom of trade within the European Community.

If we turn from the conflicting objectives of trade and the environment and we look at the means and systems whereby trade and environmental policies are formulated and enforced, we find additional elements of divergence.

Environmental protection is very much based on citizen participation, with a great deal of non-governmental organization (NGO) activity. It is therefore an area where the possibility exists of finding new ways, new instruments, new formulas for implementation, and for overcoming classic command and control ideas. In the trade area it is much more difficult to find clear involvement of the population. It is also much more difficult to find alternative approaches for the promotion and protection of trade. The only apparent optimum way is liberalization, deregulation, eliminating trade barriers and obstacles, and reducing or eliminating restrictions in the use of substances, products and techniques for companies and producers.

Regarding instruments for the definition of environmental policies, and of environmental rights, I think it will be important to take into account mutually agreed-upon principles. For example, we know that we have established the "polluter pays" principle, but we seldom discuss how this principle operates and how it is very often reflected in higher prices. So taxpayer involvement in all the environmental policies should be taken into account. In addition, we need to consider how the population can participate in the deliberation and development of environmental rules and implementation, as well as the process of demanding a real accomplishment of the objectives of the protection. That is, ensuring that trade accepts a major part of the cost of environmental protection is of some importance. To put it another way, it is important to take into account the fact that freedom of trade should consider the need to incorporate the cost of environmental protection for the business community.

But, at the same time, we find that these two issues cannot move in a context where states exist and where political organizations are trying to build international fora and international organizations. Political agreements—like the new transatlantic agenda—always confront the obstacle of state-centered, state-oriented policies which, at some point or another, tend to protect a certain area of production or recommend against another business interest putting forward another environmental agenda.

There is also the complicating problem of developing countries. The U.S. and the European Union can come closer together through the development of the new transatlantic agenda and the economic relationships between these two entities. But this relationship is also dependent on other developing countries, which may have a very different stance toward these trade and environmental issues. Basically, the two big blocs of developing countries are in a situation where freedom of trade is a basic element. It is also an element that does not allow them to take into account international measures for environmental protection.

Consequently, in the future, those measures that could be put into force due to the growing collaboration between the U.S. and the European Union can have a very negative impact on these countries and their relationship with the West. The major U.S./European Union agreements on enhancing environmental protection can make it difficult in their trade relations with developing countries. As a result this can become a new obstacle to implementing new cooperative measures for environmental protection.

U.S./EUROPEAN ENVIRONMENTAL COOPERATION

Hilary French
Worldwatch Institute, Washington, D.C.

I would first like to focus on a bit of chronology, based on my own involvement with these issues over the last several years, to share with you the way I've seen the relationship between the U.S. and the European Union on trade and environment questions evolve. It has been a changing story, and one that has important implications for where we are going to move in the future, as we try to come to resolution on these issues that have so vexed cooperative agreements over the last several years.

The first phase of intense focus on trade and environment questions and, in particular, U.S. and EU differences of opinion on these issues, came in 1993 and 1994 with the two different Tuna-Dolphin rulings. One of the things that was interesting about this stage was that in the United States there was a sense that we were the "good guys" on this issue from an environmental perspective, and that developing countries and the Europeans were creating a lot of problems for U.S. efforts to integrate the environment into international trade.

This was a biased perspective, of course, but that was the tenor of the discussions at that time within the U.S. environmental community. We had this law, which we thought was an effective law—the Marine Mammal Protection Act—and it was threatened by opposition not only from developing countries, but from the European Union, which was a party to one of the disputes. The Europeans, on the other hand, were concerned about perceived U.S. unilateralism. It was a polarized environment in which the U.S. felt that it was the one standing up for integrating environmental questions into the international trading system, in opposition to the views of most other countries around the world.

This sense of the United States as the "good guy" in the trade and environment debate was further underscored by the fact that a number of other U.S. laws were coming under challenge at about the same time. For instance, there was a challenge to the U.S. "gas guzzler" tax and fuel economy standards (the CAFE standards). In the U.S. environmental community, there was a sense that our laws were under seige and that we were the only ones that understood this threat sufficiently.

Europeans, on the other hand, tended to be of the view that U.S. public opinion was inappropriately driving not only domestic policies but international policies as well. To some extent, this was a reflection of the debate over NAFTA (the North American Free Trade Agreement) taking place at the same time as the discussions on the Uruguay Round were underway and the Tuna-Dolphin disputes were simmering. Environmental groups had secured full-page ads in major U.S. newspapers that decried what they called the faceless bureaucrats at the GATT who were ruling on the U.S. Tuna-Dophin law. Most of the Europeans that I spoke with at that time thought that the U.S. environmental groups were paranoid in their concern about the Uruguay Round and the World Trade Organization. They did not believe the GATT and later the WTO posed a significant threat to the ability of nations to implement effective environmental laws, and felt that the whole controversy was overblown.

So that was the end of the first stage. It led to the creation of the Trade and Environment Committee at the World Trade Organization, which is widely acknowledged to have accomplished little in the intervening years. No substantive steps were taken to resolve the brewing tensions. Not all that much happened. In contrast, the stage that we are now entering, what I will call the "present" of these issues as opposed to the past, is characterized by a very different landscape. A main reason is that the laws of European countries, and the European Union itself, have also come under challenge at the WTO. So, unlike in the first stage when it looked as though U.S. laws were the only ones threatened, we have recently seen a number of rulings in which the United States has challenged European laws as unfair trade barriers. Examples are the recent Beef-Hormones case and the Banana case. Although the banana case is not, strictly speaking, environmental, it is of concern to non-governmental organizations active on development issues.

One overarching issue has become of particular concern in Europe: food safety. The Beef-Hormone case is one prominent example, but there are others as well, most notably trade in genetically modified organisms (GMOs). The "Mad Cow" disease scare in Europe raised public concern about the safety of the food supplies to almost panic levels. This has contributed to a more general concern about a range of food safety issues, in particular the planting of genetically engineered crops. This new technology has swept the world at a very rapid rate. Suddenly, over the last few years, a large share of agricultural land in the United States is being planted with genetically modified corn and soybeans, some of which are destined for the European market.

The European public is skeptical of the environmental and social impacts of genetically modified organisms (GMOs). Labelling legislation has recently been introduced in the European Union that requires that these seeds, and the foodstuffs derived from them, be labelled as genetically modified. The seed companies are upset about this, particularly Monsanto, which is causing a great deal of trade tension between the U.S. and Europe. It is, in effect, the opposite of the Tuna-Dolphin era. In this case it is the U.S. that is questioning the right of the European Union, and a number of the European member states, to proceed with legislation restricting the use of genetically modified foodstuffs.

This is playing into discussions at the WTO, where there have already been a number of discussions in about it in various committees. It has also become a big issue in negotiations aimed at developing a protocol to the Convention on Biological Diversity on the issue of biosafety. This concern has been in the background for a number of years, but we now have a protocol under negotiation and the United States and Europe are taking very different positions. The European governments are responding to public concern by wanting a range of notification measures, for instance, to be included within the protocol. The United States, largely operating at the behest of companies such as Monsanto and others, does not want these provisions to be in the biosafety protocol because it is trying to ensure free movement of these goods.

Further complicating the picture is the fact that the United States is not a party to the Convention on Biological Diversity. Although we have signed the treaty which was agreed to originally in 1992 at the Rio Earth Summit, the Senate has not ratified it. So this issue of the biosafety protocol, and the differences between the United States and the European Union on it, is bringing to the forefront one of the most controversial issues within the trade and environment debate: the question of conflicts between the rules of multilateral environmental agreements and those of the GATT and the World Trade Organization.

This is an issue, of course, that has been out there for some time. It was raised by the original Tuna-Dolphin ruling. However, now we are in a situation that is quite different than it was at that time (around 1993) when the United States was generally supportive of multilateral environmental agreements which had provisions that applied to non-parties. This is the part that, arguably, violates GATT and the WTO, which calls for like treatment of different countries.

But a number of environmental treaties, in order to encourage widespread participation in the treaties, have employed trade measures that are designed to encourage all countries to join in the treaty. The most significant example is the Montreal Protocol on Ozone Depletion, which the United States strongly supported. In order to encourage widespread participation, this pathbreaking protocol included trade measures that restricted trade in ozone-depleting substances with countries that were not party to the agreement.

At that time, as noted earlier, the United States was in a position where it was trying to encourage other countries to join the treaty. The United States now finds itself in a situtation where we are the non-party, and we are wary of the provisions of the proposed biosafety protocol. The Europeans have suddenly taken quite a progressive position on this question of which treaty should trump another in cases where a multilateral environmental agreement conflicts with the WTO. They have said they think the multilateral environmental agreement should in most cases take precedence. The United States has been publicly quiet on this question, but not so behind closed doors. Suddenly they are less enthusiastic about multilateral environmental agreements taking precedence over the WTO.

So, this is the changing context to which I earlier alluded. Whereas at first we thought that the U.S. was the one defending environmental laws against the WTO threat, suddenly it seems the other way around. European laws are coming under threat and being challenged by the United States. We have a changing context of public and political opinion on this issue internationally as well. The United States has long had a public that was concerned about possible threats to environmental laws posed by trade agreements. But we now have a public and non-governmental organizations in Europe as well that are concerned and have become vocal participants in the debate. This is reflected in the fact that the European Parliament has become an important player on these issues. Of course, the European Parliament has been growing in recent years with revisions to the Treaty of Rome. The European Parliament is now issuing reports expressing concern about threats to laws, such as those on food safety, as a result of WTO rulings.

So we have growing concern in Europe, and just about the time all of this was brewing, down came the Shrimp-Turtle ruling, which reignited concerns within the United States, which had been a bit on the back burner over the last few years because there hadn't been any major rulings against the United States. Then you had coming into the political mix this ruling, which U.S. non-governmental organizations are outraged about. I don't think it is an overstatement to say that many of them consider this ruling something of a smoking gun that reveals just how damaging WTO rules have the potential to be to environmental laws.

The overarching point to bear in mind here is that sea turtles are highly endangered. In the Tuna-Dolphin case, in contrast, the dolphins at issue were not an endangered species, although the public had a strong emotional connection to them. The situation is different with the sea turtles, as their very survival as a species is at issue, and the disputed turtle excluder devices are a highly effective tool in protecting them. Environmentalists in the United States see this ruling as highly worrisome in terms of its broader implications for efforts to protect endangered species.

So to take us to the present, we have a bit of a confluence of opinion on both sides of the Atlantic that there are serious threats to various kinds of environmental laws posed by the existing rules of world trade. This changing international context has led to some of the proposals that we have been hearing about for a high level dialogue to be launched on these issues with the goal of trying to accelerate progress. As everyone recognizes, the Trade and Environment Committee at the WTO has done essentially nothing over the last few years to move the debate forward.

We thus may be at an auspicious moment in time, as more people have become convinced that that conflicts between trade rules and environmental laws are a serious concern. Earlier, there had been one or two cases that raised questions, but the Uruguay Round rules had recently been agreed to, and it was unclear what their effect would be. I think at this point the answer is: we have a problem! There have been a number of laws challenged just over this five or so year period, and this has been an equal opportunity threat, with both the United States and European countries finding their laws under threat.

So, where do we go from here? Now that there is a consensus that this is a problem, what will the proper forum be for moving us towards some kind of resolution? The transatlantic economic partnership idea that has been discussed by Jeffrey Dunoff is a very interesting one, and on one level appears to hold quite a lot of promise for breaking this logjam. Relevant parties, as I have just explained, have come to the recognition that we have a problem on our hands and want to work out some kind of a solution.

We have a shared high level of environmental concern among the U.S. and European publics, although some of the specific issues that people are concerned about are different. Nonetheless, we have environmentally aware and concerned populaces on both sides of the Atlantic, and relatively high levels of environmental protection. There should thus be quite a lot of room for common ground.

On the more negative side, it is important to realize what the motivation for this process has been. The idea of a Transatlantic Economic Partnership did not emerge from the environmental community. Rather, it is part of a long standing effort from within the trade community to further reduce barriers to trade between the United States and Europe. I refer you to an article in *The Guardian* back in March, when the idea of a transatlantic free trade zone was being floated. A European Union official was discussing the defeat in the U.S. Congress of efforts to renew fast track trade negotiating powers. A primary reason for the failure of fast-track was concerns about low-wage competition and the delusion of U.S.

environmental standards. The EU official noted that, " the issues of wage levels, labor rights and environmental standards, which nag U.S. relations with other countries, simply do not crop up with Europe."

It should be clear from the chronology I have just outlined that these issues in fact do crop up between the United States and Europe. In fact, they have cropped up repeatedly over the last five years. If the transatlantic economic partnership is going to proceed, it is important that environmental issues be one of the major issues on the table. More recently, officials involved in the process seem to be awakening to the fact that environmental issues will need to be part of this agenda. It is important for the discussions that take place to involve all of the parties to the issue. There has been extensive business involvement in the transatlantic dialogue in recent years, but the environmental community has not been at the table. They don't want to be left outside anymore. If the transatlantic environmental community is brought into this process, it could lead to some constructive results.

I will end with one cautionary note. The Transatlantic Economic Partnership could be an important venue for striking a new bargain between the United States and Europe on these issues, but we definitely cannot forget that developing countries need to be involved in the discussion. There is reason for concern that the U.S. and the European Union might try to broker a deal which will not address some of the valid concerns that developing countries are raising within the context of the Tuna-Dolphin and Shrimp-Turtle disputes. Conditions are of course different across countries and a cookie-cutter approach of effectively insisting upon the application of U.S. standards worldwide is not the best way to proceed. We need to move forward on the transatlantic partnership issue, but we need to keep this broader international context in mind.